Teton Skiing

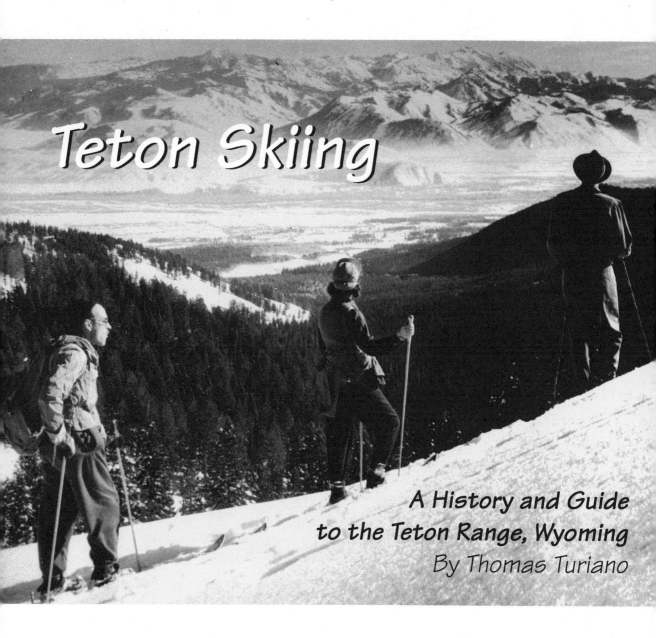

Teton Skiing

A History and Guide
to the Teton Range, Wyoming
By Thomas Turiano

HOMESTEAD PUBLISHING
Moose, Wyoming

ISBN 0-943972-43-4
Library of Congress Card Catalog Number 95-60398

Printed in the United States of America
on acid-free paper.

Cover photo: Bob Kranenberg admires the untainted winter wonderland
of Cascade Canyon during the 1930s. Roland Wolf photo courtesy of the
Teton County Historical Society.
Inside cover photo: Fred Brown, and Reddy and Willi Muller tour south
from Teton Pass during the 1930s. Photo courtesy of the
Teton County Historical Society.
Back cover photo: Forrest McCarthy makes the first turns on Peak
10,805 in upper Leigh Canyon. Photo by Tom Turiano.

Published by
HOMESTEAD PUBLISHING
Box 193, Moose, Wyoming 83012

DEDICATION

*For Bill Briggs and Leigh Ortenburger,
who trained me as a skier, climber, and as a person,
and who inspired me to share it all with others.*

ACKNOWLEDGEMENTS

Despite an earnest attempt, I could not explore every niche of the Teton Range in my quest for ski-mountaineering data. But that alone wouldn't have made this book complete anyway. I might have obtained extremely detailed route descriptions, but all the rich pioneering history would have been missing, making for a rather stale manuscript.

In piecing together the history and discovering the challenges of this legendary mountain range, I went directly to the sources; I contacted more than 300 Teton ski pioneers personally. Actually, there was a time when I thought it would be possible to contact everyone who had ever left the beaten path in the Tetons. But after eight years of networking, mailing letters, poring over books and old newspapers, and spending hours on the telephone, I realized that that was impossible. More people have ski-explored the Tetons than I ever imagined; there is no way to repeat all of the fascinating stories I've heard during my research.

Nonetheless, I think you'll find this to be a surprisingly complete record of ski descents and tours in the Tetons, dating back to the earliest ski activity this range witnessed. This endeavor certainly would not have been possible without the cooperation of all the great adventurers who enthusiastically shared their wealth of personal stories and photographs. This is their story.

My thanks to those who have contributed and my apologies to those whose names have been misplaced during my eight years of research. My gratitude to Davey Agnew, Rick Armstrong, Jerry Balint, William Barmore, Tom Bartlett, Wendy Baylor, Billy Beard, Jim Bellamy, Jack Bellorado, Tom Bennett, Scott Berkenfield, John Bernadyn, Ehmann Bernhard, Mike Best, Jeff Bjornsen, John Borstelmann, Ed Bowman, Beverly Boynton, Paul Brabenac, Brian Bradley, James Braman, Terry Brattain, Bill Briggs, Larry Bruce, Wesley Bunch, Dan Burgette, Dave Carman, Peter Carman, John Carr, Andy Carson, Skeeter Cattabriga, Blake Chapman, Wallace Cherry, John Collins, Richard Collins, Jorge Colón, Bob Comey, Tom Concannon, Doug Coombs, Barry Corbet, Jeff Crabtree, Steve Curtis, Dale Dawson, Jim Day, Larry Detrick, Doug Doyle, Ken Driese, Jim Duclos, Ted Dugan, Cindy Duncan, Bill Dyer, Jake Elkins, Steve Erickson, Frank Ewing, Mike Fischer, Roland Fleck, Ben Franklin, Leigh Fullmer, Robert Garrett, Les Gibson, Eliot Goss, John Griber, "Rody" Hagen, Robert Hammer, Todd Harley, John Harrington, Brents Hawks, Bruce Hayse, Matt Hermann, Rick Horn, Jim Huidekoper, Virginia Huidekoper, Paul Imeson, Renny Jackson, Ken Jern, Jim Kanzler, Michael Keating, Walt Kirby, Bob Kranenberg, Stephen Koch, Inga Koedt, Peter Koedt,

Gary Kofinas, Walter Kussy, Joe Larrow, Peter Lev, Rick Liu, Alex Lowe, Carole Lowe, Steve Lundy, Doug McLaren, Steve McCormick, Callum Mackay, Peter Mackay, Bill Macleod, Ted Major, Fletcher Manley, Linda Merigliano, Mike Merigliano, Greg Marin, Gregg Martell, Ron Matous, Porgy McClelland, Mike McCollister, Paul McCollister, Jack McConnell, Scott McGee, Wade McKoy, Theo Meiners, Chi Melville, Greg Miles, Dave Miller, Jay Moody, Dave Moore, Dean Moore, Bruce Morley, Stan Nelson, Mark Newcomb, Rod Newcomb, Andy Norman, Cliff Oberreit, Jim Olson, Mary Patno, Jon Patterson, Eric Peterson, Steve Piscatelli, Jay Pistono, Doris Platts, Gary Poulson, Peter Quinlan, Mike Quinn, Tim Quinn, Russell Rainey, Neil Rafferty, Clinton Reece, Elmer Reece, Jeff and Kellie Rhoads, Bill Rigby, Dave Rohrer, Jim Roscoe, Bob Rudd, Chuck Schaap, Jon Schick, Christoph Schork, Muggs Schultz, Larry Scritchfield, Peter Selkowitz, Steve Shea, Houston Simpson, Margot Snowdon, Sam Southwick, Clarence Stearns, Todd Stearns, Bob Stevenson, Pepi Stiegler, Jim Sullivan, Angus Thuermer, Whitney Thurlow, Buck Tilley, Ty Vanderpool, Jay Vanderveer, Blake Vandewater, Dustin Varga, Marty Vidak, Glenn Vitucci, Bill Wallace, Ray Warburton, Ron Watters, Ben Wilson, Tom Windle, Ray White, Mark Wolling, Rob Woodson, Charlie Woodward, Betty Woolsey, Peter Wuerslin, Rick Wyatt, Mike Yokel, Clair Yost, Jeff Zell, Jim Zell, and to countless others whose tidbits of information glued everything together.

Thanks to the staff in Grand Teton National Park for researching my many inquiries; especially Jeff Rader and Dan Burgette for your invaluable help with the sections about crossing lakes; Renny Jackson and Scott Berkenfield for being resources about mountain conditions, providing support and sharing historical information. Robin Gregory for showing me maps of Grand Teton National Park development areas. Thanks also to Jim Kanzler, Larry Livingood, and Jake Elkins for going out of their way to provide Teton Village snow-history data; Mike Commins and Larry Williamson for providing me with Grand Targhee snow-history data and other information; Christoph Schork for donating his time to fly me around the Tetons for aerial photographs; Teton Basin District of the Targhee National Forest, namely Brad Exton, Gene MacGregor and Ronnee-Sue for their help identifying sensitive wildlife areas and clearcutting history; Ashton Ranger District of the Targhee National Forest for its help identifying sensitive wildlife areas, clearcutting history, and other information; Jackson Ranger District of the Bridger-Teton National Forest; the staff at the Teton County, Wyoming Historical Center for taking time to point me in the right direction; Gretschen Notzoldt of the Teton Valley, Idaho Historical Society and historian Bill Resor for their input; and people at the Teton County, Idaho and Wyoming libraries, especially Theresa, for helping me research and order old ski articles.

Thanks also to those who helped with research and technical decisions about the book, including Nancy Arkin, Rick Black, Walter Bornemann, Steve Curtis, Gene Downer, Dick DuMais, Doug Evans, Jeff Grathwohl, Diane Henderson, Michael Kelsey, Gary Kofinas, Will McCloud, Gretschen Notzoldt, Peggy Pace, Russell Rainey, Carl Schreier, Joe Sottile, Michael Spooner, David Swift, Jon Waterman, Ron Watters, Becky Woods, and Tom Wuthritch.

Thanks to those who submitted photographs, including Todd Anderson, Ray Atkeson, Bill Barmore, Jim Bellamy, Tom Bennett, John Borstlemann, Bill Briggs, Jeff Crabtree, Frank Ewing, John Fettig, Ben and Barb Franklin, Mary Gerty, Eliot Goss, Alex Grant, the Hagen family, Rick Horn, Nancy Kessler, Stephen Koch, Joe Larrow, John Layshock, Fletcher Manley, Wade McKoy, Jay Moody, Dean Moore, Tony Morgan, Mark Newcomb, Jay Pistono, Russell Rainey, Jeff Rhoads, Teton County Historical Society, Angus Thuermer, Jr., Whitney Thurlow, Buck Tilley, Dustin Varga, Greg Von Doersten, Roland Wolf, Bob Woodall, and Betty Woolsey. Thanks to the *Jackson Hole News,* especially Angus Thuermer and Garth Dowling, for providing reference material and photo printing. And thanks to those who reviewed the history chapter, including Cindy Duncan, Peter Koedt, Rick Liu, Ted Major, Porgy McClelland, Doug McLaren, and Ray White.

Extra-special thanks go to Bruce Hayse for breathing life into this project.

Finally, this book never would have become a reality without my many ski partners who posed patiently for my photos, followed me unquestioningly to strange places, dragged me energetically behind them, and encouraged me to continue with this book. Extraspecial thanks goes to them, including Andrew Adolphsen, Todd Anderson, Nancy Arkin, Harry Beach, Tom Bennett, Andy Booth, Dave and Tracey Bowers, Wesley Bunch, Randy Bush, Sparky Colby, John Collins, Mike Collins, Dave Coon, Cathie Daniels, Art Davis, Craig Dostie, Couper Duerr, Dave Ellingson, John Fettig, Matthew Goewert, Greg Goodyear, John Griber, Rys Harriman, Diana Howell, Gail Jensen, Ken Jern, Greg Johnston, Hans and Nancy Johnstone, Michael Keating, Stephen Koch, Gary Kofinas, Mark Limage, Carole Lowe, Annie Lowery, Marcia Male, Doug Marden, Dan Marino, Ron Matous, Andy Matz, Forrest McCarthy, Steve McCormick, Scott McGee, Mike Menolascino, Minot Meser, Dave Moore, Greg Morgan, Tony Morgan, Mark Newcomb, Rod Newcomb, Jim "Hymie" Olson, Andrea Paul, Lance Peiser, Russell Rainey, Christoph and Marsha Schork, Jim Schultz, Tom Sciolino, Don Scott, Peter Selkowitz, Tracey Silberman, Mark Smith, Steve Stenger, Harry Valiente, Glenn Vitucci, Mike Whitehead, Tom Wuthritch, and Kim Young.

CONTENTS

INTRODUCTION

A ski track might be the most ephemeral and inoffensive imprint that mankind can leave in nature. This graceful evidence of a skier's passing vanishes with the ensuing storm. Whether it esses down a deep-powder slope or slices a route across a vast plateau, a ski track represents harmony between man and wilderness. And the tranquility born from swift, self-sufficient travel through the harsh mountain environment inspires skiers to return again and again. This book is, in a sense, a celebration of ski mountaineering in the Teton Range. It is a guidebook and a historical perspective, for the pleasure of both armchair mountaineers and skiers who dare to explore the challenges and mysteries of this range.

The Tetons long have been recognized for the superb hiking and climbing opportunities they offer during warmer months. In recent years, improved access into Jackson Hole and increased popularity in outdoor adventure have combined to crowd trails and climbing routes throughout the Teton Range. Effects of this heavy use are evident in the long lines at the Jenny Lake boat dock, eroded trails in Garnet Canyon, debris left behind on Baxter's Pinnacle, and trampled flora on the Lower Saddle.

With hopes of avoiding this mess, many mountain buffs enter the Tetons during winter and spring, when Mother Nature intimidates the masses and her snow hides the scars left on the summer landscape. With skis as their mode of transport, these wayward adventurers set objectives as spectacular as the Tetons. And though skiers have ventured into the Teton Range since the 1930s, each trip feels like a pioneering effort.

First glance of the Tetons' seemingly unbroken eastern front of walls and spires usually does not conjure grandiose images of wonderful ski terrain. But the Tetons are, in fact, extraordinary for ski mountaineers of all levels. Within the relatively small 50-mile-by-20-mile perimeter are couloirs and extremely steep faces, meandering valleys and ridges, wide-open plateaus and bowls, and intricate, inconspicuous passages as amazing as the scenery they afford.

Despite the intricacies of the range, Teton approaches to above-treeline areas rarely take longer than a day and usually involve minimal bushwhacking. Nonetheless, encounters with other skiers and signs of civilization are extremely rare outside the most popular areas. Unlike that in the mountains of the northwestern United States, weather in the Tetons often is quite clear, warm and dry for long intervals between vigorous snowstorms. Storms bring deep, light, dry snow for powder skiing, as well as winds that help compact the snow for cross-country touring. Unstable snow generally consolidates quickly, and those with good route-finding skills usually can avoid avalanche zones. All told, the Tetons are a ski mountaineer's paradise.

The unique geologic history of the range earns credit for the fantastic playground we have today. Fewer than 9 million years ago, 3.5-billion-year-old rocks deep in the Earth's crust were forced upward along the Teton Fault into overlying sedimentary beds. The central Teton summits—between Eagles Rest Peak and Prospectors Mountain—are eroded remnants of that massive igneous batholith. As the Tetons propelled upward, what now is Jackson Hole subsided, making for a total vertical displacement of nearly 30,000 feet at the Teton Fault. Those uprooted sedimentary beds had grown to almost 5,000 feet thick after some 500 million years of deposition from intermittent seas. Today, the lower strata of that sediment makes up most of the terrain north, south and west of the high igneous peaks. Glaciers, water runoff, and other erosional agents scoured and gouged the sedimentary and igneous portions of the range into their present shape.

The east side of the Teton Range is an imposing wall of mountains, broken only by a handful of deep canyons that were carved by glaciers. Berry, Webb, Moran, Leigh, Cascade, Death and Granite canyons are the principal approaches skiers follow to the crest of the range. Each of the some two dozen major canyons and draws has its own personality, lending novel enchantment to every visit. Between the canyons lie igneous mountain massifs with as much as 7,000 feet of relief. Steep drainages—including Glacier Gulch, Stewart Draw, and Garnet and Hanging canyons—offer skiers access to these massifs, with their classic couloirs and faces. Adventurers make technical ski descents from summits of the Grand Teton, Middle Teton, South Teton, Mount Owen, and Mount Moran. Continuously steep, sparse forests comprise the few thousand feet at the eastern base of each massif, creating a 40-mile-long skiers' playground.

In the north, Berry, Owl, and Webb canyons slice through the Owl and Ranger peak massifs to the expansive plateaus and rolling peaks of the Teton Crest. To the south, the Teton Pass Highway and the Jackson Hole Aerial Tram whisk skiers to fantastic terrain, including the bowls of Mount Glory and the chutes of Cody Peak. Long, gentle plateaus or ridges, split by parallel glacial valleys, distinguish the west side of the range. On ridgetops, such as Dry Ridge, Hovermale Ridge and Fox Creek Pinnacle, continuous downhill schusses—up to 12 miles long—lead west into Teton Valley. The north and south sides of the plateaus supply skiers with sustained, steep, wide-open and forested slopes. The eastern ends of the plateaus terminate abruptly at huge cliffs, gouged vertical by east-flowing glaciers; skiable passages through these cliffs are few and far between. Deep, light powder and great terrain on Beard, Fred's, Peaked, Fossil, and Housetop mountains bring distinction to the west side of the Tetons.

In the northwestern Tetons, ancient volcanic flows from Yellowstone widen the range, stretching approaches to the rugged crest to more than 15 miles. A complex delta of steep canyons drains the massive mountain front between Survey Peak and Dry Ridge Mountain. Sparse, high ridges, including Hominy Peak, Young's Point, Carrot Ridge and Rammel Mountain, and crest points such as Glacier Peak, Red Mountain and Peak 10,360 provide seldom-visited, wide-open, moderate ski terrain.

The diversity of terrain in the Tetons allures a corresponding variety of ski-mountaineering styles. The most audacious alpine and nordic skiers, snowboarders and mono-skiers accept the challenges tendered by the high peaks.

Some descents are as uncommitting as the four-hour climb and one-hour ski on the 30- to 40-degree slopes of Peak 10,552. Other expeditions, such as the Grand Teton, can involve risky technical ascents and descents and days of hauling gear and food from the valley to a basecamp. "Powder pigs" artfully choose their ski routes based solely on where they believe the best snow will be. You might find them "yoyoing" the sea of bowls near Teton Pass or braving the strenuous approaches to good snow on Beard Mountain or 25 Short. Shrewd powder pigs keep their favorite spots secret.

Another class of skiers dons 40-pound backpacks and dedicates two or more days to skiing every bowl visible from basecamp. The range is well-suited for such skiers because of the vast skiable terrain at the head of its every canyon.

Still other skiers concentrate on traverses and loops. Their primary goal is to ski through beautiful mountain country between access points. It's exhilarating to weave imaginative routes via inconspicuous passages of otherwise unskiable terrain; a few nice powder turns along the way are the icing on the cake. These tours take anywhere from a half day to more than 10 days.

Yet another class of skiers simply seeks out short, safe and uncommitting tours in and out of canyons and touring areas. Richard DuMais' book, *50 Ski Tours In Jackson Hole and Yellowstone*, offers in-depth descriptions of the most popular tours.

Teton Pass ski routes south of Wyoming Highway 22 are not described in this book. The topography, though excellent for skiing, is relatively uncomplicated. You need little more than a map, basic knowledge of mountain safety and avalanche awareness, and a good eye for ski terrain to have a safe, fun time there. The rolling, forested mountains in the pass region historically have been a place locals go on day trips to escape the tourist crowds and the hardpacked slopes at the ski areas.

Winter climbers often use ski equipment to simplify their trips into the mountains. Coming back down on skis is quicker than walking—and certainly more enjoyable. Likewise, some skiers and snowboarders ride up the tram and chairlifts at the Jackson Hole and Grand Targhee ski areas to enter the backcountry. When the melt-freeze cycle forms firm snow, or when long periods of stable weather allow the snowpack to consolidate, ski patrols sometimes allow skiers into terrain outside the resort boundaries. The tram supplies easy access into Granite Canyon and a myriad of slopes south to Jensen Canyon. You'll find extremely steep skiing off Cody Peak, and No Name and Rendezvous peaks. And you can access the extensive bowls of upper South Leigh and Teton canyons from the top of Grand Targhee.

Whether to allow out-of-bounds skiing at area resorts has always presented a quandary because steep, cliffy, unmarked and uncontrolled avalanche-prone terrain is readily accessible from the lifts. Those inherent dangers are exacerbated by tourists and other backcountry newcomers who lack the knowledge and experience to ascertain associated risks. Always check with ski patrols before making any plans for out-of-bounds skiing.

Whatever form of skiing suits your fancy, remember that Teton ski mountaineers have always maintained utmost respect for the natural beauty of the mountains and the oft-ruthless dangers they hold. As a result, winter travelers find pristine land and water, minimally altered by humans. This respect for nature's playground begins with ski mountaineers who enter the mountains only with precise knowledge of their abilities and the risks they will encounter. The Teton ski pioneers who have kept these ideals alive set examples for ski mountaineers of the future. In part, this book aims to document their stories of success and failure, and thus help preserve these values.

How To Use This Book

For purposes of this book, the Teton Range is defined by Teton Valley on the west, Jackson Hole on the east, Teton Pass Highway on the south and Ashton-Flagg Road on the north. The range is divided into 15 subregions, beginning with the Northern Range and progressing down the east side of the Tetons to the Mount Glory Region, then south along the west side of the range, from Rammel Mountain Massif to the Game Creek Region. Each chapter head names the most prominent geographical feature that the chapter describes. Brief chapter introductions describe skiing "suitability" and delineate the perimeter via geographical features such as access roads, valleys, and ridges not commonly breached by day skiers. Touring routes that link regions are highlighted in the text and are referenced on all pertinent maps.

Guide information is divided into three categories: approaches, peaks and bowls, and high routes. Approaches are listed from north to south and include access roads, canyons, and routes that provide entry to skiing areas. Peaks-and-bowls sections describe downhill ski routes, organized from north to south and from valley to crest. Ski routes may be on named or unnamed peaks, or ridges and faces not associated with any genuine peak. Unnamed mountain summits are identified by elevation. If they protrude more than 200 feet from all adjacent saddles, the elevation is preceded by the word "Peak," while others are preceded by the word "Point."

Ski routes off peaks known to have been skied at least once include a description, as well as a history, where available. These routes are listed in order around the mountain. For east-side peaks, routes are listed from east to northeast; for west-side peaks, they go from west to northwest. Routes not known to have been skied before are listed as potential routes.

The high-routes category describes segments of tours between two points within that region or adjoining another region.

Items labeled on maps are referenced in subsequent text. To get information about a particular route or peak, look up the feature in the index or find it on the appropriate map. Route descriptions aim to provide skiers with enough information to minimize senseless errors but still enhance adventure. Route descriptions include earliest-known descent parties and the dates of their excursions. The label "first descent" is not used, however, because there is no way to be certain of this fact in most cases. Instead, designations used are: early fixed-heel, early free-heel, and early snowboard.

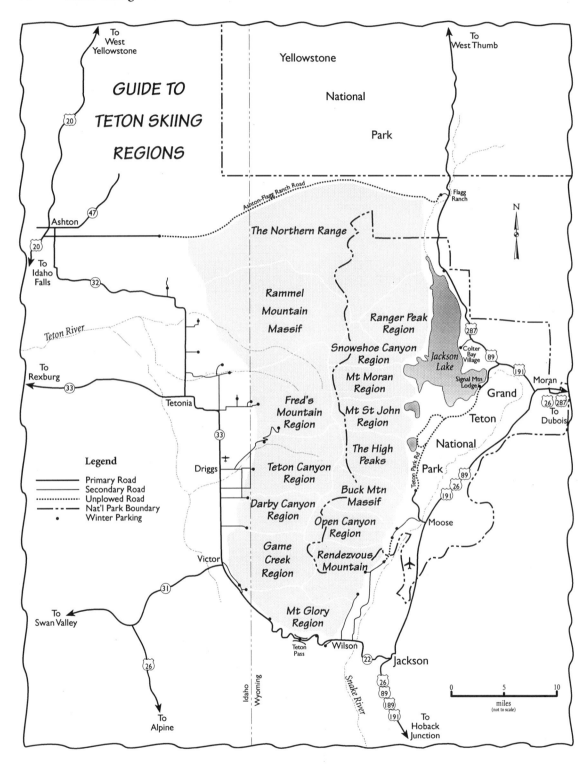

GUIDE TO
TETON SKIING
REGIONS

To
West
Yellowstone

Yellowstone

National

Park

To
West Thumb

Ashton

To Idaho
Falls

Ashton-Flagg Ranch Road

Flagg
Ranch

The Northern Range

N

Teton River

Rammel
Mountain
Massif

Ranger Peak
Region

Snowshoe Canyon
Region

Jackson
Lake

Colter
Bay
Village

To
Rexburg

Tetonia

Mt Moran
Region

Signal Mtn
Lodge

Grand

Moran

Mt St John
Region

To
Dubois

Fred's
Mountain
Region

Teton

Driggs

Teton Canyon
Region

The High
Peaks

National

Park

Teton Park Rd

Legend

Primary Road
Secondary Road
Unplowed Road
Nat'l Park Boundary
Winter Parking

Darby Canyon
Region

Buck Mtn
Massif

Open Canyon
Region

Moose

Victor

Game
Creek
Region

Rendezvous
Mountain

To
Swan Valley

Mt Glory
Region

Teton
Pass

Wilson

Jackson

Idaho

Wyoming

Snake River

To
Alpine

To
Hoback
Junction

0   5   10

miles
(not to scale)

Day-to-day changes in conditions of snowpack, weather, lake ice, river channels and topography can alter certain routes. Please send any corrections or additional route information to the author at P.O. Box 1504, Jackson, WY 83001.

SKIER GRADE SYSTEM

The following grade structure is a modified version of an ever-evolving system developed by Bill Briggs in 1967 for use at the Snow King Ski Area in the Great American Ski School. Each letter grade stands for a level of skill, ability, form, and responsibility. The author added a fifth element—avalanche awareness—because of its significance in ski mountaineering.

Ski routes listed in this book are accompanied by letter grades to help readers and potential ski mountaineers find ski outings to match their abilities. Skiers should assign themselves a grade only after meeting conditions within all five elements of that and the preceding grades.

"Skills" are precise skiing maneuvers, such as wedges or carves. At minimum, skiers must execute the required skills with balance; speed and finesse come later. If a ski route is rated {D}, for example, skiers must be proficient with skills of "checking and carving stem christies" to handle the rated terrain.

"Ability" is the degree of familiarity and quickness with which a skier executes a skill. On a {D} rated route, for example, skiers should be able to "check and carve stem christies" with proficiency on a 10- to 21-degree slope for at least 100 vertical feet. A classic paradox is a dauntless 6-year-old taking {B} snowplow turns down a {G} black-diamond slope.

"Form" is the level of efficiency skiers achieve while executing a skill. Skiers without "square shoulders to the direction of travel" may not ski a {D} slope as comfortably and effortlessly as skiers who have the appropriate form. Long {B} and {C} canyon descents and {E} east-front fault scarps become an ordeal without appropriate form.

"Responsibility" is a broad element that measures skiers' level of participation in the pursuit of ski mountaineering. How much knowledge and experience have they amassed? How much control do they have over theirs and others' circumstances? How much chaos can they manage comfortably? Are these skiers capable of protecting their partners or guiding others safely? Matching responsibility levels with ski routes is quite simply the most important decision ski mountaineers make.

"Avalanche awareness" measures familiarity with principles of snow science, avalanche physics and rescue. A very safe skier is one who has {I} avalanche awareness but only {E} skills and ability, particularly because most dangerous avalanches occur on {E} level, moderately angled slopes. A very dangerous and frighteningly common scenario is a skier with {I} skills and ability, and only {E} avalanche awareness. Certainly during the course of their adventures, skiers will encounter a volatile avalanche situation. It is to be hoped that they have at least {D} responsibility to realize that they need more intensive avalanche training.

Class K: Kindergarten
Skills: Walk, herringbone, diagonal techniques. *Ability*: Zero to three degrees. *Form*: Looking ahead to estimate effort needed. *Responsibility*: Overcoming doubt about being a skier. *Avalanche Awareness*: None.

Class A: First Timer
Skills: Sidestep, traverse, fall safely, straight run, wedge. *Ability*: One to six degrees. *Form*: Ankling forward to keep up with skis. *Responsibility*: Overcoming liability of letting skis run. *Avalanche Awareness*: Mild interest.

Class B: Beginner
Skills: Kick-turn, wedge traverse and turns. *Ability*: Three to 10 degrees. *Form*: Flexing knees to adjust edging. *Responsibility*: Overcoming uncertainty as a skier by acquiring control of speed and direction; following rules. *Avalanche Awareness*: Interested, but not knowledgeable.

Class C: Novice
Skills: Schuss, sideslip, steer skids. *Ability*: Six to 15

degrees. *Form*: Hip angulating inside to push skis sideways. *Responsibility*: Overcoming danger of solo experimentation; assuming authority for self, eclectic. *Avalanche Awareness*: Basic knowledge, limited experience.

Class D: Average

Skills: Skate step, backslip, checked and carved stem christy. *Ability*: 10 to 21 degrees. *Form*: Squaring shoulders to direction of travel. *Responsibility*: Overcoming lack of knowledge about skiing and mountaineering. *Avalanche Awareness*: Interested in learning more.

Class E: Advanced

Skills: Steered, hopped, and rebounded parallel turns. *Ability*: Skis comfortably on wide slopes between 15 and 27 degrees. *Form*: Static poising, body mass moving quietly. *Responsibility*: Stability as a skier and climber; self-determined. *Avalanche Awareness*: Solid grasp of principles, some experience.

Class F: Expert

Skills: Checked and carved parallels, shortswing. *Ability*: Skis comfortably on narrow slopes between 21 and 36 degrees with a safe runout. *Form*: Immediate readiness for next turn. *Responsibility*: Overcoming tendency to dominate others, seeking cooperation; ski instructor. *Avalanche Awareness*: Veteran of avalanche practice.

Class G: Racer

Skills: Controlling linked accelerated turns. *Ability*: Enjoys skiing 27- to 45-degree slopes of any width in most snow conditions; slopes may end in cliffs; mountaineering knowledge required. *Form*: Up motions replaced with moving skis forward, head level. *Responsibility*: Learning how to encourage and govern self determinism in others; becoming pan-determined; backcountry ski guide. *Avalanche Awareness*: Instructor of avalanche awareness.

Class H: Mountaineer

Skills: Absorbing terrain during and between turns.

Ability: Seeks 36- to 55-degree terrain of any width and any snow condition; expects jumps and/or rappels over unskiable sections; has advanced mountaineering skills. *Form*: Instant recovery, minimum reaction time. *Responsibility*: Overcoming others' resistance to empowering others; inspiring pan-determinism; skiing and climbing new routes under or at state of art; mountain guide. *Avalanche Awareness*: Snow scientist; able to use Scientific Method.

Class I: Extreme Skier

Skills: Sustaining recoveries during and when linking turns. *Ability*: Seeks any and all terrain and snow conditions of 45 degrees and steeper. *Form*: Linked recovery; sustained maximum effort. *Responsibility*: Overcoming back-off tendency by calculating risks; pioneering with reason, not luck; pervading physical, mental, and spiritual realms to obtain knowledge of situation; skiing and climbing new routes over state of art. *Avalanche Awareness*: Ph.D. in snow and avalanche science.

MOUNTAINEERING SKILLS

Difficulty ratings for rock, snow, and ice climbing have not been included in this book's descriptions of ski routes. Nonetheless, nearly all of the routes described absolutely require some degree of technical skill. These skills might be as simple as precise ski waxing, kicking steps on snow, and self-arrest, or as gear-intensive and physically and mentally taxing as extreme mixed and aid climbing. Training in mountaineering is beyond the scope of this book. Aspirants should enroll in a training program and study books about the subject.

For complete descriptions and grades of Teton climbing routes, consult Ortenburger and Jackson's *A Climbers' Guide to the Teton Range*.

TETON SKIING GUIDE

As skiing in the Tetons can be extremely dangerous, it is important that you learn as much as possible about your route and its terrain before embarking on a ski tour. Using this guide will help you learn to observe, evaluate, plan and execute successful Teton ski-mountaineering endeavors.

The goal of information preparedness is to instill in skiers confidence in their time estimates and in their ability to handle whatever surprises Mother Nature might have in store.

Most important, skiers must know their limits and not take on more than they are certain they can handle. Successful Teton ski pioneers bite off little pieces of adventure at a time, growing their confidence gradually and learning from their experience and that of others.

This guide book is not intended for field use, but it certainly can help you plan your trips—or pass away a storm while in your tent. Use this guide to locate popular bowls north of Teton Pass, on the west slope, and in Grand Teton National Park. If you're tired of the same old runs, research areas you're not familiar with. This book unveils the riches of the lesser-known treasures of this vast range.

This book is different from other guides in that it ranks specific features of the range for "skiability." By leaving it up to readers to put the pieces together and produce their own personalized tours or descents, fewer inexperienced or unprepared skiers will be influenced to enter the range.

Tour accounts from past skiing parties are included in the history chapter and, when appropriate, with route descriptions. The purposes of these stories are to help aspiring ski mountaineers design their excursions competently, to prepare them for the rigors of the Tetons in winter, and to perpetuate the traditions and values of responsible ski pioneers.

All skiers who dare to venture into the Tetons must know and be able to apply the legion of techniques involved in ski mountaineering, mountain climbing, winter survival, orienteering, emergency medical care, avalanche-hazard evaluation and rescue. Reading this book will not teach these techniques; rather, skiers should seek instruction from qualified institutions.

Contact one of the mountain-guiding services in the Teton area for assistance and, before heading out, call the Bridger-Teton National Forest avalanche hazard and mountain weather forecast at (307)733-2664.

SAFETY FIRST

Virtually everyone who ventures into the backcountry in winter accepts potential for mishaps. And no guidebook, this one included, will keep you out of danger. Never head out unless you know what you're in for and how to handle it!

Avalanches

Avalanches represent one of the more prominent hazards you'll face during winter mountain travel. Surprisingly little slope is necessary to set off avalanches; in fact, dangerous slides have occurred in the Tetons on slopes as gentle as 15 degrees. Avalanches range from harmless sloughs to cataclysmic collapses of expansive slopes precariously clinging to the highest faces of peaks.

A variety of factors escalate avalanche danger, among them heavy snowfall, persistent strong winds, and sudden warming. Weak layers within the snowpack may result from extended periods of stable weather earlier in the winter and/or temperature gradient metamorphism (TG). Dry, incohesive snow grains result when dramatic temperature differences exist between snowpack layers. Obvious signs that avalanches are imminent include recent avalanche activity in the area, "whomping," or settling in the snowpack, and/or rotted slushy snowpack. Lee slopes and gullies between 20 degrees and 45 degrees usually represent the most suspect avalanche terrain. Of course, these are very general rules for avalanche safety; the torrents that kill most often are the ones that people don't expect.

Minimize your chances of becoming involved with avalanches by choosing the day of your outing carefully. If you venture into the backcountry during or after storms, you're asking for trouble, especially if there has been considerable snowfall and wind. Wait a few days to give the snowpack a chance to stabilize. In spring, monitor the air temperature to be certain that yesterday's slush has frozen solid. And always get off mountain slopes before they turn to mush.

To identify and forecast avalanche hazards more accurately, backcountry travelers should be versed and practiced in the principles of snow science. Decide for yourself whether or not slopes are safe; don't be coerced by others to ski what you believe are questionable slopes.

Jackson Community Education Services and the American Avalanche Institute in Wilson, WY administer avalanche-awareness classes, and the National Forest Service and Jackson Hole Ski Patrol Avalanche Forecast Lab provide an avalanche forecast via recorded message at (307)733-2664. Grand Teton National Park climbing rangers also can give you the inside line on backcountry conditions. Take the time to get up-to-date conditions before you head into the backcountry.

Teton cornices are unusually weak because of dry snow and steep lee slopes; don't trust them at all. Ridge routes might be safe from avalanches but often are draped with huge cornices, so fragile that just walking nearby can trigger a sudden collapse. As cornices fail, they also can draw slabs of snow into the leeward abyss from the windward side of a ridge. Unfortunately, many skiers develop sufficient respect for these precarious cornices only after facing death in their tracks.

Frost-wedging, melting, rain, running water, creeping snow, or movement from other skiers or climbers can dislodge rocks and ice chunks, sending them into quick, deadly surges down-mountain. Reduce the hazard by entering these "bowling alleys" well before the morning sun warms the cliffs—and never after rainfall. Head protection is recommended in all areas exposed to rock and ice fall. Couloirs and snowfields below cliffs are high-suspect areas.

Weather also can present a major hazard in the Tetons. Blue skies can turn to storm quite suddenly, leaving unprepared skiers in distress. Driving winds, precipitation and frigid cold can sap struggling skiers' body heat—and take their desire to survive with it. Everyone who skis in the Tetons should be able to identify and care for hypothermia and frostbite. To prevent dire situations, pack clothing and camping gear for the worst conditions—no matter what the forecast anticipates.

All skiers who take on routes that involve glaciers must understand proper rope-team travel and crevasse rescue techniques. The Teton, Middle Teton, Falling Ice, and Triple glaciers all are crevassed. Serac collapse also is possible, especially on the Teton and Falling Ice glaciers. Always beware of moats on all snowfields, especially during spring. Running water and sun-warmed rocks erode surrounding snow and can leave deadly hidden holes. Several Teton climbers have drowned in undersnow rivers after falling into moats.

Crossing Lakes

During a geologic period in the Tetons that ended some 9,000 years ago, large glaciers carved the deep canyons we see today. The glaciers exited the canyons and skidded across the floor of Jackson Hole, gouging deep pockets and depositing large rings of debris at their termini. Long before these glaciers melted completely, though, runoff flooded morainal basins and created seven spectacular lakes. These lakes play a major role in Teton ski mountaineering. At least 13 out of some 20 major canyons that drain into Jackson Hole are accessible to skiers only via contact with a lake. In late spring, summer, and fall, most skiers cross the lakes by canoe or motor boat. Mandatory permits, as well as copies of park boating regulations are available year-round at the Grand Teton National Park visitor centers in Moose and Colter Bay.

Do all open-water canoeing in the morning, when the lakes are calm. Strong afternoon winds kick up waves that are strong enough to dump a canoe. Be sure to wear life preservers and, if you must canoe across a lake on a windy day, try to stay near the shores.

In winter and early spring, a suspicious coat of ice covers the lakes. Understandably, many leery skiers avoid those trips to canyons and peaks that require lake-ice crossings. Nonetheless, with some education and common sense, over-lake travel can be a safe, efficient means to approach Teton canyons and peaks.

Of course, skiers can bypass all lake travel when conditions obviously are hazardous or uncertain by circumnavigating on their shores or in adjacent thick forests. Certain signs that a lake is not safe for travel include areas of open water in the middle and near the shores. In such conditions, ice would be silent and appear slushy, cracked, holey, dark, and translucent.

But what if there aren't any obvious signs of danger? How can skiers be reasonably sure that a frozen lake is safe for crossing? Read on.

Formation of Lake Ice

During autumn, the surface water of the lakes cools and becomes denser than the strata below the surface. This colder, heavier water sinks and mixes with the warmer layers below. This process, called "overturn" or "turnover," continues throughout the fall, with cold surface waters gradually mixing with the deepest strata of the lakes. By winter, the entire lake reaches uniform temperature. As its temperature approaches 36 degrees Fahrenheit, water condenses, but it becomes less dense at and below this temperature. So when the frigid December air drives the lakes' surface temperatures below 36 degrees, the cold water floats on the surface and freezes instead of sinking and mixing with the uniform column below. As soon as the first skim of ice forms on the surface, wind no longer can mix the cold water into the lake. With persistent frigid temperatures and a thin, non-insulative snow cover, a strong layer of blue ice—as thick as 20 inches—forms.

If early winter temperatures are not below zero-degrees Fahrenheit consistently, the ice doesn't grow as thick and strong, especially if there is a deep insulating snow cover. On the larger lakes, such as Jackson, Jenny, Leigh and Phelps, this blue-ice layer eventually sags and cracks under weight of a deepening snow cover. Lake water seeps up through these fissures and sits between the snow and the blue ice. The bottom section of the snow layer absorbs some of the lake water and turns to slush. This layer gradually compacts and freezes into "white ice," trapping a reservoir of the remaining water between it and the blue ice. During a cold, snowy winter, this process can occur several times, forming alternate layers of water and ice below a snowpack as deep as four feet. The layers of slush-ice are weaker than the blue ice, but with thicknesses ranging from five to 10 inches, they can support a skier.

Early-season lake skiers should wait until persistent frigid temperatures (zero-degrees Fahrenheit) form a layer of blue ice three inches to five inches thick. After that, continued heavy snowfall causes ice layering that increases overall strength and thickness of the ice pack. Crackling or grumbling noises are a promising sign that ice is growing.

During an average winter, most of the lakes in Jackson Hole are safe for travel by January 1. Most alpine lakes in the Tetons usually are safe to cross through May. Many of the highest lakes, shaded by mountains to the south and east, are covered with strong ice into July. As much as 10 feet of blue ice forms on these lakes during a cold winter. Use caution near the shores, inlets and outlets, especially in spring and fall.

Anomalies in Lake Ice

The most hazardous times to venture onto the frozen lakes in the Teton Range are in early winter, when the ice begins to form, and in mid- to late spring, when ice is weakened by warm temperatures and runoff. But lake ice holds surprises for unsuspecting skiers throughout winter. Following are some of the hazards that skiers should expect:

• In fall and early winter, ice forms slower and thinner over deeper water than it does over the shallows. Strong wind can "bulldoze" this weak ice and stack it into small jumbled piles against the sounder ice closer to shore. This creates "drift ice," which has inconsistent areas that you should avoid. Drift ice commonly is observed a mile west of Colter Bay.

• During winter nights, when air temperatures drop 30 degrees to 40 degrees below zero, ice contracts and cracks in isolated areas. Lake water then spews to the surface, turning snow cover to slush. It is unlikely that skiers would break through the underlying blue ice layer, but these wet areas will make your skis ice up and collect snow, making the lake crossing miserable, if not impossible. Generally, you can skirt these slushy areas.

• Sometimes ice will crack, but no water will spill out because of low water pressure below. Cracks range in width from hairline to three or four feet. Beware of water between the larger cracks; like a crevasse, it can be hidden by new snow.

• Long, uplifted pressure ridges are formed by mass ice movement of unknown cause and generally are safe to cross.

• During mid- to late spring, ice rots and melts at different rates, depending upon exposure to wind, sun, and water. Rotting occurs especially fast if nighttime temperatures are consistently above freezing. Surprisingly, most melting and erosion occurs on the underside of the ice. Thus, the amount of firn snow on the surface of the lake provides little indication of ice thickness.

• Open water near shores, rocks, trees and weeds is the best sign that ice is on its way out. If you must cross in these conditions, give the weak ice surrounding these melted areas a wide berth. Thin skims of ice or snowfall that accumulate at night can hide open-water areas, creating deadly booby traps.

• During warm spring afternoons, skiers might be startled by deep-pitched, amplified "droplet" noises. This is the ice expanding and contracting due to warming and usually is not an immediate sign of danger. Hairline cracks in the surface firn snow actually are cracks in the ice below. They usually refreeze instantly and are safe to cross. In late spring, watch out for ice that has had standing water on its surface. Dense water bores holes downward, creating "honeycomb ice."

• In all seasons, be aware of ice that might have water currents—such as springs, inlets and outlets—running beneath it. Not only does moving water erode ice, but it hampers formation of strong ice.

Travel on Lake Ice

Taking into account the curvature of the Earth,

some might assume that the first half of a lake crossing is uphill and second half is downhill. Not true. Skiing across the frozen lakes of Jackson Hole can be among the most rewarding features of ski mountaineering in the Tetons. But it also can be harrowing, monotonous, backbreaking, and suitable only for the hardiest of skiers. Bundled with face masks and neck gaiters and caked with a white crust of frozen condensation, skiers battle extreme cold and humidity as they skate or kick and glide across endless flats of white, often amid a thick blanket of fog. Without a compass, skiers could travel in circles for hours. Snowmobile and snowplane tracks provide nice packed paths to follow, but they often lead undetectably in circles.

Ski crossings of the widest stretches of Jackson Lake may take from as little as an hour to as much as a full day if skiers are breaking trail with full packs. Using oversnow vehicles or dogsleds can reduce that time drastically but also can be more hazardous and lead to more hassles. Always look ahead for obstacles such as ice crevasses, spring holes, pressure ridges and slush ponds.

Skiers risking lake crossings should be prepared for accidents. Before each crossing, check ice strength and thickness by drilling several test holes or probing with a basketless ski pole or ice-axe spike. Wear insulated clothing under shell outer garments to trap warm air next to your body—just in case you plunge through the ice. Although weight-distributing effects of skis drastically reduce the chance of breaking through, skiers should unfasten ski-retention straps and loosen bindings before crossing a lake so that they can remove their skis in water, if necessary.

Lying flat on their stomachs in a spread-eagle position a safe distance from the hole, rescuers can extend a ski pole or stick to a victim. Once on the ice, victims should roll away from the hole to safe ice or shore. Rescuers should know how to treat victims for hypothermia and shock. Because lake-ice conditions can change so quickly, skiers should always check with local guides and park rangers for the latest conditions before heading out. Colter Bay rangers and climbing rangers at Moose travel on the lakes often and are very helpful in providing up-to-date information.

Human Hazards

Despite aforementioned hazards, most accidents are attributable to human error. Fatigue, lack of experience, poor judgment and alternative motives incite uneducated decision-making. The most common accidents attributed to human error are falls. After slipping on snow or ice, climbers or skiers can take horrifying, uncontrolled slides for thousands of feet. At least two skiers and numerous climbers have been killed or injured this way in the Teton Range. Competent skiing, climbing and self-arrest techniques and proficient use of ropes and anchors are prerequisites for travel in steep areas.

Group travel is limited by the ability and contentment of the party's weakest or most conservative member. Choose trustworthy and knowledgeable ski partners with similar abilities and risk acceptance. Good communication is key to group dynamics. Solo travel is discouraged.

To avoid exhaustion or unplanned nighttime travel, allow plenty of time for tours or descents. Poor planning often leaves freezing skiers groveling in the dark with little energy to escape from the mountains. Many ski mountaineers who party until midnight on the eves of big tours or descents can't figure out why they're moving so slowly the next day. Our bodies and minds need plenty of rest to perform with the endurance and adroitness needed for mountain treks. Marijuana, alcohol, caffeine, nicotine and other drugs inhibit mental and physical function. Eating large meals late the night before a trip can lead to a sleepless night and a nauseating alpine start.

In the Tetons, most tours and descents take one long day. To have a safe, enjoyable trip or meet a high objective, get an early start. If you're not willing to rise before dawn—between midnight and 6 a.m.—don't plan on being successful in your Teton ski-mountaineering endeavors.

Be sure to drink plenty of water the night before

your trip into the backcountry; pre-hydration is important for perspiration compensation and blood circulation. Other things you'll need to do the night before your tour include: lay out your clothes for the following day; fill water bottles; pack your backpack; have your headlamp handy; warm your boots; load your skis and poles; fuel and shuttle vehicles; and notify friends of your tour plans. In the morning, allot at least a half hour to rise, dress and eat a small snack. Allow a half hour to a full hour to meet a partner and drive to the park from Jackson. Add an extra 10 minutes to make final adjustments at the trailhead. In addition to packing full bottles of water for your trip, drink water in the car on your way to and from the trailhead.

Late in the day, deep, wet snow can make ski travel miserable and dangerous, so schedule things so that you are finished skiing before the sun warms the snowpack thoroughly. Starting and finishing early also will help you avoid late-developing avalanche danger due to wind-loading or heavy snowfall.

To schedule your day, work backward from the desired completion time, assigning intervals to each of the day's activities. For example, on a typical spring ski descent of Albright Peak, a 9 a.m. start from the summit usually offers a safe trip, with high-quality snow. So plan to arrive at the top at 8:30 a.m. The ascent from the Moose-Wilson Road takes about four hours, so reach the parking area at 3:50 a.m., including the 10 extra minutes at for last-minute adjustments at trailhead. Assuming nobody forgets their ski poles, you should be safe leaving Jackson at 3:20 a.m. If you include another half hour for home activities, you should set the alarm clock for 2:50 a.m.

For many, the glamour, adventure and excitement of ski mountaineering is irresistible. But success and survival in the game depend largely on individual skiers. Each time you go on a tour or descent, you'll learn more about how to make your trips efficient and trouble-free. Be conservative when making tough decisions—especially if you're traveling alone. If you're immobilized by an injury, it may take days before a rescue team arrives—if it arrives at all.

Your ski party must be practiced in emergency medical care and must act as a self-contained rescue team. Resort to the aid of National Park Service climbing rangers and the Teton County, Idaho and Wyoming sherrifs' departments only if you have no other choice. Expect to reimburse the park and the county in full for expenses of any rescue assistance required. Macho egos and inflated images of abilities and experience are the worst harbingers of disaster. Know the limits of your skill. Learn to feel when you're losing control. And ski with partners who know what they're doing too. Good luck.

NPS WINTER POLICY

National Park Service regulations regarding backcountry travel and overnight camping change from time to time, so get updates at the GTNP Visitor Center in Moose before venturing out. Campfires are strictly prohibited in the backcountry.

TETON WILDLIFE

Abundant wildlife is a special treasure of the Teton area. For ski mountaineers, the sight of a moose or an ermine adds vitality and variety to an otherwise motionless mountainscape. But these encounters with foraging natives should remind us that we are mere visitors to the vast Teton wilderness, and we must not disturb the delicate ecological balance that exists there.

Winter is a difficult time for many animals to survive; the highest mortality for large creatures, such as deer, moose, elk, and bighorn sheep, occurs in March and April. To conserve energy, they reduce their activity to a minimum. Human disturbance taxes their energy reserves and reduces their chances for survival. Skiers and snowmobiles elicit a locomotor response in mule deer at distances of 600 feet and 400 feet, respectively.

Dogs cause even greater distress to wild animals; dogs are permitted on Grand Teton National Park highways that are open to snowmobiles but must be leashed or in harness at all times. Dogs are prohibited in all other areas of the park. Skiers can improve the ungulates' chances for survival by avoiding close contact with them. If a chance meeting occurs, don't stop; observe the animal while moving away at a constant rate.

Wild animals also can present danger to backcountry skiers and climbers. Bear and moose might seem docile, but might attack if provoked. Black bear and moose inhabit the entire range, and it's not uncommon to encounter grizzlies in the north end of the range. In recent years, more and more grizzlies have been spotted in the south and central range as well. View these wild animals only from a distance of more than 100 yards. If a close encounter occurs, try not to disturb the animal, and leave the scene immediately. But do not run! Be especially discreet if you come upon bear cubs. Black-bear attacks are rare; their charges usually are bluffs. If a grizzly should attack, history seems to indicate that playing dead often is the best course of action. Most grizzly charges represent an effort to protect young or food. Nonetheless, there are cases in which bears see humans themselves as food sources. Moose charge unpredictably; if one comes at you, try to hide behind a tree or boulder, or use your ski poles to discourage the animal.

Other common wildlife in the Teton region include porcupine, coyote, antelope, beaver, badger, eagle, osprey, falcon, snowshoe hare, and pine marten. The National Park Service continually revises its winter wildlife policies and closures based on wildlife needs. Check with the U.S. Forest Service and National Park Service for current closures of sensitive wildlife-wintering zones.

SKI SEASON

Skiers have managed to find enough snow in the Tetons to sate their fancy during every month of the year. In fact, August and September are the only months that have little appeal to skiers. Late September and October storms usually supply enough snow to pave the way for skiing on Teton Pass by late October. Skiers must, however, exercise extreme caution to avoid stumps, deadfall and rocks that could bring a disastrous early end to their ski season.

Grand Targhee Resort in Alta, WY often opens as early as late October, while Jackson Hole Ski Area usually opens during the first or second week of December. Substantial snowfall and settlement are necessary to cover the irregular terrain and rugged boulder fields for skiing. In the most disappointing seasons, only the summer groomed and graded runs open for skiing.

Most early season snow accumulates in November, bringing excellent powder skiing to Teton Pass. Skiing over thick canyon-bottom underbrush is feasible by Christmas. Typically, weather gets drier and colder throughout December until mid-January, when moisture and higher winds move in. If the early part of the season is especially dry, weak snow layers can linger throughout winter, threatening an avalanche of the entire winter snowpack.

A mid-winter thaw usually occurs in late January or February. Statistically, the heaviest snowfall happens in January, though the same month sees its share of frigid weather too. February continues to offer loads of snow, and temperatures warm slightly; March is warmer still, with continuing heavy snows. Sun crust forms quickly on south slopes, whereas north faces hold stable powder for weeks.

Corn skiing off lower peaks usually begins in mid-April, when intermittent storms provide some of the best and safest powder skiing of the year. Excellent touring conditions prevail throughout April and May and into early June. The best time for tours such as the Teton Crest is late April to mid-May.

The south and east faces of the highest peaks do not come into skiing shape until late May and early June. In 1993, the Grand Teton offered excellent skiing conditions throughout July! The north faces of these peaks typically come into condition in late June and early July. Unfortunately, skiers have to hike on dirt higher and higher as spring turns to summer.

No two days of skiing in the Tetons are the same.

Subtle changes in the weather can transform yesterday's ice slope into today's knee-deep powder. With frigid temperatures, wet powder can metamorphose into dry surface hoar frost overnight. The following charts represent average monthly snowfall and snow depths at 8,100 feet and 9,600 feet at the Jackson Hole Ski Area:

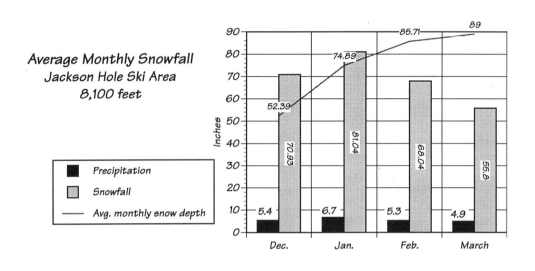

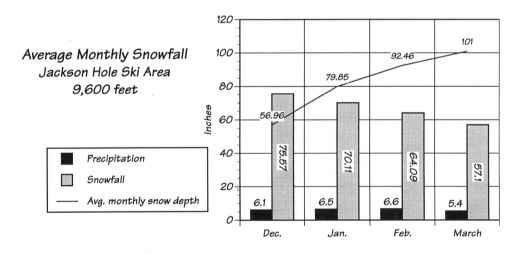

Data courtesy of the Bridger-Teton National Forest lab.

PACKING PROPER EQUIPMENT

The harsh weather and terrain in the Tetons place more demands on skiers' and snowboarders' equipment than does most any other setting. Equipment needs vary depending upon the weather, season and type of terrain you're tackling.

Following is a list of gear appropriate and necessary for the most technical of Teton excursions during a normal winter. Retail shops in the region offer full lines of backcountry equipment for sale or rental.

Recommended Equipment List

Ski Gear: Metal-edged skis or snowboard with bindings; double boots; telescoping avalanche probe poles; binding adapters; avalanche rescue beacon; shovel; climbing skins; waxes, cork, and scraper; and ski crampons.

Repair Kit: Two hose clamps; five-inch length of split ski pole; spare binding parts; duct tape; wire; wire cutters; knife; screwdrivers; flathead wrench; mini vise-grips; pliers; sewing kit; spare stove parts; tent patch kit; and spare ski tip.

Medical supplies: Moleskin; scissors; antiseptic; sterile adhesive strips; sterile gauze pads; adhesive tape; triangular bandages; Sams splint; pain killer; exothermic hand warmers; and tweezers.

Clothing and footwear: Wool or synthetic socks; vapor barrier sock liners; gaiters; thin wool or synthetic gloves; thick insulative mittens; durable waterproof mitten shells; one or two sets synthetic long underwear; durable waterproof breathable pants; thick wool or synthetic upper; durable waterproof breathable shell; wool or synthetic hat; balaclava; neck gaiter; and brim cap.

Climbing equipment: Helmet; harness; rope; hardware; slings; ice axe; ice hammer; crampons; and a backpack that will take skis.

Camping gear: Tent or bivy sac; down or synthetic sleeping bag; long thermal sleeping pad; stove with snow support; fuel; pans, bowls, utensils; lighters and waterproof matches; and a snow saw.

Miscellaneous: Wrist watch; alarm clock; barometer; altimeter; sunglasses; sunscreen; lip balm; water bottle; water-purification means; headlamp; batteries; topo maps; and a compass.

The importance of using adequate equipment cannot be overstated; it can make or break your chances of success in the backcountry. Take it seriously.

SKIERS AND SNOWMOBILES

In the early 1930s, Slim Lawrence of Jackson Hole made one of the first snowmobiles in the country; in 1938, Stan Seaton of Moran made one of the first snowplanes. Ice fishermen used these oversnow vehicles on Jackson Lake throughout the 1940s, 50s, and 60s. But it wasn't until the late 1960s that recreational snowmobiling became popular. The powered snow rigs were a blessing for those who did not ski because the machines allowed them to access the winter backcountry to take pictures and play in the snow.

Throughout the 1970s and early 80s, snowmobilers ran free in much of the Teton backcountry, until much of the west slope was designated an official wilderness area in 1984. Angered by this intrusion on their freedom, snowmobilers continued to "poach" the Jedediah Smith Wilderness, creating friction between themselves and the Park Service and Forest Service. The Park Service has resorted to using helicopters to patrol the wilderness—unfortunately, an equally disturbing nuisance. With continued patrol, however, wilderness "poaching" by snowmobilers inevitably will cease, and skiers will find fewer tracks both in the wilderness areas and in the lower non-wilderness regions.

Snowmobiles have both positive and negative attributes. On the down side, snowmobiles destroy the aesthetic value of the wilderness environment. The piercing rip of a snowmobile or snowplane engine can fetter the search for peace and quiet. And even in tranquility, skiers' enthusiasm can be paralyzed when they arrive in a meadow, cirque or lake flat that is riddled with snowmobile or snowplane tracks.

Skiers seeking a wilderness experience that is

unadultered by snowmobiles should avoid certain west-side canyons and plateaus, east-side flats, and Jackson Lake. The primary snowmobile thoroughfares on the west side are Spring Gulch, Teton Canyon, North Leigh Creek, Dry Ridge, Rammel Mountain Road, and the Ashton-Flagg Road. Less-popular areas include South Leigh Creek, Fox Creek Pinnacle Jeep Trail, Fox Creek North and South ramps, and Mud Lake Road. On the east side, traffic thoroughfares include Grassy Lake Road, Jackson Lake, Moose-Wilson Road, Jenny Lake Loop Road, Teton Park Road, and Ski Lake Trail. Jackson Lake has a snowmobile "road" system to make motorists feel safer following others' tracks. In season, you almost always can find a web of snowmobile tracks on Jackson Lake and in west-side cirques and flats, such as South Badger Creek, Green Lakes basin and Lake Valley.

At the same time that their tracks and noise may be a nuisance to some, snowmobiles also offer great advantages for ski mountaineers. Skiers can access peaks and canyons on the west side of Jackson Lake quickly with a snowmobile or snowplane and some skijoring rope. (Check with the Park Service for current policies.) If Moran Bay is your destination, oversnow vehicles could cut your one-and-a-half- to eight-hour ski crossing from Colter Bay down to a half hour. A snowmobile also can speed up access to Jenny and String lakes from Taggart Lake Trailhead. And endless slogs up west-side canyons and ridges would be eliminated during approaches to above treeline areas. In deciding whether to use oversnow vehicles, weigh convenience against ethics of self-sufficiency and wilderness preservation.

Dogsledding and doggie skijoring offer yet other alternatives to help skiers access the mountains. In April of 1984, Peter Koedt and Richard Charlesworth became some of the first modern backcountry skiers to use a dogsled assist during their tour up Moran Canyon, out Leigh Canyon to Cottonwood Creek. Keith Benefiel is the reputed master of doggie skijoring. (Check with the National Park Service for current dogsledding regulations.)

For ski mountaineers who refuse or are unable to enter the mountains with any tools besides their own will, strength, and endurance, snowmobiles still present one advantage: Packed tracks save skiers miles of trail breaking through sometimes bottomless snow. Not only do the tracks save hours or days of back-breaking work, they also allow skiers to conserve mental and physical energy normally spent on route-finding. Be careful though, snowmobile tracks sometimes can lead in circles.

Skiers usually will find packed snowmobile tracks to follow on Jackson Lake, east-side roads, and the lower sections of all major west-side canyons, except Game Creek and South Badger Creek. The wilderness boundary generally skirts the base of the steep sections of the ridges and canyons, restricting snowmobile traffic to the relatively flat areas, where skiers need packed trails the most. Descending skiers especially benefit from packed tracks on Dry Ridge, Hovermale Ridge, and Fox Creek Pinnacle.

To preserve wildlife habitat and wilderness in the Tetons, the Wyoming and Idaho parks and recreation departments, the U.S. Forest Service, and the National Park Service regulate snowmobiling. State registration, plates, and an annual fee permit are required to operate oversnow vehicles in Grand Teton National Park. Registration and plates are available for a fee at the Jackson-Teton County, Wyoming Parks and Recreation Office in Jackson. Annual park permits are available at Park Service headquarters in Moose. In the Targhee and Bridger-Teton national forests, the Forest Service simply requires that snowmobile have state registration. For most snowmobiling on the west side of the Tetons, Idaho state registration is required, in addition to Wyoming state registration. Exceptions include Rapid Creek Jeep Trail, Spring Gulch, Teton Canyon, South Leigh Creek, and North Leigh Creek, which are completely in Wyoming. Idaho residents may buy their registration at the Teton County, Idaho assessor's office or from any of several other vendors in the area.

Non-residents who plan to do considerable

snowmobiling in Idaho must buy a temporary registration at the Idaho State Parks and Recreation office in Idaho Falls.

Wyoming residents who plan to snowmobile in Idaho for just one or two days simply must tape their Wyoming registration slips inside the drivers' side of the windshields of their parked vehicles so that it is clearly visible to authorities.

Snowmobiling is prohibited in the mountainous areas of Grand Teton National Park and in the Jedediah Smith Wilderness. Get current snowmobile regulations and travel maps from the national forest offices and from Park Service headquarters.

LAND MANAGEMENT

As you plan your ski-mountaineering excursions, always keep in mind that Jackson Hole and Teton Valley are a mosaic of private, BLM, wilderness, national-forest and national-park lands. Respect government regulations and private citizens' land-use needs so that access privileges remain intact.

A
HISTORICAL
PERSPECTIVE

In 1806, John Colter left the Lewis and Clark Expedition above the Mandan villages along the Missouri. A year later, in November, 1807, he set off on foot from Lisa's fort for an eight-month journey through what is now Jackson Hole, Teton Valley, and Yellowstone. Not only did he take on unexplored ground in the dead of winter, but he did so alone. And though the specifics of his exploit are not well-documented, Colter's escapade certainly embodies the spirit of adventure that has driven Teton explorers through the years.

As long as climbers have braved the Teton Range, so too have skiers. In fact, some of the earliest Teton explorations were made in winter. To simplify their jaunts into snowy Teton canyon mouths, fur trappers and explorers procured snowshoes from Indians, who fabricated round webs for deep snow and long ski-like shoes for moving quickly across firmer snow. The term "snow shoes," as written in journals of 1800s frontiersmen, referred both to webs and skis, so we cannot be certain who the first genuine Teton skiers were. Nonetheless, we can be certain that the adventures of the early explorers, trappers and homesteaders were at least as rigorous and unpredictable as Teton ski mountaineering is today.

Skis As Tools

Passionate for isolation and adventure, fur trappers of the late 1800s were the first white men to endure bitter winters in the Teton region. Webs and long, heavy wooden skis were their sole tools of escape from the blues of cabin fever to the fortune of burgeoning traps. Skis were whittled from split lodgepole pine, and the tips bowed after a few days in a scalding wood-stove reservoir. Leather straps nailed to the sides of the skis in an arc functioned as bindings.

Skis served various purposes for early pioneers.

Fred Brown, the grandfather of Teton skiing, was one of the first to have the tools, strength, smarts and desire to explore the mountains safely on skis. Here, he and Reddy Muller reach Sunset Pass in 1941.

By 1890, Jackson Hole and Teton Valley were year-round communities, from which correspondence to the outside world was difficult. Before it would establish mail delivery to the valley, the U.S. Postal Service required that residents prove its feasibility by carrying their own mail on schedule for a year. Volunteer petitioners took turns skiing the mail back and forth over Teton Pass—with great success. In 1892, the Postal Service established the Marysvale Post Office north of Jackson and hired locals to make deliveries.

Mail carriers had to be brave and strong to ski all day through the harsh weather and avalanche terrain between Jackson Hole and Teton Valley. They stopped to rest, eat and drink in a small snow cabin at the top of Teton Pass. With elk tallow and pine pitch for wax and elk hair for climbing skins, Frank Peterson was one of the first over-the-pass mail carriers, and thus one of the first Teton skiers. But from Jackson Hole's growing population of the late 1800s grew a demand for year-round food and supply delivery, and the era of mail skiers gradually gave way to freighting.

Down in the valleys, roads were not plowed regularly for automobile use until the mid-1930s. Most people mainly trusted dog sleds, gandy wagons, and skis to accomplish their winter business. Others simply played it safe: Rather than risk freezing to death in a blizzard or deep snow, many early residents tolerated six months of cabin fever by reading and working on indoor projects.

But a few stalwart individuals refused to let harsh weather stop them; they kicked and glided miles across Jackson Hole and Teton Valley, conducting business as usual, regardless of the season. They used pine, ash, or hickory skis, seven to eight feet long and three to five inches wide. Some used leather strap bindings and others used "housings"—heavy leather boots built onto the skis—and canvas gaiters tied below the knees. Heavy wool socks and elk-hide moccasins helped protect them from the cold, and they used a sapling as a single ski pole.

Throughout the early 1900s, Rudolph "Rosy" Rosencrans—Austrian native, forest ranger and map maker—honed what he proclaimed was the fastest cross-country technique in the valley, and he skied often into Jackson from his home in Moran. On one occasion, he skied nonstop for 27 hours—covering 82 miles—to rescue cattle stranded in deep snow in the upper Green River Valley.

Beginning at age 16, Bob Kranenberg skied the 22-mile round trip from his winter home at the Square G Ranch to Moose twice a week. Occasionally, he skied to Jackson for a couple of days to get mail and attend community meetings and dances. Though he frequently had to break trail on this trip, he sometimes could follow sleigh tracks. Now and then, he was even lucky enough to hitch a ride on a sleigh.

During the 1930s, James "Jimmy" Braman of Moran spent eight consecutive days of each winter month—skiing 12 or 13 miles per day—recording snow depths between Moran and South Gate and in Yellowstone. Braman was superintendent of the Jackson Lake Dam and worked for the Bureau of Reclamation. Fellow Bureau of Reclamation workers Bennett Hill and Glenn Simmons continued the recording work through the late 1930s and 40s, logging more than 600 miles per winter in the upper Snake River watershed.

Caught in a blizzard just before Christmas of 1935, Paul and Patricia Petzoldt waited in Ashton, Idaho for the roads or the railroad to Victor to clear so they could catch a ride to Jackson Hole. They had been invited to manage a dude ranch in Moran. After waiting a week, the Petzoldts decided to ski the 70 miles to Moran—a rigorous seven-day trip. On the second day, Paul spent 12 hours breaking trail to the top of Teton Pass and Patricia, a novice skier, fell the entire way down to Wilson.

Discovery Of A Sport

With little else to do in the dead of a Jackson Hole winter, skiers began hiking up Snow King and skiing down in the 1920s. Braking with a single pole between their legs, they skied straight down through the sparse trees left by a 1879 forest fire. Forest Service worker Mike O'Neil, who came to Jackson during the winter of 1925-26, was among the first skiers in the valley to use two poles and make turns with his skis. He and C.H.

Brown, a blacksmith, invented a new binding that encased shoe soles, with irons for the toe and straps across the top and around the heel. From bamboo fishing rods, they fashioned ski poles, with an iron tip and embroidery hoops crisscrossed by riveted leather straps for baskets.

O'Neil built one of the first ski jumps on Snow King, launching a craze that would last for more than a decade. Alf and Kaarl Engen further promoted the sport when they came to Jackson in the winter of 1937 to sponsor a jumping exhibition. Jack Yokel and Grover Bassett were among the best local jumpers; Bassett made his own jumping skis, designed with three chiseled grooves in the base for stability.

At age 8, Bassett lost his right arm when a falling mailbag triggered his shotgun while he was hitching a ride on a mail truck. Amazingly, he did all his poling with one arm during ski outings with Paul Imeson in the Hobacks and Gros Ventre. Imeson sometimes had to start fires and warm the stump of Bassett's arm.

As recreational skiing gained popularity in the early 1930s, mountaineer/skier Fred Brown began to envision Jackson Hole as a famous ski destination. Accordingly, he helped form the Jackson Hole Ski Association, which launched a national campaign to promote skiing in Jackson Hole. During the summer of 1937, Brown became president of the newly formed Jackson Hole Ski Club, which aimed to provide locals with a slate of ski activities and a racing program.

The Ski Club held its first race on a horse and hiking trail that the Forest Service and the Civilian Conservation Corps cut on Snow King in 1935 and 1936. Jimmy Braman won the combined downhill and jump, using wooden skis with a stiff, ridge-shaped top. Less common were skis with metal or fiberglass edges from near the tip to less than midway down the ski. L.L. Bean snow boots were bound to the ski with leather straps and a piece of inner tube around the heel.

During Christmas week of 1937, Fred Brown hosted the Dartmouth Ski Team at his family's Teton Pass Ranch in Wilson while the team was en route to a race in Sun Valley. On Telemark Bowl near Teton Pass, the team demonstrated the latest ski techniques and the use of two ski poles and fixed-heel bindings to more than 200 spectators.

That demonstration evoked excitement about the possibilities for the sport of skiing, as did the "Hoback Boys"—Arthur "Banty" Bowlsby, and Sam, Ed and Joe Hicks. Besides being excellent racers, the Hoback Boys held ski circuses at Snow King and in Sun Valley during the late 1930s. When they weren't performing, they traveled on skis to deliver milk and mail to ranchers in the Hoback Canyon, Hoback Rim and Bondurant areas. They were master waxers, who melted phonograph records for ski bases. They used a fat, long pole to steer and owned very long homemade skis with "housings" and mukluks that came up to their knees.

Recreational Ski Touring

In the 1930s, stability and communal affluence motivated a few skiers to begin ski touring through the mountainous areas surrounding Jackson Hole and Teton Valley. These tours demanded not only proficient cross-country and downhill skiing technique but exceptional strength and varied knowledge of safe mountain travel as well. This trend represented the dawn of ski mountaineering.

Fred Brown began ski exploring the sea of bowls around Teton Pass in the 1930s and continued to do so throughout the next decade. He pioneered ski touring in "all the country behind the Tetons, from Teton Pass to Yellowstone, and from Teton Pass to the Snake River." As a youth, Fred's favorite pastime was to climb a tree and then have his friends cock the tree over like a catapult. When they let it go, Fred would hang on for dear life as the tree swung wildly back and forth. This activity earned Brown the nickname of "Tarzan of the Tetons."

Brown was a serious, bright, philosophical, and eccentric person. He worked as a mountain guide, ski instructor, over-the-pass mail skier, and for the U.S. Geologic Survey. He used a book to teach himself to ski, and soon became a well-known racer.

In 1931 or 1932, Brown, 16, joined Chief Park

Ranger Allyn Hanks on a trek into Cascade south fork, marking the earliest recorded skiing foray into Grand Teton National Park. In mid-February of 1938, Brown and Hanks returned to the park, with Park Naturalist Howard Stagner, for a four-day ski trek from Beaver Creek to Granite Canyon via Cascade Canyon, and back to Beaver Creek. During the previous fall, the trio cached food and equipment at Cascade Canyon forks, Alaska Basin and Marion Lake. They used safety ropes while surmounting steep slopes and a cornice exiting Cascade Canyon. They made the trip to "observe mountain weather and snow conditions, to study winter wildlife, and to determine the skiability of upper Teton canyons and mountain slopes."

One of Brown's longest Teton tours was a six-day trip in 1940—with Betty Woolsey, Rynie Van Evera and Katie Starratt—from Cascade Canyon to Phillips Pass. From a camp in the Cascade forks patrol cabin, they spent three days exploring the north and "middle" forks of Cascade. At their Marion Lake camp, they dug out snow from under a tree and laid pine boughs on the ground for bedding. They used their metal snow shovel to support the fire and hung the pot from the branches of the tree. That night, two feet of fresh snow fell, slowing them down the next day, as they traversed to Moose Divide. Exhausted and with little food left, they set up another elaborate lean-to near "Devil's Slide" to stay out another night. The following morning, they skied the remaining distance to the pass road below Ski Lake.

Brown continued to ski tour throughout the early 1940s, with partners including Grant Hagen, Bert Jensen, Ted Major and Herman Seherr-Thoss. But Brown was much more than a ski pioneer. On Dec. 19, 1935, when he was 19 years old, Brown joined Paul and Eldon Petzoldt on the first winter ascent of the Grand Teton! And as a result of Brown's adventurous exploits and guidance, many people were inspired to center their lives on ski mountaineering.

With the 1929 establishment of Grand Teton Monument, rangers Allyn Hanks, Dudley Hayden and Howard Stagner lived in Moose and Beaver Creek and ski toured extensively in the monument area. These skiers were some of the first to explore east-side canyons in winter. Later, other park employees, including Shorty Davis, Lyle Bressler, Pete Linn, and Bill Bartlett were active as well. Death Canyon was one of their favorite tours.

Ranger/mountaineer Phil Smith was rumored to have made the first Teton Crest traverse from Teton Pass to Grassy Lake in the 1930s. In 1930, Dudley Hayden became the second ranger in the park. To curtail illegal trapping, he patrolled the west shores of Jackson Lake on skis. For recreation, Hayden ski toured more than 1,500 miles in Yellowstone. Tenth Mountain Division skier Blake Vandewater moved to Jackson in 1945 to become one of the first year-round rescue rangers in Grand Teton National Park. He used alpine skis during his few winter patrols into the lonely Teton canyons.

With ski-touring popularity on the rise, ski instructor Fritz Brown wrote a weekly column in the *Jackson's Hole Courier* in 1937, through which he addressed ski technique and equipment. In one article entitled "Climbing Technique," Fritz explained diagonal climbing methods, waxing, and skinning, for example.

Lift-Served Skiing

The first ski lift on Snow King—Old Man Flat rope tow—began running during the winter of 1939-40. Neil Rafferty presented a plan to the Jackson Hole Club, a local commerce organization, to win the contract for its installation.

The Jackson Hole Ski Club took advantage of the lift immediately, inviting Alta, Utah racers Ted Major, Jack Major, and Virginia Guernsey Huidekoper to Snow King to compete in the first annual Tri-State Meet in 1939. The threesome received a grand welcome and were honored guests in the homes of various Ski Club members. Huidekoper and Ted Major eventually moved to Jackson Hole and became quite influential in the development of racing and touring in the valley.

Skiing at Snow King quickly became popular, and many Teton Pass tourers were drawn to the lift-served slopes. The focus was on racing, with Bill Saunders dominating locally in the 1930s and 1940s.

In 1945, Fred Toppan, Bill Jensen, Jim Huidekoper, Homer Richards and John Wort established the Jackson Hole Winter Sports Association, in response to a post-World War II ski-popularity explosion. One of the main goals of the association was to get a chair lift installed at the top of Snow King. Accordingly, the group bought an old ore tram in Salida, Colorado for $5,000 and hired Neil Rafferty to build the lift. An unprecedented community effort led to installation of the lift in 1946-47.

The next fall, Rafferty ran rope tows on Teton Pass for early-season skiing—at 10 cents per ride. The tows were driven by an old Army four-wheel-drive pickup, set on a large platform in the middle of the ski lift. The rear wheels drove one set of ropes and the front wheels drove the other. A flatbed Jeep—the Ski Jitney—picked up skiers in Jackson at 8 a.m. on holidays and took them up and down the old winding Teton Pass Road. When Snow King opened for the season, the rope tows on Telemark Bowl would close. The tows ran during early season every year until the late 1960s.

Meantime, a similar growth was occurring in Teton Valley. During the 1930s, Union Pacific named Teton Basin among possible sites for Sun Valley. At about the same time, the Teton Ski Club formed, drawing about 100 members. They built lifts and cleared runs in Moose Creek, on a hillside north of Victor, and up the Old Targhee Road. People rode the train from Rexburg, Idaho Falls, and Pocatello and were chauffeured from the station to the hills by horse-drawn sleigh.

Later, rope tows also ran on Signal Mountain, Leeks Canyon, Two Ocean Mountain, Angle Mountain, a hill near the Moran School, a hill near Catholic Bay on Jackson Lake, and Huckleberry Ridge on the Moose-Wilson Road.

With lift-served, packed-snow skiing now available throughout the Teton area, ski touring in the Teton backcountry became stagnant. No longer did skiers have to climb to enjoy downhill skiing. The racing technique displayed by the Dartmouth Ski Team and local Olympians and racers such as Katie Starratt, Virginia Huidekoper, and Betty Woolsey, became a craze. The pole-drag and telemark turns that had sustained early Teton skiers now were obsolete.

The advent of lift-served terrain, along with stem and parallel christie technique, redefined the sport of skiing from the late 1930s through the 1960s.

Equipment Follows Suit

As lift-served skiing became popular, equipment developed to meet associated needs. It included tip-to-tail ski edges, greater ankle support in boots, and releasable bindings. Skis of the 1940s and 50s were wooden, like the Groswolds, Northlands and military surplus skis. Later, metal skis, such as Head

Endowed with the proficiency of an Olympian, Betty Woolsey pursued a lifetime of mountain adventure. She introduced countless others to the sport as well.

Standards, dominated the market. Haderer and Molitor made over-the-ankle, full-shank, lace-leather boots. Bindings varied, including around-the-heel cable systems with front throws, bear-trap toe plates, and fixed/free heel conversion cable hitches. The Ramy binding had a releasable bear-trap toe plate and a breakaway front throw.

Long thongs were crampon-strap-like bindings the French introduced to the United States in the mid-1950s. In the simplest version, the thongs were threaded into holes that were drilled horizontally through the ski—the ultimate non-releasable binding. Before they became obsolete in the mid-1960s, long thongs were combined with bear-trap toe and various heel pieces for extra stability. One Marker model had a turntable heel plate to which the thongs attached with a releasable toe piece.

The Renegades

A small community of skiers resisted the novelty of lift-served terrain and the allure of racing; they had northwest Wyoming and eastern Idaho to themselves and accomplished some fantastic tours. They used seal skins and a free heel to climb, then hitched their cable to fix their heel for a parallel or stem-christie descent.

Like Fred Brown, and influenced very much by him, Grant Hagen became possessed to ski the backcountry. Before he left Jackson for service in the Tenth Mountain Division in 1943, Hagen made numerous tours, including two long spring trips into Cascade Canyon headwaters with Fred Brown, Herman Seherr-Thoss and others in 1941 and 1942. When he returned from the war, he toured extensively in the Gros Ventres with Grover Bassett and others.

Despite the Jackson Hole Ski Club's primary focus on developing lift-served racing, Austrian immigrant Walter Kussy convinced Dick Lang and Neil Rafferty that building a remote ski cabin would benefit the skiing community. In 1953, the Ski Club secured a Forest Service special-use permit and began construction of the cabin in the Sheep Creek drainage, northeast of Jackson Peak. Still standing today, the 16-foot-by-20-foot structure sleeps as many as 20 people. Volunteers Dave Page, Gib Scott, Ed Hodson, Dean Driskell, and many others built the cabin.

The true renegade of the era was Betty Woolsey, who first came to Jackson Hole in 1936 to train on Teton Pass. She was a member of the 1936 U.S. Olympic Ski Team, and served as team captain between 1937 and 1940. Woolsey and her friends hitched rides to the top of Teton Pass on the 8:30 a.m. mail truck bound for Victor, Idaho. "It was the best powder snow I had ever skied, including five years in Europe, Alta, Aspen, and Sun Valley," Woolsey recalled.

In 1943, Woolsey bought the Trail Creek Ranch; in 1947, she became a full-time Jackson Hole resident. She and Margaret "Muggs" Schultz took guests skiing on the pass as a courtesy during the late 1940s, 50s, and into the 60s. Schultz recalls that the townspeople "all kind of thought we were out of our minds. If anyone climbed to go skiing, they had to be crazy." Woolsey named some of the ridges and bowls of Teton Pass after friends and guests of the ranch, many of whom later moved to Jackson Hole and got involved with the skiing community.

"We had the joys of doing certain things for the first time," Woolsey said. "I think that is exciting; skiing was a completely different cup of tea. Then, it was mostly untracked snow and exploration. Now, you have groomed trails and lifts. It was an adventure."

In the late 1940s, Woolsey made some of the first skiing forays into the Granite Hot Springs area of the Gros Ventre with Herman Seherr-Thoss and others. With alpine gear, they skied "Palmer Peak," now known as Flying Buttress. During the 1940s, Woolsey also organized at least three trips into the Dinwoody Glacier area of the Wind Rivers.

Another resolute ski tourer was mountain runner Frank Ewing, who made three trips up Berry Creek in 1957-58. Ewing arrived in the valley in 1955 and learned about ski mountaineering and avalanche hazards from seasonal ranger Keith Jones. Ewing, Jones, and seasonal ranger Don Williams skied Survey, Red, and Forellen peaks together. During one tour, they crossed over Conant Pass, where Ewing zipped out of some trees and headed straight for a moose standing in a clearing. Unfortunately, skiers didn't know how to turn their skis in those days, so Ewing had to grab trees to gain control. He split the hairs of the moose as he zoomed by, making every effort not to fall down.

Ewing eventually became an expert downhill skier, with years of skiing at Snow King and on Teton Pass. He made other major tours in the area, including traverses from Dubois to Pinedale with Dick Pittman in the late 1950s, and from Moran to Cody and Teton Pass to Rendezvous Peak with Rod Newcomb in the early 1960s. Ewing made at least four trips into Gannett Peak and the Dinwoody Glacier for spring skiing with partners Rod Newcomb, Pete Sinclair, Barry Corbet, Dick Pittman, Jake Breitenbach. Tragically, Pittman was killed in an avalanche on Snow King and Breitenbach died on Everest shortly after these excursions.

Idahoans Joe Gale and Dean Millsap began making regular backcountry ski trips to the Tetons in the late 1950s. In 1964, co-worker Robert Hammer joined the group, which skied more in the Tetons during the subsequent 30 years than did most local skiers. At first, the trio skied in the vicinity of Teton Pass, where the only other skiers they saw were Clarence "Stearnie" Stearns and groups from Trail Creek Ranch. But as the pass became more popular in the early 1970s, Gale, Millsap and Hammer ventured west into Mail Cabin Creek and north into Grand Teton National Park. They made two of the earliest width traverses of the range, one from Targhee to Cascade north fork and the other from Teton Canyon Roaring Fork to Cascade south fork. With national park research biologist Bill Barmore, they toured to Taylor Mountain, Rendezvous Peak, Amphitheater Lake, and Garnet Canyon, and made early descents of 25 Short and Peak 10,696.

Setting Sights On High Peaks

Buck Mountain was the first high Teton peak that skiers took on. On May 29, 1961, Barry Corbet—with encouragement from fellow ski instructor and mountain guide Bill Briggs—guided clients Eliot Goss and Ann LaFarge on the descent. The feat didn't stir much attention at the time, as it was beyond the understanding of most local skiers. Actually, Barry didn't think much of the descent himself, having skied it with his boots unbuckled.

By the mid- to late 1960s, winter mountaineering in the high peaks became popular. Climbers including Rick Horn, and George, Greg, and Mike Lowe skied approaches to Grand Teton routes, including the north ridge and face, Black Ice Couloir, west face and the east ridge. In the winter of 1968, Peter Koedt, Frank Ewing, Rick Horn, and half a dozen others teamed up for successful climbs of the Grand, the Middle, and the South Tetons. They used snowmobiles to haul heavy food and equipment from Moose to the base of the mountains. Using mountaineering boots and Silvrettas, George Lowe was among the earliest Teton ski mountaineers to master both skiing and climbing.

Paul Petzoldt began an annual New Year's Day Grand Teton ascent attempt in December of 1965. Using skis and snowshoes to approach, he guided fellow National Outdoor Leadership School instructors at first but eventually took students along as well.

INDUSTRIALIZATION OF SKIING

Jackson Hole Ski Resort

Retired California ad exec Paul McCollister came to Jackson Hole in 1957 to try his hand at cattle ranching. Inspired by a ski-area development concept in Cache Creek, however, McCollister envisioned a ski resort that could rival the complexes in the Alps. McCollister bought the Crystal Springs Ranch and obtained a Forest Service lease, then began scoping Peak 10,450 on horseback in the late 1950s and early 1960s.

In the late 1950s, Jim Huidekoper and John Harrington made some of the earliest reconnaissance ski tours on Crystal Springs Mountain. In the early 60s, Frank Ewing, Rod Newcomb, Barry Corbet, Jake Breitenbach, Alex Morley and others joined McCollister in climbing Peak 10,450. During one ascent, they climbed straight up the couloirs of the Laramie Headwall. Later, McCollister bought a Christy Cat snow tractor to carry skiers partway up the mountain. Working closely with Alex Morley, Willi Schafer, Gordy Wren, and the U.S. Forest Service, McCollister began building the Jackson Hole Ski Area in 1964. The mountain opened to the public in the winter of 1965.

During the first year of operation, skiers used Apres Vous, Eagle's Rest and Teewinot chair lifts, while a work tram took patrolmen to Peak 10,450 to investigate avalanche-control routes. From Apres Vous, skiers traversed as far as Jackson Face and Sundance Gully in the south and to Saratoga Bowl in the north.

In 1966, the aerial tram and Thunder chair lift opened to the public. Thunder ran inconsistently for two years while repair crews worked out design flaws in the lift-tower foundations. Casper and Crystal Springs chair lifts were installed in the early 1970s. Despite $75 season-pass rates, few skiers skied at the resort in its early days.

Grand Targhee Ski Resort

In the late 1950s, Guy Bush of the Soil Conservation Service and Jim Huidekoper teamed with Fritz Kaufman and John Wilson for ski tours on Mount Baldy above Alta, Wyoming. By the early 1960s, other Teton Valley residents, including Bill Rigby, and Rex and Jim Christensen, got hooked on the idea of opening a ski area on Mount Baldy—later named Fred's Mountain and the Grand Targhee Ski Resort. To stir interest in the concept, Rigby led ski-industry notables such as Sverre Engen, Clarence Stearns and Dr. Don MacLeod up Mount Baldy and Lightning Mountain via Dry Creek and Rick's Basin.

The Big Valley Corporation formed in 1964, with help from 400 Idaho and Wyoming residents who bought membership certificates. Sales of the certificates garnered enough money to qualify the corporation for a $600,000 loan that supplied capital for resort construction in 1966, under the direction of Bob Blank. The resort opened to the public with 25 Driggs ski patrollers in December of 1969.

In the beginning, Grand Targhee Ski Resort included the Bannock and Shoshone lifts, along with a day lodge, restaurant, bar and overnight lodging. The Blackfoot lift was added in 1973.

Original investors later sold the resort to Ohio investor Bill Robinson, who upgraded the buildings at the base area by 1978. Robinson died the next year, though, and his trust ran the ski area until Mory Bergmeyer took over in 1987. Bergmeyer's goal was to make the resort a national destination by expanding base facilities and sending lifts into surrounding backcountry areas.

Resort Skiing vs. Ski Mountaineering

With development of two world-class ski resorts, skiers from throughout the world moved to Jackson Hole and Teton Valley. Newcomers and locals alike bought season passes or worked for the resorts. Skiers were treated to uncrowded sanctuaries of lift-served ski terrain and powder that lasted for days after storms. For most, backcountry skiing either became a forgotten endeavor or never had any appeal at all. Except for a few sporadic spring tours, backcountry skiing remained stagnant through the second half of the 1960s.

For the few spring tourers that remained, ski-lift access into the backcountry via the Jackson Hole Ski Area uphill facilities nurtured a growing interest in touring and mountaineering. In the spring of 1966, Peter Koedt led a party of four from the tram to the north fork Avalanche Canyon on alpine gear. The next spring, Koedt and Bill Briggs led an alpine tour with six others from the top of the tram to the south fork of Darby Canyon. Butch Williams, Jerry Balint and friends chose that same route during a separate outing.

Ray White was another exception to resort fanatacism. In 1967, White moved from New York to Jackson Hole to ski at Teton Village, but instead got hooked on ski touring. In December of his first winter, White joined Robbie Fuller, Rick Horn, and Dave Reinmann in breaking trail from Jackson to Granite Hot Springs in one day. Exhausted, they soaked their aching bodies in the hot springs and spent the night at the Granite Creek Ranch.

That winter, White slept in the mountain station at the top of the tram in exchange for $10 a night and an "A pass." Although he was a ski patrolman from 1970-1979, White spent much of his time skiing on Teton Pass and making long loops and traverses in surrounding mountains. He applied pine tar to the raw wood of his Splitkin hickory skis to keep the bases moist; the skis had screwed metal edges, and he used Galibier double-leather mountaineering boots with Silvretta touring bindings.

A Higher Level Of Commitment

In April of 1966, an uncontrollable urge drove Jackson Hole Ski School Director and three-time Olympic Gold Medalist Pepi Stiegler to ski Buck Mountain. Stiegler had little mountaineering experience, but he was totally committed. He didn't know about Stewart Draw in those days, so he approached from Beaver Creek. With an amazing solo push, he climbed 25 Short and Peak 10,696 before arriving on Buck Mountain well after the snow turned to slush.

Thanks to a combination of skill, stamina, and luck, Stiegler narrowly escaped death in an avalanche and returned to the valley safely. With his success bloomed a new era in Teton skiing, fathered by Bill Briggs. Throughout the rest of the 1960s and 70s, hundreds of skiers challenged the steep faces and couloirs of the Teton peaks.

Bill Briggs first came to Jackson Hole in 1951 and, in the subsequent 30 years, engaged in ski tours and descents never before realized in America. Briggs left Dartmouth College in 1953 and began teaching skiing at Cannon Mountain in 1955.

By 1963, Briggs made three expeditions to the Canadian Rockies, plus an early descent of Mount Rainier and three long ski tours in the Tetons. Using Dovre cable bear-trap bindings and Head Standard skis, Briggs was joined by Rod Dornan, Jim Greig, Julie Briggs, Peter Koedt, and Ann Williams during the Teton tours—in 1960, 1961, and 1962—covering the entire Teton Crest in three segments.

Born with no cartilage in his right hip joint, Briggs was saddled with painful, frustrating complications throughout his years of skiing. He planned to ski Mount Rainier, then have Dr. Hans Kraus fuse his hip joint in place. He participated in the Rainier trip, accepting it as his last ski-mountaineering endeavor. But to his joy, the surgery was a great success and Briggs soon was skiing again, his hip fused at an angle that would tolerate skiing and climbing. After teaching skiing for a year

at the Jackson Hole Ski Area, Briggs became director of the ski school at Snow King in 1966.

After a descent of Buck Mountain in 1966, Briggs continued to blaze ski routes off the Teton peaks throughout the 60s, including descents of the Middle

---

Ski patrolman Frank Ewing consults with Snow King Mountain Manager Neil Rafferty in the late 1950s. Ewing made early ski tours in the Tetons and toured extensively in the Wind Rivers and Gros Ventres. Rafferty was instrumental in developing Jackson Hole's ski industry.

Teton and Mount Moran. On June 16, 1971, Briggs shocked the country when—on the heels of three years of disappointing attempts—he became the first to ski the Grand Teton. In this huge success, Briggs achieved his goal of "creating a noteworthy effect by setting the first in any field of endeavor," and he widened the scope of the ski-mountaineering movement.

Throughout the mid- to late 1900s, Briggs discovered, documented, and passed on to his apprentices and students a progression of ski maneuvers that allowed developing skiers controlled access to more difficult terrain and snow conditions. His techniques gave many local skiers the self confidence to tackle descents of Teton peaks. Briggs also passed on his knowledge of skiing to the public in 1969-70 via a *Jackson Hole Guide* newspaper column called "Brigger's Basics." In the words of Whitney Thurlow, "Because of Briggs, you knew it could be done, whatever it was you wanted to do."

Instrumental in supporting Briggs during his descent of the Grand Teton was Jorge Colón, who arrived in the valley in the late 1960s and became perhaps the most active Teton skier of the 70s. He captained a ski-fanatics gang called the "Alpine Liberation Army." Besides his enthusiasm at the ski area and his interest in winter touring, Colón was driven to ski aesthetic lines off high Teton peaks in spring. Using Lowa mountaineering boots and Silvretta bindings, he skied Mount Hunt, Prospectors Mountain, Static Peak, Buck Mountain, and the South and Middle Tetons with partners including Tom Raymer, Davey Agnew, Mark Wolling and many others. He also made first ski descents of routes on Mount Moran, Teewinot Mountain and Mount St. John, among others.

A New Order

Throughout the 1970s, most backcountry skiers used alpine touring equipment, but a small society of nordic skiers grew steadily and inconspicuously. These skiers rebelled against industry establishment and manifested their freedom with lightweight, less-robotic

tools. Even as late as 1979, Mike Quinn recalled being the only participant in an American Avalanche Institute course on Teton Pass who was using cross-country boots and edgeless skis. Everyone else had Silvrettas or some variation thereof and either Galibier or Kastinger mountaineering boots.

But unorthodox equipment needs created a dilemma for these renegade skiers. The only common nordic boots available in the 1970s were the flimsy Alfa touring shoe and its high-top relative, the Norrona. These boots provided neither the support nor the warmth required for backcountry skiing in the Tetons. Skinny, wooden skis of the day, such as the Bonnas, Asnes, Splitkins, and Birkebiners, were notorious for breaking. They were simply ill-equipped for their game and were too few to legitimize a bona fide nordic downhill boot and ski market. Unswayed, though, these skiers improvised with whatever gear they could muster.

One of the earliest modern nordic backcountry skiers was Bob Stevenson. He began skiing with edgeless birch skis in the Snowy Range near Laramie, where he went to school from 1964-69. When the sole-nails of his single layer, unlined leather ski boots began wearing through and impaling his feet and his flimsy skis broke, he knew it was time to upgrade. He found some sturdy hickory Army skis at a surplus store in Laramie and planed down the sides to make them skinny. He drilled three holes in the nailed leather soles of some Falk oxford-like ski sneakers to use with his Rottefella pin bindings. Voila! With this system, Stevenson skied throughout the Tetons for years. In fact, on one eight-day Absaroka traverse attempt from Turpin Meadow to Cody in the spring of 1970, Stevenson's staunch loyalty to the pin nordic system was reaffirmed when partner John Corcoran broke four Silvretta cables!

When Stevenson arrived in Jackson in 1969, only a handful of skiers were daring to venture into the backcountry. Trail-breaking was a constant chore for him and his partners, Alice Stevenson and Chuck Schaap. If they saw tracks, they probably belonged to Rick Horn. Young Stevenson anticipated a boom in backcountry skiing and convinced John Horn of

Powderhorn Mountaineering to order a crate of the Army skis. Horn took the request to heart, then hired Stevenson to plane the sides of the skis to make them skinnier and the top to expose the nice hickory wood. They were heavy, but Stevenson's prediction was on target: The skis sold like hotcakes.

Colorado Outward Bound instructor Davey Agnew moved to the Tetons in the early 1970s. Like most of the ski mountaineers of the era, he used alpine touring equipment. With a nudge from friends in Colorado, however, Agnew tapped his cobbling skills to modify the welt of his Galibier mountaineering boots, which had a square toe and a heel cable groove for an alpine touring bind-ing. Like many Teton skiers to fol-low, Agnew converted his alpine touring boots to fit pin bindings by grinding down the welt and attaching pinhole plates to the bottom of the boots.

With fine-tuned parallel tech-nique, Agnew and Wilson partners Todd Stearns, Wes Fox, Carson Hubbard, Donny Black, Gary Beebe, and Callum Mackay bagged free-heel descents of the Banana Couloir and the east face of Taylor Mountain, proving that you didn't need fixed heels to ski the steeps. With blazing trail-breaking speed, they also established usefulness of light skinny skis and supple boots for yoyoing on Teton Pass and touring to other peaks and bowls throughout the range.

In 1977, local tinker Peter Wuerslin decided he wanted a nordic boot—for steep ski-area skiing and spring descents—that had even more support than the converted European imports. At a Jackson secondhand shop, he found two pairs of 1960s lace-leather alpine boots. One pair fit him well and the other was four sizes too big. He attached the larger soles onto the smaller uppers, then water-softened and creased the leather toe for boot flexibility,

thereby creating a modestly stiff boot with a welt for a pin binding.

Still, some skiers were perfectly content with the flimsy gear of the day. In May of 1973, Jim Roscoe made an amazing first nordic descent of Buck Mountain on Alfas and Bonnas. Jim Day and Bob Graham "crashed and burned" down Edelweiss Bowl with Alfa boots and Bonna 2000s during the winter of 1974-75. Graham's secret to staying dry was not to fall, and his technique for not falling was not turning. So while his friends

struggled to learn to turn in the deep snow, Graham simply made a high-speed, figure-11 to the bottom of the run. In May of 1979, Jeff Crabtree, Owen Ander-son, and Greg Lawley used Norronas during their tour between Teton Pass and Flagg Ranch. Crabtree used edgeless Rossignol cross-country skis! This equipment actually worked well but definitely added a little excitement when the team had to traverse steep slopes and downclimb a couloir to bypass Doubtful Peak.

Bill Briggs and Peter Koedt return after a successful first ski descent of Mount Moran, on the left. Briggs went on to become the first to ski the Grand Teton and Mount Owen. Koedt (right) pioneered numerous nordic-tour-ing routes in the range during the 1980s and 90s.

Mavericks And Other Maggots

As backcountry skiing popularized in the early 1970s, skiers explored variations of the sport. Wearing one of the valley's first pairs of Bonnas with underfoot metal edges, Frank Venutti became one of the earliest nordic skiers to enjoy long ski tours into remote areas of the Tetons. Venutti tried to excite people about touring but did many solo trips because he could find no one to join him.

John Carr was a rarity in the early 1970s as well. He was interested in both alpine and nordic mountain skiing. In addition to pioneering many touring routes in the northern Tetons throughout the 70s and 80s, Carr made numerous spring alpine descents of the high peaks, including his 1971 descent of Skillet Glacier.

Davey Agnew, Jim Roscoe, and Mike Burns pioneered the idea of setting up camp in a remote cirque and skiing the surrounding bowls thoroughly. The trio lived near Ski Lake one winter and explored the terrain of the east-side cirques north of Mount Glory. Especially enchanted with the Wind Rivers, Agnew made five long trips to ski in the Gannett Peak area and, in 1971, explored terrain in Cirque of the Towers.

With inspiration from climbing ranger Pete Hart, Grand Teton National Park rangers Jim "Olie" Olson, Ralph Tingey, Pete Armington, Bill Conrod and Tom Milligan ski toured extensively throughout the eastern Teton front during the 1970s and 80s. With real seal skins glued with pine tar for climbing, the rangers moved fast and light during one- and two-day east-side loops and traverses to Idaho.

In the early 1970s, Fred Mugler opened Mountaineering Outfitters in Driggs and stocked up on old Army surplus gear and Bonna skis. Mugler's store was a sign of changing times in Teton Valley. Grand Targhee's management coined the label "mountain maggots" or "snow maggots" for the nordic skiers that infiltrated Teton Valley during the 1970s. They were a well-educated, earthy lot—like a mountain version of the 60's hippies, wearing baggy wool pants. Ben Franklin, Richard "Rico" Young, Tom Warren, Gregg Amalong, Bob "Bub" Talbot, and Dan Daigh skied all over west slope, including Beard, Table, bowls east of Targhee, Peaked Mountain, Spring Gulch, Darby Canyon, and Battleship Mountain. They also were among the first skiers to explore the bowls of Oliver Peak, Mail Cabin and Burbank creeks thoroughly.

Amalong, who moved to Teton Valley in 1974, was one of the earliest modern backcountry skiers to live there. He and other dedicated "mountain maggots" spent winters throughout the 70s living in straw-lined snow caves at the base of Grand Targhee in Dry Creek Basin and Rick's Basin. Amalong bathed in the Targhee swimming pool and dried his socks by the fire in the lodge. With his simple lifestyle, bull-like strength, commitment to skiing, and tranquil personality, he inspired many a Teton Valley skier and set an example for a backcountry way of life that persists in Teton Valley today.

In about 1977, Grand Targhee banned free-heel skiers from its slopes. Jackson skier Jim Day charged that Targhee management made the rule to keep its family resort atmosphere free of "mountain maggots." The resort said the reason for the rule change was that skinny-skiers disregarded closed-area and ski-area boundary signs, thereby jeopardizing the safety of patrollers and guests.

When Teton Village closed for the season that winter and Day was denied access to lifts at Grand Targhee, he became quite perturbed. Under the slogan, "Free the Ghee!," Day spent the next three years campaigning to persuade the mountain to allow free-heel skiers. He and Dave Titcomb even hired lawyer Cabell Venable to help them gather pertinent evidence that would convince the Forest Service to force Grand Targhee to comply.

Day made a video of Les Gibson figure-eighting his own tracks, both with nordic and alpine equipment. After viewing the video, the Forest Service agreed that there was no difference between fixed-and free-heel equipment and that Targhee had no right to discriminate. In the spring of 1981, Targhee reopened to nordic skiers.

Rebirth Of The Telemark Turn

For some skiers, including Bob Stevenson and Art Becker, learning to turn with long, skinny skis and flimsy boots became an obsession. They hid away in less-popular areas, such as Stewart Draw, Togwotee Pass, and Burnt Wagon Gulch, for hours of frustrating practice that included plenty of face-plants. One day in the early 1970s, Becker watched in amazement as a skier from Washington linked smooth turns on Teton Pass, doing "something weird" with his inside leg—the telemark turn!

In its rudimentary early 20th-century form, the telemark turn began to re-popularize in the 1970s in isolated pockets throughout America. The turn revolutionized backcountry skiing by allowing skinny-skiers to handle deep, sometimes inconsistent mountain snow. Some contended that skiers used alpine touring gear and the telemark turn because they lacked the skill and balance to make parallel turns on nordic equipment. But skiers such as Jack Bellorado, John Walker, Jim Eckberg, Don Hultz, and Mike Murphy didn't care what anyone else thought. They kept their fancy, old-fashioned turn hidden on backcountry slopes and got thrills from skiing deep untracked powder in the early and mid-1970s.

The telemark turn didn't become really popular until skiers used it at the ski areas. During a two-year Colorado stint, Jim Day and Dave Titcomb became very proficient telemarkers and attracted a lot of attention. Day returned to Jackson in the winter of 1977-78; as a ski guide for Powderhound Nordic, he got a free season pass to the Jackson Hole Ski Area. There were only 10 days that winter that it didn't snow, and Day skied every day. As proficient skiers including Day, Titcomb, and Tom Russo telemarked at Jackson Hole Ski Area, the turn caught on quickly.

That spring, skeptics challenged Titcomb and Day to ski Glory Bowl in firm conditions with the telemark turn and gear. They did so with ease. The pair went on to win three tele powder-eight competitions together, beginning in 1980. The merits of the telemark turn were proven, and the technique had taken root in Jackson Hole.

After 1978, more Teton skiers converted to free-heel backcountry skiing and the telemark turn. The first pin-binding eights were held on West Gros Ventre Butte in 1978, at which time telemark races were run at the ski areas and pin-binding gelunde competitions were run on Teton Pass! Whitney Thurlow, Craig Tanner, Dan McKay, and Bob Comey were among the most active, skilled telemarkers of the day.

As telemark and backcountry skiing popularized during the late 70s and early 80s, Phil Leeds, Jim Barry, Wayne Hanson, Steve Beedle, Steve Hendrickson and Keith Benefiel each had a ski-related column in a local newspaper. They addressed ski-touring gear, waxing, telemarking technique, parallel technique, tricks, tele-eights, avalanche awareness, and winter camping. The *Jackson Hole News* even excerpted tours from Horn and LaVake's, *The Guide to Ski Touring in Jackson Hole*, published in 1975.

Genesis Of Avalanche Awareness

Despite the increase in backcountry skiing popularity, many skiers wisely avoided everything but the flattest backcountry terrain because they feared avalanches; others operated under the "ignorance is bliss" theory. A scant few chose their ski routes based on sound knowledge and decision making.

In 1974, a tragic avalanche accident in Glacier Gulch killed three NOLS students and initiated an extensive educational movement. The National Park Service augmented its winter-ranger staff, upgrading Jim "Olie" Olson and Bill Conrod from seasonal duty to nine-month stints. Ralph Tingey and Pete Armington joined them soon after. In 1975, Bridger-Teton National Forest Avalanche Forecaster Gary Poulson instituted a public phone line to offer current avalanche and weather forecasts.

Former Jackson Hole ski patrolman Rod Newcomb filled a business niche to educate skiers when he founded the American Avalanche Institute in the fall of 1974. One focus of Newcomb's program was rescue training.

Although rescue beacons such as the Skadi Hot Dog and Pieps were available in the early 1970s, they weren't used widely until the mid-1980s. Local ski patrols didn't even start using them until the Skadi Flat Pack became available in the mid- to late 1970s. Before then, patrolmen simply trailed 50 feet of red avalanche cord on avalanche-hazard-reduction mornings. Through the years, Newcomb taught thousands of people about snow and avalanche physics, backcountry travel, and effective use of rescue transceivers. This knowledge increased confidence substantially and gave skiers skills to explore more-precipitous areas of the Tetons.

A Lifetime Devotion

Like many other alpine tourers of the 60s and 70s, Ray White switched to nordic equipment in 1979. With partners including John Carr, Robbie Fuller and Tom Raymer, White ski toured ranges of northwest

A pioneer in alpine and nordic downhill technique, Dan McKay experienced his greatest thrills while launching air and skiing fast. He died while attempting to ski the Grand Teton.

Wyoming like no one before or since. He holds many tours to his credit in the Beartooths, Absarokas, Wind Rivers, Gros Ventres, Big Holes, Hobacks, and Salt River ranges but is most renowned for his multi-day and multi-week winter ski tours in Yellowstone. He and partners Dave Adams, Bill Morrow, Gregg Smith, and a few others kept other commitments in their lives minimal so that they could, for example, leave on a seven-day trip with just a couple days of notice. On one of White's six-day trips over the Pitchstone Plateau—with Adams and Smith—the temperature never rose above 35 degrees below zero and reached lows of 55 below at night! During the late 1970s, White taped felt inner liners from a pair of Sorrel boots to the outside of his Alfas to help him bear such cold spells.

Peter Koedt was another Teton ski pioneer who used alpine touring equipment exclusively during his tours and descents of the 1960s. But after a stint in Canada from 1968-1978, he reentered the Teton scene as a nordic skier. Skinny Skis, an outdoor-equipment shop, sponsored a nordic-skiing promotion day at Snow King in 1980 and, with encouragement from friends, Koedt attended; he was hooked.

Very few skiers had more enthusiasm or were more focused on ski mountaineering than Koedt. Throughout the 1980s, he skied numerous Teton summits and logged hundreds of miles of touring in the range. In the course of his tours, he traveled Death Canyon and crossed the Death Canyon Shelf at least six times each, traveled Stewart Draw as many as 10 times, Avalanche Canyon at least five times, and Cascade Canyon at least 11 times. He used these primary routes to access more remote areas, such as Rimrock Lake, Mica Lake, Icefloe Lake, Snowdrift Lake, The Jaw, Doane Peak, Ranger Peak, Peak 11,094, Alpha and Omega Lakes, Peak 10,650, and the Wigwams. He also skied the entire Teton crest alone in late December of 1985. Many of Koedt's partners skied with him only once, before they realized how arduous his tours were. Koedt never took along a tent—only a snow saw to build igloos.

A Labor Of Love

A sundry of ski-touring guide services have come and gone since the 1960s. Besides the Trail Creek Ranch, the earliest was Dick Person's Skiing Unlimited, which dawned during the winter of 1966. Sundance Ski Tours and Powderhound Nordic originated in the 1970s, and Peter Koedt began his sideline ski-touring guide service, Timberline Tours, in the early 1980s, specializing in rugged multi-day mountain trips.

In 1974, Robin "Boomer" McClure and Dave Miller launched High Mountain Helicopter Skiing, with help from Jerry Tapp, Frank Werner, and Dr. Richard Sugden. From 1974-76, they did only two or three flights a year, with Kjerstad Helicopters. During the drought year of 1977, they flew only once on 16 inches of snow!

Determined to make the business successful, however, Miller printed a brochure and rented an office in 1978. Business improved throughout the early 80s until 1984, when the Wyoming Wilderness Act established the Jedediah Smith and Gros Ventre wilderness areas, ousting the heli-ski service from its best terrain.

In 1980, Sun Valley ski guides Kirk Bachman and Chi Melville moved to Teton Valley to start a ski-touring guide service. Bachman invited Ben Franklin to bring his thorough knowledge of the local mountains to the partnership, while Clair Yost rounded out the team that made up Teton Mountain Touring. The group did most of its trips in the Big Hole Mountains, where it built three yurts for overnight stays. Unfortunately, a lack of interest forced the business to fold in 1988.

Bachman was a consummate skier with a relaxed philosophy. He provided jobs for skinny-skiers, cooperated with Grand Targhee Resort, and injected new ideas into the sport. As a result, the Idaho backcountry bunch grew more sophisticated—and gained more respect.

In 1987, former Teton Mountain Touring guides Glenn Vitucci and Carole Lowe obtained insurance and permits to build a yurt at the top of Plummer Canyon. With previously unmatched commitment to making a living at ski guiding, the pair founded Rendezvous Ski Tours, which was highly successful.

Advanced Gear, Technique And Skiers

Ski areas offered perfect training grounds for learning techniques of the steep and deep. Competitions like the Serendipity Bump contest of 1975 and the Gelunde jumping of the mid-1970s prompted skiers to push their limits. The beginning of "extreme skiing" perhaps could be marked by two movies produced in the area. The first one, produced by Bob Carmichael with cohorts Larry Bruce and Greg Lowe, was filmed during the springs of 1978 and 1979; *Fall Line* aired on "National Geographic," and featured Aspen skier, guide and renowned ice climber Steve Shea skiing the Grand Teton and steep couloirs on the Middle Teton. Salomon's *Rhythms* highlighted local skiers Joe Larrow and Bill "Mad Dog" Danford launching at full speed into Corbet's Couloir.

Shea arrived in the Tetons in 1977, in search of an American ski area comparable to Chamonix, France, where he spent four years climbing and skiing. In addition to nordic touring, Shea had a flair for spotting unskied lines in the Tetons and made first alpine descents of routes on Bivouac Peak, Mount Moran, and Middle Teton in the late 1970s. In June of 1978, he became the second person to ski the Grand Teton.

Ski mountaineer Robin "Boomer" McClure came to Jackson Hole in 1973 and loved sharing his sport with others. He worked as a ski instructor at Snow King and co-founded High Mountain Helicopter Skiing. McClure was driven to test his expert skiing skills on the Teton peaks; most notably, he made first descents of the Koven Couloir and the northeast snowfields of Mount Owen, the latter with Bill Briggs.

McClure's life dream was to make the first ski descent of the Matterhorn. He studied the mountain and trained hard for three years before making an attempt with Glen Conarroe in July of 1977. Tragically, though, both of them were killed in a fall from near the summit to the base of the north face. McClure is remembered most for his stalwart companionship and his unfaltering optimism.

In the early to late 1970s, diehard Jackson Hole Ski

Corp employees and their cohorts rode the Jackson Hole Aerial Tram—on Memorial Day weekend—to ski the remaining north-facing snow patches. The tram operated for Pepi Stiegler's summer race camps on Cody Bowl and Four Shadows from 1968 to about 1974. Taking advantage of their seasonal unemployment, Victor Gerdin, Mike Quinn, Mike Fitzpatrick, Steve Lundy, Larry Detrick, Glen Jaques, Frank Barrows and others broke new ground in couloirs including Endless, Mile Long, Space Walk, Zero G, Once is Enough, Twice is Nice, and even Central Chute. These skiers carried their prowess into the higher Teton peaks, with descents of steep routes on Peak 10,552, Rendezvous Peak, Teewinot, Buck Mountain, Mount Moran, Mount Hunt, and Rockchuck Peak.

A company of highly active skiers ventured onto the steep Teton flanks during the early to mid-1980s; on that team were Whitney Thurlow, Theo Meiners, Richard Collins, Mike Fischer, Jeff Bjornsen, Greg Miles, Brian Bradley, Jim Duclos, Jay Moody, Dan McKay, and Les Gibson. As masters of both alpine and nordic skiing, these men pushed the limits of both persuasions with early alpine descents of the north face of Static Peak, the northeast ramp of Mount Saint John and the southeast face of the South Teton, and early nordic descents of the Skillet.

But the true pioneer of free-heel skiing on the high Teton peaks was Salt Lake City ski patrolman Rick Wyatt, who entered the Teton scene in 1974 during a winter ascent of the Middle Teton. Throughout the 1970s and early 1980s, Wyatt made first nordic descents on the Middle Teton, Mount Moran, Teewinot, and the Grand Teton. He began his peak skiing spree with a nordic descent of Buck Mountain in the late 1970s, using Epoke 1400 edgeless skis. Wyatt brought a pure style of ski mountaineering to the Tetons. He made his Grand Teton descent without any rappels, by downclimbing ice chimneys unroped! And after sloshing through deep, wet snow during his first descent of Teewinot, Wyatt vowed to return in better conditions. He credits persistence, patience, and knowledge of when to turn around for his success.

Another skier who was fascinated with Teton skiing was Pocatello mountain guide Jeff Rhoads. Under the wing of Pacific Colorado Outward Bound instructor Ike Gayfield—along with friends Rocky Shaver and Brad Peck—Rhoads was only 19 years old when he skied the Skillet Glacier. The following year, Rhoads, Peck, Diane Jerman, and Chris Barnes tried to ski the Grand Teton, but weather turned them back. Then, on July 4-5, 1978, Rhoads, 21, skied the Grand Teton twice! One of the descents, which he made with Peck, marked the first ski descent of the Ford Couloir.

"Dangerous Downhill" Dan McKay began skiing at Teton Village in 1975. He was an exceptional skier who got his greatest thrills from jumping and skiing fast. McKay was one of the best local gelunde jumpers, won the Town Downhill, and skied in the world speed-skiing trials in Silverton, Colorado.

The vanity with which McKay burst into the Jackson Hole skiing scene angered many. But his exuberance and uncanny skiing ability would create a friendly, competitive atmosphere. He helped organize various skiing events and wrote outlandish ski articles for various publications. His late 1970s *Jackson Hole Guide* column, "Skiing in the Hole," discussed Wintersticks, nordic technique, para-skiing, and ski repair.

In 1980, McKay focused on nordic backcountry skiing and made numerous Teton Pass tours. His associations with mountaineers such as Jay Moody, Whitney Thurlow, and Brian Bradley inspired McKay to challenge the high peaks. He began with an April, 1981 nordic descent of Peak 10,552, along with Jay Moody. With Brian Bradley, McKay made the second ski descent of Mount Owen. With these successes behind him, McKay's ambitions mushroomed, and he sought first nordic descents of Buck Mountain and the Grand Teton.

But McKay became frustrated when he learned that Skeeter and Lenny Cattabriga and Rick Wyatt had already skied Buck and the Grand on nordic equipment. But he kept his energy high enough to attempt the first continuous ski descent of the Grand.

On July 11, 1982, McKay fell while climbing slabs on the east face. Sprawled helpless at the bottom of the Teepe Glacier, he died of exposure.

It's unclear what drove McKay to his fateful climb. Several people showed him the exact location of the Stettner Couloir, and others warned him not to go at all.

Alternatives To Skiing

During Barry Corbet's 1963 visit to Innsbruck, Dr. Burkhard Hussl—a friend of Dr. Roland Fleck of Jackson—gave Corbet a pair of figls. Figls are mini-skis, about two feet long and five inches wide. Europeans used them to descend from early-season rock climbs. Fleck used them for several Teton descents.

World-class surfer Mike Doyle brought monoskiing to Jackson Hole in 1972. Fletcher Manley and Pat Derouin made a monoski video of Doyle at the Jackson Hole Ski Area. Outside the ski area, monoskiers frequented Mount Glory throughout the 1970s. Davey Agnew and Jerry Balint made a frightful downclimb over the Four Shadows cornice and monoskied the couloir during the spring of 1972. And in the early 1980s, the pair carried monoskis to Edelweiss and played in the powder.

In the mid-1970s, the wooden Brunswick Snurfer and the plastic Coleco board became the first snowboards to appear in the Tetons. Snow surfers would stand on their boards and hold onto a rope that kept the tips from diving. In the late 1970s, GAR Skis made a snowboard with a bungy-cord binding. The first modern snowboard was the Performer by Burton, which appeared in the early 1980s and was made with plastic buckle bindings and under-board fins for stability. At about the same time, Wintersticks came out with metal edges, p-tex bases, and bizarre shapes. Chris Pappas launched the snowboarding program at the Jackson Hole Ski School in 1986.

Leaving Their Mark

In light of the harsh winter conditions of the Tetons, many local skiers turned to ingenuity to fill unique equipment needs and to augment or replace run-of-the-mill equipment. Peter Carman invented the super-gaiter; and Clair Yost purchased the original cast for Earl Miller's ski called "The Noodle," renamed it the "Yöstmark Mountain Noodle," and used it for greater flotation in deep Teton powder. Yost convinced his partners at Teton Mountain Touring to buy about 40 Noodles to rent to clients.

As the number of backcountry skiers grew and skiers became more advanced technically, manufacturers developed numerous new bindings. By the early 1990s, the race to create the ultimate nordic binding was on.

Jackson Hole skiers were instrumental in development of the binding. In the mid-1980s, Rick Liu helped develop the Chouinard cable binding, which reigned as the most popular binding for more than five years. Liu also developed a binding adapter for the Chouinard cable binding to accommodate plastic mountaineering

Stephen Koch snowboards the Owen-Spalding route on the Grand Teton. Koch brought a super-alpinist style to the Tetons, making numerous first descents of highly technical routes, including two on the Grand.

boots. This allowed climbers to approach the Tetons with rigid mountain boots bound to light nordic skis.

In 1985, transplanted Arkansas skier and climbing guide Russell Rainey began development of the SuperLoop tubing and clamp bindings. The tubing version was a revival of the 1930s bicycle inner-tube binding but with a more advanced toe plate. The clamp version was the first to use a compression spring instead of an extension spring to absorb cable tension.

Good Things Never Last

As a booming tourism industry jammed the Jackson Hole Ski Area during the 1980s, so too did ski tracks obliterate the pristine powder slopes that once lasted for weeks after storms. Numerous skiers abandoned the ski area altogether to take on untracked backcountry. Their principal tools were the telemark turn and Chouinard front throw cable binding.

An exhaustive marketing program launched in the late 1980s helped turn Jackson Hole into a winter-destination resort. The cost of living rose sharply; wealthy vacationers bought second homes in the valley, ousting hard-core ski mountaineers or forcing them to work more jobs. Many of them compromised by moving to Teton Valley, where the cost of living was dramatically lower.

Despite financial constraints, nordic skiers including Jim "Hymie" Olson, Ray Warburton, Greg Marin, Jay Pistono, Marty Vidak, Peter Quinlan, and Skeeter and Lenny Cattabriga devoted most of their winters to backcountry skiing during the 1980s and into the 90s. In the spring of 1987 or 1988, Vidak and Quinlan made their first of three crest traverses of the Wind Rivers!

Free-heel skiers began racing and skiing the steeper flanks of the Teton peaks in the late 1980s and early 90s. Ahead of his time in 1987, Peter Wuerslin designed a lightweight, supportive boot that provided control in such situations. He used the shell of a Garmont alpine boot and handcrafted the toe box out of wood and fiberglass. The plastic uppers came down to the heel and forward to the ball, leaving the toe to flex for telemarking. Merrill didn't come out with its comparable Super Comp until a couple of years later.

Similar to Wuerslin's boot, the Scarpa Terminator plastic nordic downhill boot appeared on the scene in 1992, allowing more nordic skiers—including Forrest McCarthy and Pete Romaine—to brave the steep flanks of the peaks.

In the early 1990s, Mike Best set new standards for speed and courage with mid-winter nordic descents of major Teton peaks, including the Skillet Glacier and the Banana Couloir. Best also made numerous first descents of steep couloirs and faces in the Moose and Granite creek headwaters. He dug snow study pits every time he went skiing and kept a snowpack log book. Despite his precautions, however, Best miscalculated in January of 1992 and was carried over some cliffs in a Glory Bowl avalanche. Somehow, he emerged unharmed.

Between 1989 and 1994, transplanted San Diego surfer Stephen Koch successfully snowboarded the Grand Teton, Middle Teton, South Teton, Teewinot, Buck Mountain, Mount Moran, and Mount Owen. Koch sported a euro-super-alpinist style for speed ascents and first descents of new, highly technical routes. Among his routes are the southeast couloir of the South Teton, the Bubble Fun Couloir (north couloir left) of Buck, the Apocalypse Couloir of Prospectors, the northwest ice gully of the Middle Teton, and the Black Ice Couloir on the Grand Teton. These five accomplishments stand as the most extreme skiing ever achieved in the United States. On the heel of these, Koch continued to push the limits of "surf mountaineering" with descents in the Wind Rivers, Oregon Cascades, Chamonix Alps, Argentine Cordillera, Alaska Range and Nepal Himalaya.

Skiers and snowboarders persist in stretching their limits, as witnessed by an attempted descent of the 2,500-foot icy and rocky Hossack-MacGowen Couloir on the Grand Teton by Koch and this author, as well as Alex Lowe's second descent of the icy, exposed Enclosure Couloir and Frishman Couloir on the Middle Teton, plus Koch, Mark Newcomb, and Hans Johnstone's descent of Nez Perce and Koch and Newcomb's technical descent of the formidable Black Ice Couloir. Only time will tell how far skiers can push the bounds of their skills in the Tetons.

THE
NORTHERN
RANGE

Bordered by Carrot Ridge and Webb Canyon on the south and Ashton-Flagg Road on the north, this vast area comprises about one-sixth of the entire Teton Range. But the difficulty and inconvenience of the approaches keep the scores of beautiful ski routes here relatively untracked. In drought years, the prospect of dangerous crossings of the exposed Snake River channel in the northern end of the Jackson Lake basin has kept many skiers away, while a resident grizzly-bear population wards off spring skiers. And the sheer remoteness of places like North Bitch Creek and upper Berry Creek keeps the Teton Pass day crowds away.

The northern range is harsh, more akin to the Alaskan wilderness than to the rest of the Teton Range. Be prepared for more arduous, unforgiving tours than

Velvety open bowls grace the upper slopes of Owl Peak. The Owl/Elk massif offers perhaps the greatest variety of ski terrain of any massif in the range. Bighorn sheep also winter here; be careful not to disturb them.

you find in southern and central ranges.

For detailed reference to the Northern Range region, use USGS maps for Rammel Mountain, Ranger Peak, Hominy Peak, Survey Peak, Flagg Ranch, McRenolds Reservoir, and Lamont.

APPROACHES

Ashton-Flagg Ranch Road (Targhee National Forest Road No. 261/Grassy Lake Road): {A} Following a natural 48-mile route over the mountains between Teton Valley and Jackson Hole, this historic road forms the northern boundary of the Teton Range. Although the route was used by Indians for hundreds of years, John Colter might have been the first white man to use it. At about the turn of the century, freight wagons shuttled mining materials and supplies for construction of the Jackson Lake Dam. Trappers George Fitzmeyer and Mr. Huckman ran a year-round roadhouse near Cascade Creek. In 1913, Huckman died in an avalanche while skiing to a trap.

To reach the road from the west side of the Tetons,

51

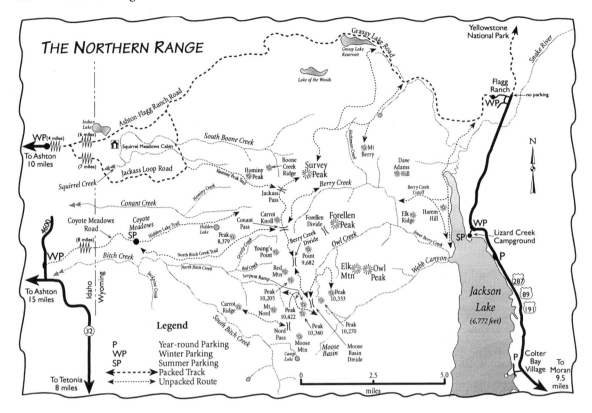

THE NORTHERN RANGE

turn east onto Ashton-Flagg Road a mile south of Ashton, Idaho on Highway 32. Drive 9.25 miles to a large parking lot at the end of the plowed road. From Jackson Hole, turn west at Flagg Ranch Junction and follow signs to the snowmobile parking area. Ski on the snowmobile-packed track across a bridge, along the Snake River, and over a broad ridge, into Glade Creek. Follow the north side of the drainage nine miles to Grassy Lake Reservoir. The east end of the reservoir is the northern tip of the Teton Range and the start or finish of a complete Teton crest traverse.

Grassy Lake Road no longer gets plowed. The National Park Service used to open it to vehicles when all the snow had melted off. The road closes to all vehicles between April 1 and May 31 each year. The road closure begins at Rockefeller Parkway Ranger Station junction and continues nine miles west to the Targhee National Forest boundary. Call Grand Teton National Park for current conditions and closures.

Highway 287/89/191: Improved in the mid-1950s, this scenic highway is plowed in winter between Moran and Flagg Ranch.

Lizard Creek Road and Campground: Although this campground and road on Fonda Point are closed annually between June and September, skiers may pass through to get to Jackson Lake and the mouths of Webb and Berry canyons. Park in a pullout on Highway 287/89/191 and follow the road for a quarter mile until you can drop onto the lake ice in the small bay formed by Fonda Point. During low water, ski over small creeks to Fonda Point and the main body of the lake.

Jackson Lake: See Ranger Peak Region.

Grassy Lake Reservoir-Survey Peak: {C} Though this 11-mile stretch of the Teton hydrologic crest is relatively uninteresting, you should include it if you intend to ski a complete traverse of the range. In June of 1962, Bill Briggs, Rod Dornan, and Jim Greig became the first skiers to use this laborious route, as they toured from Grassy Lake to Cascade Canyon.

The route is not an aimless trash through the forest, as a map might indicate; it actually follows natural boundaries. The first four miles follows the edge of the 800-foot east-facing escarpment above Glade Creek. The remaining seven miles follows a broad, undulating ridge that separates Hechtman Creek from the Cascade and Boone Creek drainages. The forest is mostly old- to medium-growth trees, so travel is easy.

Flagg Ranch-Mount Berry: {D} Wesley Bunch, Rod "Rocket Man" Barnes, and Judd Stewart first used this route in April of 1994 during their exit from a Teton Crest traverse. To find their way through the thick forest, Stewart set compass bearings on Bunch, who skied slightly ahead. Stewart then would yell directions: "left, right, or straight."

Coming from Survey Peak, the crew followed the hydrologic crest northeast, contoured the headwaters of Hechtman Creek, and climbed to the north ridge of Mount Berry. They dropped east off of a large escarpment to a tarn and followed discontinuous creek beds until they popped out of the woods right on the Grassy Lake Road!

Berry Creek mouth-Flagg Ranch: {B} This tedious route is not recommended. But if you haven't made provisions to cross Jackson Lake and the Snake River channel after they thaw, you might have to use it. Skiers who have used the route include White, Carr, Connors, Crabtree, Lawley and Koedt in the 70s. The eight- or nine-mile route is a less-favorable beginning or end to a Teton Crest traverse.

Follow the west side of the floodplain to the Grassy Lake Road bridge, crossing to Flagg Ranch. In the worst scenario, expect willow-whacking, stream crossings, swamps, waist-deep mud, and at least one climb up a hillside where the river bank is too steep.

Lower Berry Cutoff: {B} This convenient route provides easy access into upper Berry Creek Canyon.

From Fonda Point, cross Jackson Lake and trend north toward the break between Harem Hill and Elk Ridge. Connect open meadows just south of an unnamed creek for three miles or so to an indistinct divide. In the next half mile, you'll drop 80 feet into Berry Creek.

Berry Creek Canyon: Some of the first skiers to explore Berry Creek—in the late 1950s—were Frank Ewing, Keith Jones, and Don Williams.

The main and south forks of upper Berry Creek offer premier easy ski terrain. Park rangers traditionally have been the primary skiers in Berry Creek because of their privilege to stay in the patrol cabin. Until the mid-1960s, the cabin was high on the northeast shoulder of Survey Peak. Now, the deluxe cottage sits on the canyon floor, just north of Forellen Peak.

Skiers who are familiar with the short, steep eastern Teton approaches will find this long, flat canyon quite tedious. The upper canyon's flat meadow floor includes a meandering stream, easily skirted on either side {K}.

Ranger John Carr was one of the first skiers to use lower Berry Creek to access the Berry Creek patrol cabin. This narrow, V-shaped section of the canyon is flanked by demanding cliffs, steep slopes, and thick forest {D}. If you must use the lower canyon, stay on the north side, above the cliffy creek chasm, especially near the canyon mouth. Farther up this narrow canyon, it is perhaps easier to drop into the creek bed rather than traverse the north flank. When the canyon opens near the Owl Creek confluence, continue on the north side of the creek to avoid steep hillsides {K}.

The middle stretch of the drainage between Elk Ridge and Forellen Peak also is difficult to ski. The most feasible route follows the line of the summer trail north into upper Berry Creek {B}.

You must use lower Berry Creek to reach Owl Canyon, from Lizard Creek Campground. Otherwise, bypass the hassles of lower Berry Creek by using Lower Berry Cutoff.

Owl Creek Canyon: {B} This long canyon is difficult to access from Jackson Hole because the easiest route requires travel in narrow lower Berry Creek.

Once you reach the upper canyon, however, access to peaks including Forellen and Red Mountain is easy.

Webb Canyon: See Ranger Peak Region.

Squirrel Meadows Guard Station: Some 24 miles east of Ashton is a cabin, available for public winter rental from the Ashton Ranger District of the U.S. Forest Service. From the Ashton-Flagg Road, turn south on the Squirrel Meadows Spur Road and you'll find the cabin near the west end of Squirrel Meadows. Built in 1924, it provides convenient access for tours in the northwestern Tetons. Call or write to the Ashton Ranger District for further details: P.O. Box 858, Ashton, Idaho 83420. (208) 652-7442.

Jackass Loop Road (Targhee National Forest Road No. 264): {B} Use this snowmobile track to approach Hominy Peak and South Boone Creek. Park at the end of the plowed section of the Ashton-Flagg Road, then ski or snowmobile four miles east and fork right onto the Conant-Fall River Road. After two miles, the Jackass Loop Road turns left (east) 14.4 miles to its junction with Ashton-Flagg Road, a mile northeast of Squirrel Meadows.

South Boone Creek: {A} A mile and a half south of the Ashton-Flagg Road/Jackass Loop Road junction, this canyon and trail strikes east, culminating at Survey Peak some six miles upstream.

Hominy Peak Trail: {D} From the southeast corner of Jackass Loop Road, two trails strike east through the thick forest of Hominy Peak's west ridge. The northeastern of the two trails leads 4.5 miles to the summit. Also use this trail to reach Boone Creek Ridge and Jackass Pass.

Coyote Meadows Road (Targhee National Forest Road No. 265): {B} A half mile west of Lamont, Idaho, head north on 4600 Street. After driving a mile, dig out a parking spot near the Coyote Meadows sign. This road is difficult to follow in winter because it's not a popular snowmobiling area. It follows the general line of Cart Hollow, gains a ridge, then drops to Coyote Meadows at the head of Coyote Creek.

Hidden Lake Trail: {D} Use this route to reach Hidden Lake and the headwaters of Conant Creek.

From Coyote Meadows, follow upper Coyote Creek to the ridge south of Conant Creek. Continue east past Hidden Lake and traverse down to Conant Basin.

North Bitch Creek Trail: {C} Follow the South Bitch Creek approach to the top of the second short ridge. Scale this low-angle ridge east, then cross a shallow draw and follow the north rim of North Bitch Creek Canyon to the head of Grizzly Creek and Conant Pass.

North Bitch Creek: {C} Follow the approach to South Bitch Creek but bear left at the canyon fork. Most skiing in this remote, thick-forested canyon is across its headwaters, nestled between Mount Nord and the peaks above Moose Basin.

South Bitch Creek: See Rammel Mountain Massif.

PEAKS AND BOWLS

Harem Hill (7,326 feet): {D} Bruce Hayse made a short day tour on this bump just west of the narrows in the north end of Jackson Lake. Approach from Lizard Creek.

Dave Adams Hill (9,004 feet): This relatively high ridge marks the south end of the long escarpment that starts at Grassy Lake Reservoir. Beginning with a steep 400-foot ridge that drops from the southeast end of the summit plateau, five- to 10-degree slopes lead through forest—nearly 2,300 feet in two miles—to Jackson Lake, near Steamboat Mountain. Approach from Lizard Creek.

Survey Peak (9,277 feet): A favorite ski area of Grand Teton Park rangers, this snow dome offers plenty of moderate wide-open and gladed skiing. This mountain is sensitive bighorn sheep winter range. Approach from Berry or South Boone creek or Grassy Lake Reservoir-Survey Peak.

East Face: {E} This yoyoing classic is a mile-long wall of 30-degree treeless slopes, 500 feet tall. Watch out for dangerous wind-slab conditions.

South Face: {E} This 1,700-foot face is a spectacular ski route in good conditions, which are rare.

West Face: {C} Often climbed during south-to-north

Teton Crest traverses, this face offers some 500 feet of easy gladed slopes.

(Early fixed-heel: Frank Ewing, Keith Jones, and Don Williams; December, 1957.)

North Face: {D} This wide open 1,000-foot face is used primarily during Teton Crest traverses.

Elk Ridge (8,451 feet): This high ridge might have been part of Forellen Peak before Berry Creek carved a gap between them. Approach from Lizard Creek.

Northeast Face: {D} A favorite day tour of Bruce Hayse, this face offers 1,200 feet of interesting gladed terrain.

(Early free-heel: Bruce Hayse; mid-1980s.)

Forellen Peak (9,772 feet): This broad massif offers a diverse selection of ski terrain and astonishing summit views of Elk Mountain, Mount Moran, and the Grand Teton. Approach from Owl or Berry creek.

East Ridge: {D} In *The Best Ski Touring in America*, Steve Barnett describes a propitious way to finish a Teton Crest traverse. His route avoids laborious flat-tracking in Berry and Owl canyons by climbing the 900-foot west face of Forellen from Berry Creek Divide, then skiing the 2,400-foot, four-mile-long east ridge to Lower Berry cutoff. Be careful not to lose your partners in this vast forest.

Jay Pistono and Ron Labatte made perhaps the first ski ascent of this ridge in the early 1980s.

(Early free-heel: Steve Barnett, et al; 1980s.)

West Bowls: {D} Jim "Olie" Olson describes gladed powder slopes below the northwest face, which drop into a southern tributary of Berry Creek.

(Early free-heel: Frank Ewing, Keith Jones, and Don Williams; 1957 or 1958.)

Northeast Forest: {D} As you begin a descent of the east ridge, the enormous potential of this forested face unfolds below. Between the north and east ridges, sparse forest and random clearings sweep more than 2,000 feet—three-plus miles wide—into Berry Creek. Although a day trip to this face is not unreasonable for a very strong party, staying at the Berry patrol cabin or camping at Berry Creek would allow more skiing time.

(Early free-heel: Bruce Hayse.)

Other potential routes: From the summit, the classic south gully drops nearly 2,500 feet into Owl Creek.

Point 9,682: This insignificant point along the Red-Forellen ridge makes a great campsite with astonishing views and has lashings of easy terrain off all sides. Approach from Owl or Berry canyon.

Red Mountain (10,177 feet): This remarkable ski mountain stands out from Driggs, Idaho as the northernmost high ridge in the Teton Range. It also is arguably the northernmost crest peak—other than Survey Peak—that deserves attention from ordinary ski mountaineers. This mountain is sensitive bighorn sheep winter range. Approach from Red, Berry, or Owl creek.

East Side: {E} Expansive, treeless, windy bowls that drain into Berry and Owl creeks grace the east and northeast flanks of the mountain.

(Early free-heel: Bill and Woody Barmore, Mike Whitfield, Shari Gregory, Donny Black, and one other; Feb. 10, 1980.)

North Ridge: {C} From Conant Pass, climb this gradual undulating ridge two miles to the summit.

(Early fixed-heel: Frank Ewing, Keith Jones, and Don Williams; 1957.)

Other potential routes: The west ridge boasts 15-degree slopes that drop more than 3,000 feet in just more than two miles, to the confluence of Grizzly Creek and North Bitch Creek. Use Serpent Ramp to return to Moose Basin, or use Red Creek to regain the crest above the Berry Creek patrol cabin. The vast southwest face is not recommended for skiing; it is steep, with intermittent cliffs, and often is strewn with avalanche debris.

Peak 10,205: The highest point on the Red Mountain massif, this jewel of the northern crest offers three great ski routes. From the east, climb the mountain from its northeast shoulder via the northeast ridge. Approach from Owl or Berry creek.

Southeast Face: {E} This classic bowl drops more than 600 feet into upper Owl Creek.

(Early free-heel: Tom Turiano; April 15, 1994.)

North Couloir: {F} One of four north couloirs, this drops precipitously for 500 feet into upper Owl Creek.

(Early free-heel: Dave Moore and Tom Turiano; April 15, 1994.)

Other potential routes: The consistent 2,000-foot west face is perhaps the only enjoyable way to ski the vast west wall of the Red Mountain massif. Have a plan of escape before you arrive in remote North Bitch Creek.

Owl Peak (10,612 feet): Jackson school teacher Marty Krueter was instrumental in establishing the Special Olympics. As a fund-raiser, Krueter and others climbed Jackson Peak in the winter of 1978, accepting pledges for each vertical foot they climbed. After each 100-foot gain, they transmitted to the local radio station, which announced their progress to the public.

Locals made donations that contributed greatly to the viability of the Special Olympics. The following year, the group made a similar fund-raising trip up Owl Peak and encountered bighorn sheep on the windswept summit.

The Owl/Elk massif offers perhaps the greatest variety of ski terrain of any massif in the range. Near the granite domes in the mouth of Webb Canyon, where

---

Flat-bottomed Berry Creek makes a tedious trek to Survey Peak, but vast bowls of all exposures make the trip well worth the effort. Among the first skiers to explore Berry Creek were Frank Ewing, Keith Jones and Don Williams.

the trail descends to the creek, branch northeast and make an ascending traverse on a ramp. Climb this ramp and creek directly east past windswept bowls and along an undulating ridge to the summit. This open plateau is a highly sensitive bighorn sheep winter range. You also may approach from lower Berry Creek.

East Ridge: {D} Vast open bowls and a variety of snow conditions make this a classic Teton tour. Skiing north off the ridge usually offers the best snow.

(Early free-heel: Ray White, Robbie Fuller, Ken Thomasma, Marty Krueter, and Gary Marple; Feb. 10, 1979.)

Northern Cwm: {E} and {F} Dropping directly north from the summit, these steep, wide gullies and rolling bowls outclass the best of Teton Pass. Explore!

(Early free-heel: Tom Turiano, Mark Newcomb, and Hans Johnstone; March 2, 1994.)

Northeast Ridge: {D} Follow the approach to the east ridge but gain the northeast ridge at the 9,000-foot level. An interesting notch at 9,920 feet often is guarded by bighorn sheep and offers the only passage through cliffs to reach the upper plateau. Many Owl skiers use this scenic ridge for their ascent.

Other potential routes: The south couloirs are a series of long, steep chutes that plunge south from the east ridge into Webb Canyon.

Elk Mountain (10,720-plus feet): Viewed from Forellen and other points north, this remote double peak is quite impressive. Approach from Owl Peak, Webb or Owl canyon.

East Ridge: {E} After climbing both summits, the first and only known descent pair skied this rather dull ridge route to regain the summit of Owl Peak.

(Early free-heel: Dave Moore and Dave Coon; March 26, 1994.)

Other potential routes: Elk may yield interesting ski routes on the north, northeast, and southeast sides, but none of these have yet been skied. The 2,600-foot Elk/Owl Couloir drops into Webb Canyon with some tricky maneuvering to bypass a cliff band.

Peak 10,333: This high point on the long west ridge of Elk Mountain offers great skiing on two flanks. Approach from Owl or Webb canyon.

East-Northeast Face: {E} 700-plus-foot powder bowls, a mile wide, drain skiers into the south fork of Owl Creek. Use Peak 10,333-Owl Creek to return to Moose Basin.

(Early free-heel: Dave Moore, Tom Turiano, and Mike Whitehead; April 14, 1994.)

Other potential routes include the windblown northwest bowl, which ends at a cliff.

Peak 10,270: This beautiful cliff-striped mountain stands just east of Moose Basin Divide. A cave was discovered in the west-face cliff. Approach from Webb or Owl canyon.

East Face: {E} This 35-degree, 500-foot bowl leads into a steep basin between Peak 10,270 and Peak 10,333 and is the best ski route on the mountain.

(Early free-heel: Dave Moore, Tom Turiano, and Mike Whitehead; April 14, 1994.)

Peak 10,422: This reptile-shaped mountain has little to offer the average nordic tourer, as it is nearly ringed by unskiable cliffs. Only a few couloirs connect the upper bowls with the lower ones but none of them are very aesthetic. Approach from North Bitch, Webb, or Owl canyon.

East Ridge: {E} On April 7, 1993, Tom Turiano, Forrest McCarthy and John Fettig skied the east ridge to Moose Basin Divide, around the north side of the monolith, which they climbed as well.

(Early free-heel: Tom Turiano, Forrest McCarthy and John Fettig; April 7, 1993.)

Peak 10,360: This classic conical peak has no trees and sits at the top of Moose Basin. Approach from Webb Canyon or North Bitch Creek.

East Side: {D} or {E} Skiing is superb anywhere off the east side.

(Early free-heel: Tom Turiano, Forrest McCarthy and John Fettig; April 7, 1993.)

Moose Mountain (10,054 feet): Approach this insignificant bump from North Bitch, South Bitch, or Webb canyon.

East Bowl: This wide but short, cornice-capped, windy bowl rises from upper Moose Basin.

(Early free-heel: Norm Larson and Martha Clarke; Jan. 20, 1985.)

South Ridge: Ron Matous skied this scenic ridge in February, 1986.

Other potential route: The 1,600-foot southwest face is Moose Mountain Slide, which can offer good skiing when conditions are safe.

Boone Creek ridge: The west side of this South Boone Creek ridge offers good skiing.

Hominy Peak (8,362 feet): Approached via Hominy Peak Trail, this rather dull peak might have good skiing on the northwest side.

Point 8,379: Approached from the North Bitch Creek Trail, this interesting ridge provides a scenic view and good skiing on its west face, above Hidden Lake. Check out the northeast face for deeper wind-loaded powder.

Carrot Knoll (8,800-plus feet): This mound separates Grizzly Creek from Conant Creek and offers easy corn skiing on its south face.

Young's Point (9,337 feet): This remote low ridge offers 2,000 feet of fantastic easy skiing on its long, broad west ridge to the fork of Red and Grizzly creeks. Approach from Coyote Meadows via North Bitch Creek and Red or Grizzly creek, or from upper Berry Creek.

Carrot Ridge: (9,636 feet): {C} This five-mile-long ridge is an excellent approach to or return from Coyote Meadows for a tour in the North Bitch Creek headwaters. Approach from Coyote Meadows and climb straight between the north and south forks of Bitch Creek.

Mount Nord (9,720-plus feet): Limestone towers, cliffs, huge boulders, hanging snowfields, steep chutes, inconspicuous passages, and a northwest-facing bowl make this stumpy ancient sea-floor remnant very interesting to explore. Approach from South Bitch, North Bitch, or Webb canyon.

HIGH ROUTES

Berry Creek Divide-Survey Peak: {D} From Berry Creek Divide, traverse northwest, staying high across several draws to reach the crest. Follow the broad crest across Conant Pass and the forested isthmus separating Berry Creek from Conant and South Boone creeks. Climb the west face of Survey.

Berry Creek patrol cabin-Conant Pass: {C} To reach Conant Pass, leave Berry Creek near Knoll 8,220, about a mile upstream of the patrol cabin. Climb around the knoll to the west to gain the large bench below Carrot Knoll and Conant Pass.

Moose Basin Divide-Berry Creek Divide: {D} This scenic leg of the Teton Crest follows a bench on the east side of Peak 10,422 and is the best route between Webb and Berry canyons. It most easily contours below the rocky east buttress of Peak 10,205. John Carr was one of the first skiers to make a loop from Berry Creek into Webb Canyon via this route, and he's completed the tour several times since then.

Peak 10,333-Upper Owl Creek: {E} Use this route to return to Moose Basin after yoyoing the east-northeast side of Peak 10,333. Dave Moore, Mike Whitehead, and this author traversed north along the base of Peak 10,333 in a howling blizzard until we reached the long north ridge. After contouring west around the north ridge, we then skied into Owl Creek via the only break in the two-mile cliff band that rings the head of Owl Creek.

Serpent Ramp: {E} This fascinating route allows skiers to enjoy the west-facing ski routes of Red Mountain and return to camp in Moose Basin. Climb arduously east out of North Bitch Creek and bypass Peak 10,360 via the pass on its north side.

Carrot Ridge-Nord Pass: {D} Following the basic line of a summer trail, this scenic route skirts the craggy ridge of Point 9,657 on a bench to the southwest. You'll have to cross one steep avalanche gully on this route.

RANGER
PEAK
REGION

The empire of Ranger Peak is not dominated solely by its namesake. Doane and Eagles Rest peaks share the spotlight for skiing potential. Surrounded by Webb Canyon to the west and north, Snowshoe Canyon to the south, and Jackson Lake to the east, this winding massif is breached only by three major canyons, which culminate at magnificent snowbound basins.

The region's peaks are graced with long couloirs, wide-open bowls and long scenic ridges. Approaches to the area entail tranquil, contemplative lake-ice crossings that may be as long as three miles.

For detailed reference to the Ranger Peak Region, use USGS maps for Ranger Peak and Colter Bay.

Lance Peiser telemarks through the wet powder in the Gendarme Couloir of Mount Robie after an unsuccessful summit bid from the east ridge. The couloir has a dogleg and descends precipitously into Colter Canyon.

APPROACHES

Lizard Creek Road and Campground: See The Northern Range.

Highway 287/89/191: See The Northern Range.

Jackson Lake (6,742 feet-6,770 feet): This 400-foot-deep lake formed as a result of the combined gouging of the Moran Canyon, Snowshoe Canyon, and Jackson Lake glaciers. When these glaciers dissipated, residual water formed a lake in the deepest section of the glacial basin, leaving all higher ground as hills and marshes. In 1906, the Jackson Lake Dam was erected on the Snake River, just north of Signal Mountain, to provide reservoir water for Idaho farms. Water flooded the ancient marshes and was contained by the morainal hills of the Jackson Lake Glacier, thus tripling the size of the lake.

Because of fluctuations in precipitation and downstream water demand, Jackson Lake's level can vary by as much as 30 feet. Consequently, the area of the lake is as much as 8,000 acres (30 percent) smaller at low water than at high water. High water fills the entire lake

59

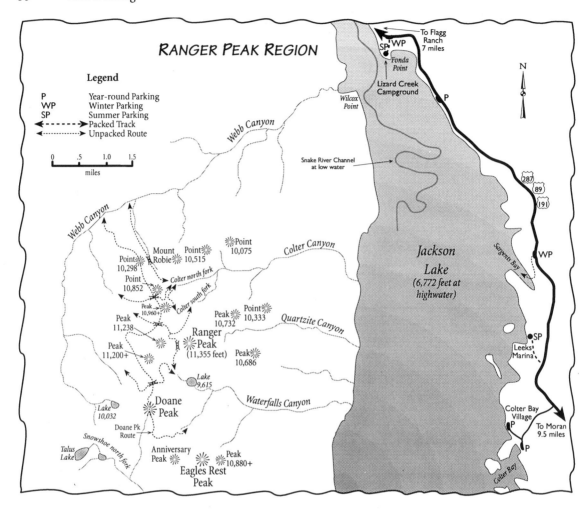

basin, from Steamboat Mountain to Spalding Bay. Low water changes the southern shores only slightly, while the northern shores shift by as many as seven miles. In these circumstances, the Snake River meanders through the northern lake basin. Call the Bureau of Reclamation for current lake levels (307)543-2519.

On Feb. 20, 1960—in low water—rangers Gale Wilcox, John Fonda, and Stan Spurgeon tried to cross the river just west of Lizard Creek inlet on what seemed to be hard ice. Spurgeon made it safely to the other side and Wilcox was halfway across when Fonda fell through near the east bank. Wilcox and Spurgeon rushed quickly to Fonda's aid, lying on their stomachs in a chain fashion and stretching a ski pole to him. The ice on the edge of the hole kept breaking as Fonda tried to get out, and soon the other two rangers fell through the ice as well. Spurgeon was able to remove his skis quickly and climb onto the ice, but Wilcox's and Fonda's ski safety straps were attached, preventing them from moving effectively. With a desperate effort, Spurgeon pulled Wilcox out, but Fonda drowned in the cold current. Wilcox died soon after from shock and exposure.

In another instance during the late 1980s, Bill Hopkins tried to ford the river after a week-long spring ski tour from Grand Targhee to Lizard Creek. He lost his poles and nearly drowned in the deep, swift current. During a reconnaissance before his trip, he concluded that the iced-over lake would be safe to cross. When he arrived a week later at the mouth of Moose Creek, however, the ice on the river was gone. He hitchhiked to Jackson fully drenched.

Skiers must seriously deliberate plans to cross the lake flat when the water is at the Snake River level. If you must cross, be certain that the aerated ice is thick enough to support weight, keeping in mind the inconsistency of over-current ice. If the river is free from ice, which usually is the case, consider fording the river with chest waders or crossing in a raft or canoe. Remember, the current is swift and can vary from 30 feet to 60 feet wide and from two feet to six feet deep. The most oft-used riffle is marked with posts about 200 feet northwest of Lizard Creek campground. The southern post, if visible above the snow, marks the easier crossing.

When the north end of the lake basin, near Lizard Creek, is iced over, crossing to or from Webb, Owl and Berry canyons usually is relatively safe. Because the lake is shallow there, the ice grows quite thick. And the Snake River does not erode the ice here as it does north of Harem Hill. Nonetheless, always use extreme caution, particularly near the Moose and Berry creek inlets on the west shore.

At times, increased current at the Snake River inlet and drastic ice sag in the northern end of Jackson Lake cause water to flow over the ice, creating a lake on the surface of the ice. In the rest of the lake, such flooding is caused by ice sag and water seeping up through the cracks. These situations create severe slush problems and "honeycomb ice," which you should avoid.

Small areas of open water, or "spring holes," sometimes develop near Hermitage Point, Spalding Bay, Half Moon Bay, and the mouths of Colter and Webb canyons. Spring holes are formed by circulating water from lake floor vents and other currents. Surprisingly, the surrounding ice usually is solid. Be careful not to ski into these holes, as they often are hidden by just a thin skim of ice!

The "Big Hole" area refers to the deepest section of the lake, more than a mile west of Colter Bay and extending as far as three miles in both directions. The overturn process occurs more slowly there, allowing extensive areas of open water to last into late December.

Along the shore south of Wilcox Point and north of the mouth of Colter Canyon is a string of warm-water vents. The ice here is very thin or nonexistent. In some years, however, ice strangely forms above these vents with little effect on thickness and strength.

Use caution in Moran Bay, where ice may be weakened by currents from Moran and North Moran creeks. The direct southern exposure of the north shore also absorbs heat that weakens the ice. In spring, however, Moran Bay sometimes holds ice for weeks longer than the main body of the lake. This ice is not for travel, though. Avoid ice in Willow Flats as well.

Even strong lake ice usually becomes dangerous for skiers by mid- to late April, two to three weeks before the lake is clear enough for boating. For spring crossings by canoe, park at Spalding or Colter bay, or hire the Signal Mountain Lodge Marina to shuttle as many as five people and gear across and back in a motor boat. If you don't own or can't borrow a canoe and the shuttle is too expensive, hobble along the cobble shores of Spalding, Bearpaw, and Moran bays. They provide excellent bushwhacking-free routes around the southwest side of the lake during low water. The Leigh Lake-Bearpaw Bay route affords the best overland course from the south.

Webb Canyon: {D} This vast drainage offers exceptional scenery and superb terrain of all difficulties. Use Webb Canyon to access peaks including Owl, Elk, Peak 10,360, Mount Robie, and Glacier. Random bowls abound in Moose Basin, north of Peak 10,880-plus and on the west side of the Ranger-Doane ridge. Bruce Hayse is perhaps the only person to ski the entire length of the canyon, from Jackson Lake to Pass 10,320-plus.

Park at Lizard Creek and cross Jackson Lake to access the canyon. Be especially careful to avoid moose here. Navigate the web of creeks near the mouth and ski up the north side of the canyon. Three to four miles from the lake, you'll encounter a strenuous series of gullies and granite hummocks that make the route inconspicuous. The most efficient way follows the summer trail up a gully, over some hummocks and back down into the creek. Farther up, cross to the south side to avoid steep banks and cliffs. You'll find a patrol cabin and latrine on a lower bench of Moose Basin.

Colter Canyon: {C} This spectacular but seldom-visited canyon provides a mecca of relatively unexplored ski terrain and straightforward access to Ranger Peak and Mount Robie. Bruce Hayse made one of the earliest ski tours here in 1990. While approaching from Colter Bay, be aware of spring holes in Jackson Lake near the canyon mouth. The easiest route in the lower canyon follows clearings north of the creek. To enter or exit the north fork of the canyon most easily, avoid cliffs by following the south fork creek, then traverse north by way of Lake 9,367. On Jan. 30, 1995, Forrest McCarthy, Mike Menolascino and this author tackled this cliffy headwall en route to an unsuccessful Mount Robie climb. We climbed a deep gully on the south end of the cliff, then McCarthy skied a steep, narrow chute in the center. The upper north and south forks are rimmed by impressive bowls and couloirs of all exposures.

Quartzite Canyon (Falcon Draw): {F} This draw drains due east from Ranger Peak. For skiers, few Teton drainages match this terrain. After a marvelous descent of the east face of Ranger Peak, you'll encounter huge gullies, couloirs, long traverses, short meadows and extensive bowls during the lengthy descent to Jackson Lake. Keep a map handy to avoid cliff bands and to discern the best ski terrain. Approach from Colter Bay.

Waterfalls Canyon: {D} This canyon renders the primary access to Eagles Rest, Doane, and Ranger peaks. Two major waterfalls in the canyon flow over headwalls that impose the only obstacles during ascents or descents. Pass both waterfalls on the north side. Large, burned forest areas make travel in the lower canyon easy. Approach from Colter Bay.

Snowshoe Canyon: See Snowshoe Canyon Region.

PEAKS AND BOWLS

Point 10,515: This is the obscure point along the east ridge of Mount Robie. Approach from the mouth of Colter Canyon and gain the ridge to the north. You can follow this ridge easily to the summit, passing Point 10,075 to the north. Gently angled, wide-open slopes grace this scenic ridge.

East Side: {E} Terrific east-facing bowls stretch along the one-mile ridge between Point 10,180 and the east ridge of Point 10,515.

(Early free-heel: Bruce Hayse; late 1980s.)

Peak 10,881 (Mount Robie): Undistinguished from the east and south, craggy walls and steep couloirs surprise climbers and skiers who view the mountain from the north and west. Approach from Webb or Colter canyon.

Gendarme Couloir: {F} Three skiers tried to ascend Mount Robie from the east, via the five-mile ridge that extends from Jackson Lake, over Point 10,075 and Point 10,515, to the summit. Some 200 feet below the summit, the team encountered a gendarme that proved too difficult to bypass without a rope. In retreat, they happened upon a couloir with a dogleg that descended precipitously into Colter Canyon.

(Early free-heel: Tom Turiano, Dave Moore, and Lance Peiser; March 4, 1994.)

Other potential routes: While the west face often is wind-scoured and cliff-encumbered, the northeast face boasts spectacular couloirs that drop directly from the summit into Webb Canyon, via a heavenly glacial drainage with a nunatak. The primary route on Mount Robie probably is the hourglass-shaped southeast couloir, which drops at a 45-degree angle for almost 800 feet into the north fork of Colter Canyon.

Point 10,852: Sitting at the head of Colter Canyon north fork, this sharp peak offers two potential ski routes. The southeast face is a large bowl, dropping 450 feet into Colter Canyon. The north couloir and gully are a surprising treasure, plummeting 3,200 feet into Webb Canyon. Approach from Colter or Webb canyon.

Peak 10,960-plus: This horn stands on the triple

divide between Webb Canyon and the forks of Colter Canyon. Two north-facing couloirs lead 500 feet from the summit to the upper north fork of Colter Canyon and are separated by an impressive gneiss buttress. Approach from Colter or Webb canyon.

Point 10,333: This high point is destined to be a classic, vaunting a straightforward approach, grandiose views and great ski terrain. Approach from Colter Bay.

Northeast Ridge: {D} This aesthetic spur is broad, rounded and extends smoothly from Jackson Lake to the summit. The summit actually is just a small bump on the northeast ridge of Ranger Peak, but still represents a worthy objective. Snow on the mile-long upper northeast ridge often is sastrugi or wind slab, but its position is spectacular for touring. The lower ridge and east face offer moderate terrain of all but western exposures through sparse trees burned by a September, 1987 fire.

(Early free-heel: Bruce Hayse; late 1980s.)

Other potential routes: The north face sports two Endless Couloir-like chutes that open into one of the largest avalanche faces in the Tetons—encompassing two miles of a 3,000-foot slope. Both couloirs drop off the northeast ridge, east of a diagonal cliff band. Ski them only in the most stable conditions. The west face often is wind-scoured at the top but you'll find plenty of snow in the scenic cirque below.

Peak 10,732: This sub-summit on the long northeast ridge of Ranger Peak sustains one potential ski route. The 20-foot-wide northeast couloir includes straight rock walls and plummets 1,000 feet directly off the summit, into a southern tributary of Colter Canyon. Approach directly from Colter Canyon.

Ranger Peak (11,355 feet): From the highway north of Moran Junction, this undistinguished peak doesn't strike laymen as the highest Teton peak north of Mount Moran. But skiers' eyes are drawn like a magnet to its massive east-facing snow bowl. Approach from Waterfalls Canyon north fork, Colter Canyon south fork, Quartzite, or Webb canyon.

East Face: {E} Strong west winds commonly scour all but the deepest gullies on the north, west and south faces of the mountain, depositing all of the snow on this face, which is one of the classics that the range offers. Weak wind-slab conditions often exist in winter, so it's safest in spring. Continue skiing down Quartzite Canyon for a top-10 run.

(Early fixed-heel: Davey Agnew, not from summit; mid-1970s. Early free-heel: Dave Moore and Bill Stanley; Feb. 3, 1991.)

Diagonal Couloir: {F} or {G} Ski the southeast ridge for at least a quarter mile until this couloir drops sheerly southwest. Walk over a short section of wind-scoured rocks to the top of this classic double-falline challenge.

(Early free-heel: Forrest McCarthy and Bill Iorio; March 15, 1994.)

South Side: {D} Ski the west ridge past wind-scoured south slopes until you can drop onto a snow face.

(Early free-heel: Peter Koedt; March, 1984.)

Other potential routes: The north couloir drops into Colter Canyon from the first saddle northeast of the summit. The northeast ridge couloir pierces into Colter Canyon a mile northeast of the summit. Straight-sided and consistent, two other couloirs lead almost 2,000 feet from the southeast ridge into Waterfalls Canyon below Wilderness Falls.

Peak 11,238: Often wind-scoured and slabby, this peak offers little to skiers except a bowl at the head of Waterfalls Canyon.

Peak 11,200-plus: Of the two insignificant peaks at the head of the northwest basin of Waterfalls Canyon, this one offers the better ski terrain. Several steep chutes and bowls lead southeast from the summit.

Peak 10,686: From its position as the easternmost extension of Ranger Peak's southeast ridge, this minor summit serves up an excellent view of the entire Eagles Rest/Doane/Ranger massif. Despite a three-mile lake crossing and a 4,000-foot approach climb, this is the most popular ski descent north of Mount Moran. And with increasing crowds on mountains like Peak 10,552 and 25 Short, its popularity will continue to grow. Approach from Colter Bay.

East Side: {E} or {F} From this summit, you can find at least four fantastic ski lines. To the southeast drops a continuous gully, topped by the mountain's main feature—a Glory-like bowl. The lower section of this gully is quite narrow and usually is filled with avalanche debris. You can avoid it by traversing south to the adjacent face.

Slightly northeast from the summit lies a fabulous bowl that funnels into a steep, narrow gully, joining the main one just below midpoint. Another nice route, "The Burn," is a large triangular face directly below the

east sub-summit. In July of 1974, a forest fire left nothing but stumps on this steep face.

Other potential routes: Dropping into Quartzite Canyon to the north, one moderate gully leads from the east ridge, whereas a steep, broken face leads directly from the summit. One couloir on the face leads straight off the summit for 1,500 feet.

Doane Peak (11,355 feet): This snow dome was

Ranger Peak's east face offers some of the best accessible moderate ski terrain in the north half of the range. West winds often scour all but the deepest gullies on the three other faces of the mountain, depositing all of the snow here.

named after Lt. Gustavus Doane, who made a December expedition along the base of the Tetons in 1876. It shares with Ranger Peak the distinction of being the highest peak north of Mount Moran. Its flanks and summit are, however, even less conspicuous from the valley's highway than is Ranger Peak. Yet Doane boasts some of the best moderate ski terrain of any Teton peak. Only the northwest side of the mountain conforms to the area's wind-scoured standard. Approach from Waterfalls, Snowshoe, or Webb canyon.

Southeast Couloir: {F} This steep couloir drops 1,000 feet from the south end of the summit plateau into the basin between Anniversary and Doane peaks. Christoph Schork, Jim Schultz and this author climbed the route on our way from Eagles Rest to Doane in March of 1991.

(Early free-heel: Forrest McCarthy and Bill Iorio; March 14, 1994.)

Southwestern Cwm: {E} After honing in by helicopter on a radio-collared bighorn sheep that was presumed dead, a park biologist and ranger skied this 3,000-foot bowl into Snowshoe north fork. The carcass was not recovered, but some great skiing was had.

(Early free-heel: Mason Reid and Renny Jackson; March 28, 1995.)

North Ridge: {C} Wind thrashes this broad ridge into bizarre snow sculptures along its one-mile, 1,000-foot descent to the head of Waterfalls Canyon.

(Early free-heel: Peter Koedt and John Silverman; March, 1984.)

Other potential routes: The windblown northwest ridge leads to Lake 10,032 and Webb Canyon. The northeast face presents three wonderful wind-loaded cirques in safe skiing conditions. The central cirque has a steep exit.

Peak 10,880-plus: Disparaged as the east summit of Eagles Rest Peak, this mount nevertheless stands alone as a prime ski-mountaineering objective. The continuously challenging east face leads 4,000 feet to Jackson Lake. Approach from Colter Bay.

(Early fixed-heel: Christoph Schork; March 28, 1995. Early free-heel: Tom Turiano and Forrest McCarthy; March 28, 1995.)

Eagles Rest Peak (11,258 feet): This peak, with its igneous summit, stands out like a tower among a sea of rolling plateaus. Approach from North Moran Bay or Waterfalls Canyon.

North Couloir: {F} In late February of 1991, just before starting up the north ridge with Jim Schultz and this author, Christoph Schork cached his skis at the base of the north couloir. The trio climbed the technical north ridge to the summit and plunge-stepped down the north couloir. Arriving at the base of the couloir at 5 p.m., Schork grabbed his skis and reclimbed the 900-foot couloir to ski it! Approach from Waterfalls Canyon south fork.

(Early fixed-heel: Christoph Schork, on randonnée; Feb. 27, 1991. Early free-heel: Forrest McCarthy and Bill Iorio; March 14, 1994.)

Other potential routes: The south face has many gullies, but the 3,000-foot couloir that descends directly from the summit looks the best, and it corns up in early spring because of the mountain's eastern protrusion from the range. Ski this only during exceptional snow years. The huge northeast-facing cirque below Eagles Rest can offer fantastic skiing into Waterfalls Canyon.

Peak 11,253 (Anniversary Peak): Sharing the crown of Waterfalls Canyon south fork with Eagles Rest Peak, this hidden crest offers two potential ski routes. The south couloir spirals 4,000 feet to Snow-

shoe Canyon, and the wind-hammered west bowl empties into a 15-foot-wide chute above the forks of Snowshoe Canyon.

HIGH ROUTES

Colter Canyon north fork-Webb Canyon: {E} Pass 10,480-plus accesses the north gully of Point 10,852 and can be reached with moderate difficulty from Colter Canyon. You can use Pass 10,720-plus between Point 10,852 and Peak 10,960-plus to reach upper Webb Canyon.

Colter Canyon north fork-south fork: {E} This requires a strenuous high traverse via the east shoulder of Peak 10,960-plus.

Colter Canyon south fork-Webb Canyon: {D} Skiers can traverse easily between these two canyons, a quarter mile north of Peak 11,238.

Colter Canyon south fork-Waterfalls Canyon: {E} An ice axe might be helpful in surmounting the huge cornice below Col 10,960-plus, just west of Ranger Peak.

Webb Canyon-Doane Peak: {D} In March of 1984, Peter Koedt and John Silverman made a classic ski loop from the Moose Basin patrol cabin. They traversed the entire ridge south from Point 10,298, passing Peaks 10,852 and 11,238 to Doane Peak and skiing Ranger Peak along the way. After skiing the north ridge of Doane Peak, they "cut an endless descending traverse north" into Webb Canyon. The descent follows a gully formed by Point 10,020, then climbs to a spur and traverses sparse forest to the 7,700-foot level of Webb Canyon.

Waterfalls Canyon-Webb Canyon: {C} Pass 10,800-plus north of Doane Peak is quite gentle.

Doane Peak Route: This high route crosses over Doane's summit plateau via the southeast couloir and north ridge to allow a traverse of Eagles Rest and Doane and Ranger peaks.

SNOWSHOE CANYON REGION

This paradisiacal region has no summer trails, few visitors, and is ringed by stellar peaks. Bounded by Moran Canyon in the south, Bitch Creek in the west, Webb Canyon in the north, and Jackson Lake in the east, the region bestows a diverse lot of ski terrain. The six-mile mountain chain between Bivouac and Doubtful peaks is draped by an impressive array of bowls and couloirs. Glacier Peak and the Webb Canyon highlands present a sensational environment for touring and yoyoing. Rolling Thunder, a majestic island mountain, provides a beautiful backdrop while you're skiing the nearby bowls and domes. But the seven-mile approach across Jackson Lake keeps all but the most determined ski mountaineers away.

For detailed reference to the Snowshoe Canyon

Dave Moore enjoys wet June powder on Crocodile Crag (Point 10,732), perhaps the nicest peak for skiing in the vicinity of Glacier Peak, which provides an impressive backdrop here.

Region, use USGS maps for Ranger Peak, Mount Moran, Colter Bay and Jenny Lake.

APPROACHES

Jackson Lake: See Ranger Peak Region.

Webb Canyon: See Ranger Peak Region.

Snowshoe Canyon: This hidden valley is perhaps the least-visited major canyon in the range. The peaks at its head are some of the highest and most formidable on the crest. Craggy summits, such as the Images, Raynolds and Doubtful peaks and Rolling Thunder Mountain defend the valley from travelers seeking easy passage from adjacent points.

Except for skiers who traversed the canyon head during Teton Crest traverses, Peter Koedt and Larry Young were among the first skiers to explore the south fork—in the early 1980s—during a tour to Cascade Canyon. John Carr was one of the earliest skiers to take on the Talus Lake area, which he did during a loop from Berry Creek in the late 1970s or early 80s.

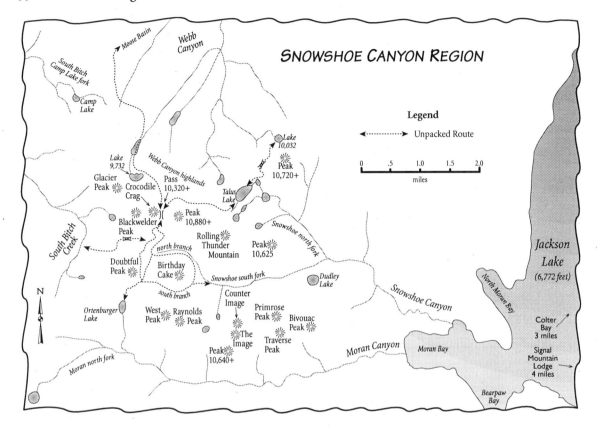

After surmounting a moraine above Moran Bay, winter travel through the lower canyon is straightforward; the easiest route is on the north side of North Moran Creek {D}. During spring, follow the south side of the creek through the bog to the base of a headwall. A steep, faint trail leads up through granite hummocks until a cliff forces a difficult stream fording. Once you're on the north side of the creek, easy bushwhacking will lead you to the forks.

To reach Talus Lake at the head of the north fork, however, you must negotiate three headwalls {E}. Excellent terrain abounds here.

The entrance into the south fork is a quarter-mile chasm that channels a raging cascade bordered by sheer walls. In mid-winter, this gorge fills with snow to provide an easy corridor into the upper canyon {D}. In spring, however, using the gorge route is not recommended. Loose rock, moats, and a swift current can mean disaster. The alternate route involves bushwhacking uphill to the south from the forks to Dudley Lake, then traversing through thick forest and crossing steep ledges into the south fork above the gorge {E}.

When you reach the south fork, your labors are rewarded with an unmatched mecca of terrain. You'll find numerous cirques on the south side of the canyon, steep couloirs on the north, and vast bowls at the headwaters.

Approach from Colter Bay or Signal Mountain by crossing Jackson Lake to Moran Bay. Cutting through the thick forest between North Moran Bay and Snowshoe Canyon is not recommended.

Moran Canyon: See Mount Moran Region.

South Bitch Canyon: See Rammel Mountain Massif.

PEAKS AND BOWLS

Peak 10,720-plus: This broad mountain just west of Doane Peak sports spectacular bowls on the west and east faces and an impressive southwest couloir. Approach from Snowshoe, Webb, or Waterfalls canyon.

Peak 10,625: This obscure, elegant mountain a mile east of Rolling Thunder Mountain has seen just a few ascents, none in winter. Potential ski routes include the south couloir, which drops into Snowshoe Canyon south fork, and the northwest face, which includes a system of chutes leading into the northeast scoop of Rolling Thunder.

Rolling Thunder Mountain (10,908 feet): Although this author and Tom Bennett skied from the 10,560-foot level of the north glacier on March 20, 1990, no skiers have descended from the summit.

Potential routes: The 2,400-foot south couloir drops into Snowshoe Canyon from the southeast end of the summit ridge and ends at a 60-foot frozen waterfall. In some years, it might be possible to avoid technicalities by traversing west just above the waterfall. The north couloir extends at 50 degrees from a notch in the west ridge. The northeast scoop would make a long moderate run from near summit.

Peak 10,880-plus: This long Colorado-like high ridge stretches between Rolling Thunder Mountain and Pass 10,320-plus. Approach from Snowshoe or Webb canyon.

Northeast Ridge: {D} Climbing from Talus Lake, the first descent party groped its way in a storm along the half-mile east ridge to the summit. The descent back to Talus Lake was on heavy powder.

(Early free-heel: Dave Moore and Tom Turiano; June 3, 1993.)

Other potential routes: The mile-wide, 1,600-foot south face would make an excellent corn run, whereas the equally wide north face—though often wind-scoured or crusted—would make an excellent powder run.

Point 10,732 (Crocodile Crag): This is perhaps the nicest peak for skiing in the Glacier Peak vicinity. Dave Moore and this author might have been the first to ski extensively on its flanks—in early June of 1993—though we didn't ski from the summit.

The northeast face of the summit cone and the several bowls on the north ridge are long enough to allow plenty of turns but short enough to make the climb up for second and third runs desirable. Approach from Snowshoe or Webb canyon.

Peak 10,800-plus (Blackwelder Peak): This sharp horn stands at the triple divide between Bitch, Snowshoe, and Webb canyons.

North Glacier: {E} Although you cannot ski it from the summit, this small glacier below the north face of the peak is one of the nicest snowbowls in the northern range, offering nearly 100 turns. The first descent pair climbed out of Snowshoe Canyon up steep couloirs to the rocky saddle between Blackwelder and Point 10,732.

(Early free-heel: Dave Moore and Tom Turiano; June 4, 1993.)

Other potential routes: The planar, triangular southeast face is plainly visible from the summit of the Grand Teton. Closer inspection reveals cliffs and chutes near the bottom, which interrupt what might have been a very clean line.

Glacier Peak (10,927 feet): Representing the highest crest point north of Table Mountain, this massive mountain is a prize ski-mountaineering objective. By Teton standards, however, it is so remote that it gets very little traffic. Each of the three commonly used approaches requires a day and a half for most parties. Use South Bitch Creek, Webb Canyon, or the Talus Lake-Pass 10,320-plus-Moose Basin high route.

North Ridge: {D} This scenic ridge is the standard ascent and descent route. Skiers encounter no major difficulties but the exposure is impressive for the northern Tetons. The ridge is narrow with wind-blown snow.

(Early free-heel: John Carr, Susan Enger, Ted

Shimo, and George Bloom; April 4, 1974. Bill Conrod and Jim Barmore; March 5, 1976.)

Other potential routes: The northeast scoop drops east from the north ridge. The southwest face—a jumble of couloirs and ridges that stretches a mile and a half long and 3,000 feet high—is among the most imposing walls in the northern range. The Camp Lake glacial scoop drops off the northwest end of the north-ridge plateau to Camp Lake. The lower northeast face, overhung by a cornice, drops northeast off the lower north-ridge plateau. The exposed falline of the direct northeast face spirals 1,200 feet to Lake 9,732.

Point 10,214 (Birthday Cake): This is the monolith at the eastern extension of Doubtful Peak's east ridge. You'll find wonderful faces off the north side of this long ridge and on the northwest side of the monolith itself. Approach from Snowshoe Canyon south fork.

Peak 10,852 (Doubtful Peak): Hidden from many familiar Teton vistas, this remarkable horn stands at the apex of four drainages. Viewed from Pass 10,320-plus, east of Blackwelder Peak, Doubtful's defined ridges and cliffy triangular faces are especially impressive. Approach from Snowshoe south fork, Moran north fork, Webb, or South Bitch canyon.

South Couloirs: {F} After two previous attempts on the peak, this author finally skied this couloir-striped face from a camp in Snowshoe south fork. Some 1,200 feet of 40-degree narrow chutes lead to Ortenburger Lake (Lake 9,610).

(Early fixed-heel: Wes Bunch; Jan. 4, 1995. Early free-heel: Tom Turiano; Jan. 4, 1995.)

Other potential routes: The north side has a harrowing route descending northwest from the summit—on steep slopes—toward a 400-foot cliff, then traverses north above the cliff into a couloir and South Bitch Creek.

Bivouac Peak (10,825 feet): Although seemingly insignificant next to Mount Moran, Bivouac offers three superb ski routes. The mountain's name gained deep meaning for Tom Bennett and this author when we bivouacked on the summit during the calm night of Feb. 9, 1991, as we attempted to traverse Raynolds Peak. We ended up downclimbing the slabby snow in the southeast couloir and continuing our traverse into Idaho via Moran Canyon, Green Lakes Mountain, and Dry Ridge. Approach from Moran Bay, or Snowshoe or Moran canyon.

Southeast Couloir: {G} This couloir extends from the flat summit for more than 4,000 feet toward Moran Bay, thus representing one of the longest continuous couloirs in the range. Jorge Colón made the first attempt on this couloir in the mid-1970s, but weather and poor snow turned him back.

The route's major obstacle is a huge chockstone in the narrows at the bottom. Steve Shea skied over the chockstone without rappelling during the first and only descent of this route. But more than 40 feet of snow must fill the void before it requires no rappels or jumps. Solid rappel anchors are available on the couloir's north side.

Surmounting the chockstone on the ascent is the crux of this expedition. You might be able to scramble around the chockstone via the exposed ledges of the wall to the south if the obstacle itself is impassable. The snow in the couloir often is high-quality neve, on 35- to 50-degree slopes.

(Early fixed-heel: Steve Shea; spring of 1979.)

Northeast Face: {E} This broad face extends nearly 4,000 feet, from a small pinnacle on the east ridge of Bivouac Peak to Moran Bay; it's one of the longest continuous faces in the range. Reaching the true summit from the pinnacle involves time-consuming, third-class climbing and one 30-foot rappel.

Two large bowls near the top provide the best skiing on the face. Nonetheless, you can find excellent winter powder on the lower forested slopes of the east ridge. In the middle elevations of the face, skiers encounter at least two major avalanche gullies, divided by steep, forested ridglets. Most skiers work their way east by traversing the gullies and skiing the ridglets.

This ascent and descent continually exposes skiers to avalanche terrain, so attempt it only in the most stable conditions. Approach from Snowshoe Canyon.

(Early free-heel: Mike Best; Feb. 25, 1991. Greg Marin; Jan. 31, 1993.)

(Early fixed-heel: Christoph Schork and Tilley; March 29, 1995.)

Peak 10,800-plus (Primrose Peak): The first descent party on this splendid peak ended up here after discovering that the north ridge of Traverse Peak was too technical for a ropeless ascent. Approach from Snowshoe Canyon south fork.

Primrose Couloir: {F} During exceptional snow years, you can ski this 800-plus-foot dike couloir from the summit, dropping west into the remote cirque northwest of Traverse Peak at angles of 40 degrees to 45 degrees.

(Early fixed-heel, not from summit: Wes Bunch, Christoph Schork and dog "Tilley;" March 15, 1994. Early free-heel, not from summit: Tom Turiano and Scott McGee; March 15, 1994.)

Traverse Peak (11,051 feet): Only two ski routes  seem possible from this hard-to-reach summit plateau. The southeast face includes several steep, narrow couloirs that lead into the main gully between Traverse and Bivouac. On the north side of the mountain, a steep, broken ramp leads from near the summit northeast into the glacial cirque above Dudley Lake. Approach from Moran or Snowshoe canyon.

Peak 10,750 (The Image): After realizing a ropeless ascent and ski descent of Traverse Peak via its cliffy northwest side was unthinkable, the first descent party spotted an exposed ski line on this minor, but impressive peak. Approach from Snowshoe Canyon south fork.

East Face: {G} Skiers took a 45- to 50-degree hanging snowfield east off the summit, then traversed into a large northeast-facing bowl on the southeast side of the mountain.

(Early fixed-heel: Wes Bunch [only one who skied from summit], Christoph Schork and dog "Tilley;" March 15, 1994. Early free-heel: Tom Turiano and Scott McGee; March 15, 1994.)

Peak 10,640-plus: The northwest face of this insignificant horn—just south of The Image—offers good skiing into an unnamed lake-filled basin above Snowshoe Canyon south fork.

Raynolds Peak (10,910 feet): Wes Bunch, Christoph Schork and dog "Tilley," and Tom Turiano attempted to ski this beautiful, remote mountain from the northeast on March 16, 1994. After conquering a difficult overhanging cornice just west of a red tower on the east ridge of the peak, we cached our skis and continued to scramble to the summit. Tilley was hauled over the cornice by hooking her leash with an ice axe. Bunch dislocated his shoulder during the ski descent of the 50-degree couloir below the cornice, but the injury was reduced. Approach from Snowshoe Canyon south fork or Moran Canyon north fork.

Potential routes: The southwest and south couloirs drop into Moran Canyon, much like the south face

---

The southeast couloir and northeast face stand out in this aerial view of Bivouac Peak from the east. The broad northeast face is one of the longest continuous faces in the range, extending nearly 4,000 feet to Moran Bay.

of Maidenform Peak. The extreme east face involves cliffs, chutes, and exposed ramps. The northwestern cwm is a large bowl between Raynolds and its west peak.

Peak 10,800-plus (Raynolds West Peak): This impressive unlabeled sub-summit of Raynolds Peak offers skiers at least two superb ski routes. Approach from Snowshoe Canyon south fork or Moran Canyon north fork.

Racing-the-Sun Couloir: {F} After a successful but time-consuming descent of Doubtful Peak earlier in the day, Wes Bunch and this author decided to race up this 1,000-foot route, as the January sun set on the horizon. Reaching angles of more than 45 degrees near the top and channeling skiers between sheer walls no more than 30 feet apart, this northwest-facing couloir is one of the most striking mountain features north of Mount Moran.

(Early fixed-heel: Wes Bunch; Jan. 4, 1995. Early free-heel: Tom Turiano; Jan. 4, 1995.)

Other potential routes: The southwest face drops 2,400 feet into the north fork of Moran Canyon.

HIGH ROUTES

Talus Lake-Lake 10,032: {D} Tom Bennett and this author pioneered the easy one-mile traverse between these two cirques on March 20, 1990. From Talus Lake, drop to the next lake and climb to Pass 9,920-plus. Contour easy slopes west of Peak 10,720-plus, over a ridge to Lake 10,032.

Talus Lake-Pass 10,320-plus: {D} This high pass and traverse provides excellent views of Webb Canyon and is the most efficient route to the crest in the Glacier Peak region. Follow a gully southwest from Talus Lake and climb moderate bowls to the northeast shoulder of Peak 10,880-plus. Contour on easy terrain across the Webb Canyon headwaters and climb to Pass 10,320-plus.

Pass 10,320-plus-Moose Basin: {E} Use this route during Teton Crest traverses or for approaches to Glacier Peak. Ski north from the pass, a few hundred yards down a gully until you can traverse northwest to

a flat shoulder on the long north ridge of Point 10,732. Ski the 400-foot bowl below, west to Lake 9,732 at the base of Glacier Peak. From the lake, either climb or contour northwest until you can begin one of the classic downhill traverses of the range. Use the same route coming from Moose Basin.

Snowshoe Canyon south fork-South Bitch Creek: {F} A 100-foot, 50-degree couloir above the northern cirque of the Snowshoe Canyon south fork provides the only difficulty during this passage. This couloir rarely is capped by cornices, as is a deceptively docile-looking couloir to the south. Dave Moore and this author used both chutes during an attempted climb of Doubtful Peak's north ridge on June 4, 1993.

Lake 9,610 (Ortenburger Lake)-Pass 10,320-plus: {E} or {F} Two variations are possible during this stretch of a Teton Crest traverse, which bypasses the precipitous Doubtful Peak massif on the east side. During a tour between Grassy Lake Reservoir and Cascade Canyon in June of 1962, Bill Briggs, Rod Dornan and Jim Greig skied over Pass 10,320-plus into Snowshoe south fork. They reached Ortenburger Lake by skiing down and around the east side of Birthday Cake and back up to the southeast shoulder of Doubtful Peak.

In May of 1979, Jeff Crabtree, Peter Koedt and Greg Lawley pioneered a complex two-mile route that traverses high from the southeast shoulder of Doubtful Peak, across avalanche terrain on its east side. They plunge-stepped into the north branch of Snowshoe south fork via a steep chute, then climbed easy slopes to Pass 10,320-plus. Crabtree used edgeless Rossignol cross-country skis but followed easily across the steep traverse in Koedt's randonnée track. You can avoid the steep chute by dropping directly into the north branch of Snowshoe south fork from the southeast shoulder of Doubtful Peak.

Moran Canyon north fork-Snowshoe Canyon south fork: {E} Tim Quinn and friend skied this straightforward loop in the mid- to late 1980s. From Ortenburger Lake, climb northeast to the high divide and enjoy the 1,600-foot wind-loaded run into Snowshoe Canyon.

None of the eight major Teton peaks that tower above 12,000 feet has seen more skiing than the stunning Mount Moran. And considering the time and effort it requires, it's remarkable that some 300 people have skied it. Still, the mountain's satellite peaks—including Cleaver, Peak 10,952, Maidenform, and Thor—didn't see first winter ascents and descents until 1993-95.

Confined by remote Leigh and Moran canyons to the south and north, Leigh and Jackson lakes to the east, and a high stretch of Teton crest on the west, this bastion of obscurity remains one of the Tetons' great treasures.

For detailed reference to the Mount Moran Region, use USGS maps for Mount Moran, Jenny Lake and Moran.

The beautiful 12,000-foot Thor Peak gets its first ski track as Tom Turiano turns cautiously off the precipitous summit. Mystery surrounds this incredible mountain.

APPROACHES

Moran Canyon: {B} This broad, glacier-carved valley is bordered by peaks of spectacular relief. Mount Moran, Peak 10,952, Cleaver Peak, and Dragon Peak line up along the southern side of the canyon, with three major tributary forks separating the massifs. On the north side of the canyon, a long, broken wall leads from Bivouac Peak to Dry Ridge Mountain.

Travel in the lower canyon can be arduous because of deadfall, thick brush, and rolling terrain. Enter through a clearing some 100 yards south of the mouth of Moran Creek. During cold, heavy snow years, the easiest route from Moran Bay might be directly up the creek gorge. About a half mile up the canyon, cross to the north side of the creek to avoid excessive ups and downs. Just above the confluence of the Triple Glacier drainages, you'll find easy travel north of Moran Creek. Farther up, the canyon widens and the forests consist primarily of older, massive trees, making for fast, scenic touring. Approach from Colter Bay or Signal Mountain Lodge.

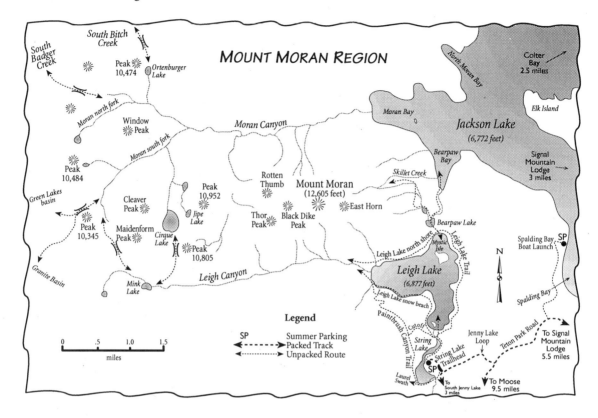

Leigh Lake-Bearpaw Bay: {A} This isthmus requires some of the most rigorous bushwhacking in the range. Nonetheless, the route is crucial to connect Cottonwood Creek drainage with Jackson Lake. From Leigh Lake patrol cabin, ski across a large meadow to Bearpaw Lake. Cross the lake and follow the west side of the outlet stream to Bearpaw Bay.

To access Skillet Creek, ski to Trapper Lake, climb a couple hundred vertical feet up the forested slope of Mount Moran, then make a tedious traverse north into the drainage. In spring, follow animal and climber trails most of the way.

Spalding Bay Boat Launch: From a point two miles north of North Jenny Lake Junction—where the Teton Park Road turns east and descends across the Burned Ridge moraine—turn north on a marked road that winds two miles to Spalding Bay. Launching

motorboats at Spalding Bay currently is prohibited.

Jackson Lake: See Ranger Peak Region.

Leigh Lake Trail: {K} In fall and spring, when the ice is dangerous, follow this trail around the east side of Leigh Lake to reach points north.

Leigh Lake north shore: {D} Again, use this when Leigh Lake ice is unsafe. This tedious route traverses and bushwhacks from the Leigh Lake patrol cabin to the mouth of Leigh Canyon.

Leigh Lake (6,878 feet): Ski or canoe across this 250-foot-deep lake to access Leigh Canyon and points north. Approach from String Lake trailhead by skiing the length of String Lake, or via the String Lake Trail. Exercise caution near the Leigh and Paintbrush creek inlets and near the outlet at the south end of the lake.

Mystic Isle currently is closed to humans for revegetation from effects of the 1981 fire.

Leigh Canyon: {C} The mouth of Leigh Canyon is nine miles from the nearest parking area in winter, making it the most remote canyon on the east side of the range. Approach from String Lake trailhead by skiing across String and Leigh lakes or by dropping north from the Paintbrush Canyon Trail. From Colter Bay or Signal Mountain Lodge, use the Leigh Lake-Bearpaw Bay route.

Rivaling Death Canyon in sheerness, this canyon is rimmed by the south buttress of Mount Moran and the north face of Mount Woodring and has no major forks. The canyon bottom also is relatively steep, which makes exiting the mountains quick and enjoyable.

Leigh Lake Snow Beach: {A} In spring, when the ice on Leigh Lake is dangerous, cross the bridge at the north end of String Lake and follow a summer trail as it skirts the southwest shore of Leigh Lake. When the shore turns west, you might be able to ski along the bank on a precarious "snow beach" up until late spring.

String Lake: See Mount St. John Region.

Paintbrush Canyon Trail: {B} See Mount St. John Region.

PEAKS AND BOWLS

Peak 10,474: This insignificant peak above Ortenburger Lake might offer nice skiing on its south and southwest faces. A striking couloir dives off the summit plateau toward Ortenburger Lake.

Window Peak (10,508 feet): This isolated peak between the forks of Moran Canyon might offer good skiing on its west face and in a pair of couloirs on its southeast face.

Peak 10,484: See Fred's Mountain Region.

Mount Moran (12,605 feet): Although Skillet Glacier offers the only ski route from Moran's true summit, numerous sub-summits, glaciers, couloirs, and faces give this mountain incredible ski potential. Approach from Jackson Lake, Leigh Canyon, or Moran Canyon.

Skillet Glacier: {F} or {G} This is *the* classic Teton descent. In the best conditions, you'll find almost 6,000 feet of skiing on slopes of up to 50 degrees. High altitude, slight northeastern exposure, and its position in the shadow of the East Horn, however, combine to reduce the probability of skiing the route in safe, enjoyable snow conditions. Early spring parties have a good chance to ski from the summit all the way to the lake but likely will have to start at Colter Bay and cross the ice-covered lake. Those skiers might be lucky enough to find stable powder but are more likely to meet with breakable crust or dangerous avalanche conditions. Snowpack on the mountain usually is safer and more consistent in late season, but skiable vertical terrain is diminished and, if the faint approach trail is lost, bushwhacking to snowline can be loathsome.

From the shores of Bearpaw Bay, follow game and climber trails on the lateral moraines north of Skillet Creek until you reach snow. From the glacier, climb to the south side of the large rock island, unless the bergschrund on the north side looks easily passable. Climb the interminable handle, then bear left into the upper handle to a small notch north of the rounded summit. Beware of rock fall.

From the summit, some have skied a short distance north on easy snow and jumped or downclimbed to the notch at the top of the Skillet. Others have been content with starting their descent at the notch. But the essence of the descent is the first turn off the notch! One spring day during the mid-1980s, Chris Hoeft jumped more than 10 feet off the notch cornice onto the 50-degree slopes of the upper handle. During most years, the cornice is more manageable.

A deep avalanche runnel invariably forms in the center of the handle, thus restricting skiers to one side or the other. Crossing or jumping the runnel is more difficult and dangerous than it may seem. To avoid avalanches on this extremely prone route, air temperatures must reach freezing at night and you *must* get an early start. During the first descent climb, Peter Koedt and Dick Person were caught in a small, wet-snow avalanche near the top of the handle. Koedt plunged his poles upside down into the soft snow and held on until the slide passed. And in late July of 1993, three climbers were swept 2,000 feet down the glacier by a wet-snow avalanche. Remarkably, no one was hurt seriously.

Most parties make the descent in two days so as to be at the summit early enough for the safest snow conditions. The best camp spots are on the shore of Bearpaw Bay or on Dixie's Nipple, a small morainal summit at the base of the glacier.

The aesthetics of this route and the challenge of skiing the mountain's full 5,850 feet drives skiers back again and again. Throughout the 1970s and 80s, Jorge Colón skied the Skillet five times, with partners including Pepi Stiegler, Mark Wolling, Tom Raymer, Nick Anderson, Eric Cutting, Bob Yanden, and Rick Walters. One year, the ultimate skiers' dream came true when Colón and Wolling skied in perfect corn from the summit to the lake!

Several skiers made free-heel attempts before Rick Wyatt's successful autumn descent on exceptional early-season powder. During the first attempt, in the spring of 1978, Dan McKay and Whitney Thurlow pushed toward the summit despite horrific weather and icy snow. McKay began skiing from the top of the handle. In 1979, Jeff Crabtree made the second nordic attempt with soft boots and Europa 77s. He and alpine skier Jeanetta Brown had climbed to the summit but decided to downclimb to the midpoint of the Skillet handle before putting on their skis. They anchored to a deadman and belayed each other for one pitch to be certain that they could ski without sliding for life. Jim Duclos and Walt Kirby made another nordic attempt and began skiing 200 feet below the top.

(Early fixed-heel: Bill Briggs, Peter Koedt, Dick Person, and Fletcher Manley; June 2, 1968. Early free-heel descents: Rick Wyatt; October, 1980; Brian Bradley and Whitney Thurlow; June, 1982; Jay Moody and Les Gibson; late June, 1982. Early snowboard: Stephen Koch with skier Christoph Schork; May 22, 1991.)

Falling Ice Glacier: {F} During the first ski-descent attempt in February of 1974, Jorge Colón, Hugo Lucic and "Tap" encountered a large slab and ice avalanche, which ran down the Falling Ice drainage a quarter mile onto the Leigh Lake ice. They camped in subzero temperatures below the West Horn and were climbing in the avalanche path when it came through. They quickly ran to the side of the path, but Lucic lost a ski in the process.

Although this route starts 1,100 feet below the summit, beautiful views, challenging terrain and excellent snow abound. The crux of the descent undoubtedly is the ice fall. Steve Shea and Larry Bruce passed on the north side. In lesser snow years, passing might require rappels.

(Early fixed-heel: Steve Shea and Larry Bruce; spring of 1978 or 1979.)

Southwest Couloir: {F} When viewing Mount Moran from the southwest, this couloir is the most striking feature on the mountain, and perhaps in the range. Although 200 feet of easy fifth-class rock separates the top of the couloir from the summit, more than 4,800 feet of skiing will lead you into Leigh Canyon.

During the first descent of this couloir, skiers found that the high rock walls of the couloir shaded the snow for most of the day, keeping the rough snow surface frozen solid. But below the couloir, they enjoyed 3,300 feet of vast south-facing slopes in perfect corn.

(Early fixed-heel: Jorge Colón, Mark Wolling, and Dean Moore; spring of 1980.)

Triple Glaciers: Although a ski route from the summit down the north side of Mount Moran is not feasible in typical conditions, vast potential exists in this huge glacially carved triple amphitheater above Moran Canyon. Some of the first skiers here were Jim Gates and Tom Bennett, in the early 1980s.

Photographer Wade McKoy, snowboarders John Griber and John Recchio, and skiers Steve Jones and Kevin Brazell made a three-day trip into the area June 20-22, 1993. After two gear-hauling trips from their canoe at Moran Bay, the team settled into camp at the base of the East Triple Glacier {E}. On day two, they skied an east-facing couloir off the ridge to the west of the glacier and called it the "Broom Handle" {G}. They counted at least four other enticing couloirs.

After a long run down the east glacier, the party climbed into the larger Middle Triple Glacier {E} for countless slushy turns back to camp. The next morning, rainy skies foiled their hopes of skiing the West Triple Glacier, and they bushwhacked to their canoes in the rain.

A large snow face extends off the west ridge of Mount Moran toward the East Triple Glacier, ending abruptly at 500 feet of broken cliffs. In exceptional snow years, these cliffs might be buried, offering a 5,200-foot run into Moran Canyon. Approach directly from Moran Canyon, or by traversing under the north buttress from Sickle Glacier.

Sickle Couloir: {G} This route catches the eye of many a ski mountaineer. Jeff Rhoads first spotted it in 1979 and knew he'd be back someday. In 1991, he returned to find the route in bad condition. Its shaded position under the northeast ridge makes it a late-season descent.

The bottom half of the couloir is blocked by an extremely steep constriction, which is not known to have a ski descent. The first descent party traversed skiers' right on very exposed terrain into another sickle-shaped couloir that drops off the northeast ridge into a basin on the northeast side of Mount Moran, above Moran Bay.

(Early fixed-heel: Jeff Rhoads and Cory Flandrow; June, 1992.)

Other potential routes: The east face of the East Horn has sustained 40- to 50-degree slopes for 4,700 feet to either Leigh or Jackson lake. The southeast face of the Drizzlepus is a spectacular 35-degree ramp that leads to the CMC high camp via a short 50-degree couloir. The northeast ridge is a prize descent, boasting almost 6,000 feet of extreme terrain. The Sandinista Couloir would make an exciting diversion off the west side of the south buttress. Steve Shea theorizes that combining the Falling Ice with the upper Skillet might

make a superb ski route from the summit to Leigh Lake. The north-buttress couloir drops precipitously west from the north buttress onto the East Triple Glacier. A forest fire ravaged the triangular buttress on the lower southeast slopes of the mountain before 1960. Today, much of this slope consists of densely packed dwarf conifers that offer challenging glade skiing.

Peak 11,658 (Rotten Thumb): This is the northernmost of three obscure peaks along a curving ridge north of Thor Peak. The northeast face, southwest couloir and west face all await ski descents. Finding a continuous snow route from the summit might be a challenge.

Peak 12,000-plus (Black Dike Peak): This diabase high summit between Thor and Moran has at least three potential ski routes, including one from the summit that plummets more than 4,000 feet into Leigh Canyon.

Thor Peak (12,028 feet): Mystery surrounds this beautiful 12,000-foot mountain. Through the years,

---

Bill Briggs, the father of American ski mountaineering, cuts first tracks on Mount Moran's Skillet Glacier (right), a 6,000-foot run from the summit to Jackson Lake.

skiing pioneers including Davey Agnew and Harry Frishman have dreamed of finding themselves on the west- and south-facing snow routes. Jorge Colón and Hugo Lucic actually made an attempt on the peak in the 1970s but were foiled by bad weather. Forrest McCarthy and this author suffered the same malady during another ski attempt that began at Grand Targhee in mid-April, 1993. Approach from Leigh or Moran canyon.

Standard Route: {F} The broad, aesthetic, west gully stretches 1,200 feet to a bench west of the peak. From the bench, a short walk over rocks to the south leads to the 2,800-foot southwest couloir, where you'll find a variety of terrain—ranging from vast bowls to 25-foot-wide narrows and angles near 45 degrees.

To access Moran Canyon from the bench west of the peak, ski north and plummet 1,000 feet down a sustained couloir that leads into the unnamed southeast fork of Moran Canyon {F}.

(Early fixed-heel: Christoph Schork with dog Tilley, Peter Selkowitz, and Tom Turiano; May 19, 1993. Early free-heel: Russell Rainey; May 19, 1993.)

Other potential routes: A route on the south face has become known as the Spiral Face because it begins as an east-facing couloir south of the top of the Hidden Couloir, turns to face west, then widens to a vast south-facing bowl. The bowl ends abruptly at a huge cliff, broken only by two skiable couloirs. The western one ends at a 30-foot waterfall, while the eastern one is passable with very narrow and steep skiing. The

Seemingly undaunted by steepness and exposure, Dick Person and Peter Koedt prepare for their descent of the upper Skiller Glacier. Skillet Glacier is the classic Teton descent.

extreme Hidden Couloir descends to the northeast, at 50 degrees to 55 degrees, to a large bowl. The bowl is extremely steep and broken by cliff bands, resembling the direct northeast snowfields of Mount Owen. Rappels most likely will be required.

Peak 10,952: This is the high point along the spectacular north-south ridge that separates Cirque Lake valley from the unnamed valley west of the Moran/Thor massif. Other than the one route that has been skied from the summit, several nice bowls and couloirs grace its flanks. Approach from Moran Canyon.

East Couloir: {F} This splendid couloir begins at a notch just north of the main summit and stretches for 2,000 feet into the unnamed valley west of the Moran/Thor massif.

(Early fixed-heel: Wesley Bunch [randonnée]; Jan. 25, 1994. Early free-heel: Tom Turiano and David Bowers; Jan. 25, 1994.)

Point 10,805: This insignificant but high point lies a mile east of Maidenform Peak, above the southeast corner of the Cirque Lake basin and marks the east end of the vast south wall of Maidenform.

South Face: {F} This steep face is avalanche-prone on spring afternoons and crusty during winter but offers 2,200 feet of fall-line skiing to Leigh Canyon.

(Early free-heel: Tom Turiano and Forrest McCarthy; April 15, 1993.)

Cleaver Peak (11,055 feet): First climbed in winter on Jan. 26, 1994 by this author, David Bowers, and Wesley Bunch, this miniature Ogre in the remote reaches of Moran Canyon had seen several winter-ascent attempts.

Potential routes: The peak offers little interest to skiers, except snowfields on the lower flanks of the mountain; summit bidders have skied these extensively. Also, a technical route might be possible from the south summit to Cirque Lake. Approach from Leigh Canyon, Moran Canyon, or the Granite or Green Lakes basin-Moran Canyon south fork route.

Maidenform Peak (11,137 feet): One of the highest peaks in the interior range, Maidenform Peak is a worthy objective for ski mountaineers, despite its long approach. From Grand Targhee, use Fred's Mountain High Route-10,686 Plateau-Littles Peak, then Littles Plateau-Mink Lake or Littles Peak-South Badger Creek. Or approach from Moran Canyon or South Leigh Creek via Granite Basin. Leigh Canyon provides the best access in spring, when the String Lake trailhead is open.

With a 5:30 a.m. start from the base of the Grand Targhee Resort on April 7, 1990, Tom Bennett, Gary Kofinas and this author struck off for Maidenform. After a long ridge traverse, we arrived at the base of the mountain at 2 p.m., snow rotting in the afternoon sun. With more than 35 years of backcountry skiing experience between us, we wisely decided to camp and wait until morning—when the snow would be safer—to climb the peak.

But after waiting about and hour and a half on that perfect day beneath a perfect peak, we foolishly decided to go for the summit. Postholing to the waist on 20-degree slopes, we arrived at the east ridge, one mile east of the summit, an hour later. On the ridge, we encountered steep fourth-class rock climbing, waist deep slush, and knife-edge exposure.

On one snow knife-edge, Kofinas kicked off a ball of snow that propagated a five-foot slab avalanche, 100 feet wide, which ran full-track, 1,200 feet to Mink Lake! Quivering in fright and cursing our decision to climb, we ran to the summit, wondering how we would get down. Operating on the theory that an avalanched slope, like a broken rubber band, is free of tension, we took turns jumping the crown and plunge-stepping down the icy avalanche track to Mink Lake. The lesson was well-relearned.

South Couloirs: {E} and {F} The south face is a three-mile wall of couloirs and faces. The most westerly couloirs are narrower and steeper, while the easterly ones are wider and lower-angled. The earliest known descent party skied the couloir directly southeast off the summit.

(Early fixed-heel: Christoph Schork [randonnée], with dogs Tilley and Emma; March 31, 1994.)

Other potential routes: The northeast bowl would be one of the primary skiing attractions from a camp at inaccessible Cirque Lake.

Peak 10,345: See Fred's Mountain Region.

HIGH ROUTES

Lake 9,610 (Ortenburger Lake)-South Bitch Creek: {E} This avalanche-prone route climbs north to the pass west of Doubtful Peak, then drops sharply into South Bitch.

South Badger Creek-Moran Canyon north fork: See Rammel Mountain Region.

Mink Lake-Cirque Lake: {E} Backcountry enthusiasts long have searched for easy access to Cirque Lake from points south. Although this arduous route climbs nearly 2,000 feet from Mink Lake to the long east ridge of Maidenform, near Point 10,805, it's quite straightforward and offers a 1,200-foot powder run on 25-degree slopes to Cirque Lake.

Leigh Canyon-Moran Canyon south fork: {D} Jim Olson and fellow rangers used this safe, scenic link during a loop from Moran to Leigh in the late 1970s.

Granite or Green Lakes basin-Moran Canyon south fork: See Fred's Mountain Region.

Isolation and avalanche danger account for limited winter skiing in this region. In spring, however, stalwart skiers park their bikes or cars at the foot of the mountains and climb on firm snow to 11,000-foot summits in less than four hours. Bordered by Leigh Canyon on the north and Cascade Canyon on the south, the Mount St. John region encompasses a wide variety of terrain. Tranquil high cirques in the head of Leigh and Paintbrush canyons hold snow into midsummer. Hone your steep skills on eastern front peaks, including The Jaw, Mount St. John, Rockchuck Peak, and Mount Woodring. Their routes offer steep, but not death-defying, skiing from jagged summits.

For detailed reference to the Mount St. John Region, use USGS maps for Mount Moran and Jenny Lake.

This photograph offers a view of the precipitous southeast face of Mount Woodring, which is nestled at the head of remote Paintbrush Canyon. The seldom-skied south face drops to the left off the summit.

APPROACHES

Leigh Lake: See Mount Moran Region.

Leigh Lake Snow Beach: See Mount Moran Region.

Leigh Canyon: See Mount Moran Region.

Teton Park Road: See High Peaks Region.

Jenny Lake Loop Road: Although this road has never been plowed in winter, it is open to snowmobiling. The Park Service plows the road in early spring for non-motorized traffic use only. Ride your bicycle on this road to access String Lake.

String Lake Trail: {A} The summer trail's swath through the thick forest makes a good route for by-passing String Lake on the east side when the ice is unsafe for travel.

String-Paintbrush Cutoff: {C} From the north end of String Lake, cross the bridge and ski due west, following the summer trail until you reach Paintbrush Canyon Trail.

String Lake (6,870 feet): Formerly called Beaver Dick Lake, String "lake" can almost be considered a

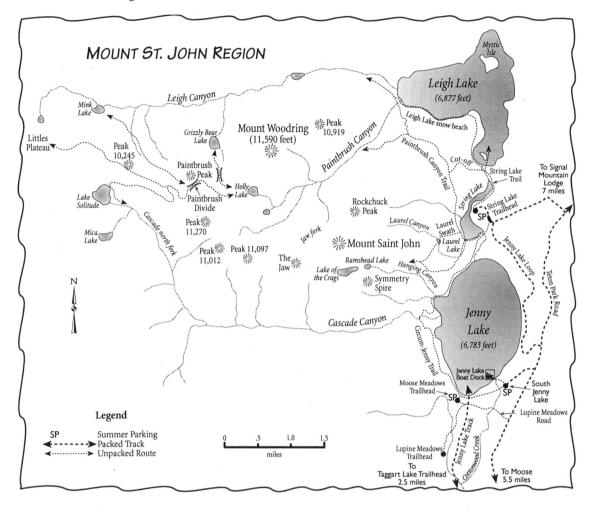

MOUNT ST. JOHN REGION

Mystic Isle

Leigh Lake
(6,877 feet)

Leigh Canyon

Mink Lake

Littles Plateau

Grizzly Bear Lake

Mount Woodring
(11,590 feet)

Peak 10,919

Leigh Lake snow beach

Paintbrush Canyon

Paintbrush Canyon Trail

Cut-off

To Signal Mountain Lodge 7 miles

Peak 10,245

Paintbrush Peak

Holly Lake

Paintbrush Divide

Lake Solitude

Peak 11,270

Mica Lake

Peak 11,012

Peak 11,097

Jaw fork

The Jaw

Mount Saint John

Lake of the Crags

Ramshead Lake

Symmetry Spire

Rockchuck Peak

Laurel Canyon

Laurel Swath

Laurel Lake

Hanging Canyon

String Lake

String Lake Trail

String Lake Trailhead

SP

Jenny Lake Loop

Teton Park Road

Cascade north fork

Cascade Canyon

Jenny Lake
(6,783 feet)

Circum-Jenny Trail

N

Jenny Lake Boat Dock

Moose Meadows Trailhead

SP

SP

South Jenny Lake

Lupine Meadows Road

Legend

SP — Summer Parking
←- - - -→ Packed Track
←· · · ·→ Unpacked Route

0   .5   1.0   1.5
miles

Lupine Meadows Trailhead

To Taggart Lake Trailhead 2.5 miles

Cottonwood Creek

Jenny Lake Track

To Moose 5.5 miles

---

wide section in the creek between Leigh and Jenny lakes, because a slight current is detectable. This current has little effect on ice formation and strength except during spring runoff, when water entering from Leigh Lake increases the under-ice current and erodes channels along the lake. Also, String is so shallow that the lake floor absorbs solar energy, causing the ice below to erode. Consequently, String Lake usually is the first lake to become unsafe for travel in spring. The shores seem to melt out especially early. In winter, use caution near the inlet and outlet.

While approaching Mount Woodring and Thor

Peak at 2 a.m. in May of 1990, this author broke through a thin skim of ice, which had formed near a log overnight and stood screeching in shock from the frigidity of waist-deep water.

In late spring, park at either end of the String Lake parking lot, depending upon your destination. Otherwise, either bicycle, snowmobile, or ski from Taggart Lake trailhead. Hand-propelled boats are permitted on this lake.

Paintbrush Canyon Trail: {B} This corridor through thick forest provides access to Paintbrush and Leigh canyons when String and Leigh lakes are unsafe for travel. Park at String Lake and use the String Lake trailhead-Laurel Swath route to join this route. To reach Leigh Canyon, bushwhack down to the north, off the moraine and to the mouth as the trail curls around Rockchuck Peak into Paintbrush Canyon. String-Paintbrush cutoff also meets Paintbrush Trail.

Paintbrush Canyon: {C} In 1938, Bob Kranenberg and Roland Wolf made the earliest ski tour in Paintbrush Canyon, when they skied to Holly Lake. Like Leigh Canyon, Paintbrush is quite remote in winter. In spring, however, you can access it easily on Paintbrush Canyon Trail from the String Lake trailhead.

In 1939, the Jackson Hole Ski Club considered running summer racing camps on the vast northeast-facing snowfields at the head of this canyon. Today, these bowls remain popular, offering some of the most reliable spring and summer skiing in the range.

String Lake trailhead-Laurel Swath: {A} This is a quick way to access the mountains in spring, when String Lake is unsafe to cross. Park your bike or car at the lot near the southern end of String Lake. Cross the bridge near the outlet but don't follow the trail to Jenny Lake. Instead, turn right and follow the south shore of String Lake to the base of the Laurel Swath. This shore holds snow late into spring because it is well-shaded.

String Lake-Hanging Canyon: {D} Use this route to access Hanging Canyon when Jenny Lake is unsafe for ski or boat travel and the Circum-Jenny Trail remains snowbound. From Laurel Lake, traverse up and south across moderate slopes and gullies into Hanging Canyon. Or skin south up the Laurel Creek gully from the south end of String Lake. Continue southwest up this gully or ramp when the creek turns west and gain the Hanging Canyon lateral moraine. Drop slightly into the canyon.

Hanging Canyon: {E} Ski this wonderful, steep draw to approach Mount St. John, The Jaw, and a passel of unskied peaks and chutes. In about 1970, a huge spring avalanche ripped down the canyon, uprooting a path of trees and depositing them in Jenny Lake.

From the northwest side of Jenny Lake, follow the summer trail from a footbridge on the circum-lake trail. In early spring or winter, climb the draw directly. Pass steep slabs near the base of the canyon to the north. Or approach via String Lake-Hanging Canyon.

Circum-Jenny Trail: {B} This scenic trail winds along the west shore moraines of Jenny Lake, between the String Lake and Moose Meadow parking areas.

Jenny Lake (6,779 feet): {K} Skiers commonly cross this famous lake en route to Cascade or Hanging canyon. Approach from Taggart Lake trailhead via Jenny Lake Track during winter and by bicycle on the Teton Park Road during April. When the lake ice thaws, use the Circum-Jenny Trail from Moose Meadow or String Lake to reach the canyons. Teton Boating begins a shuttle service across the lake in early June. Private hand-propelled boats and motorboats with less than 7.5 horsepower also are permitted.

When traveling on lake ice, use caution near the inlet, outlet, and the mouths of Cascade and Hanging creeks. Ski at least 100 feet from the west shore in early and late season, as direct sun and runoff springs weaken ice there.

Cascade Canyon: See The High Peaks.

PEAKS AND BOWLS

Mount Woodring (11,590 feet): Nestled at the head of remote Paintbrush Canyon, this peak sees little skiing. Smooth, moderate slopes make the descent worthy of the tedious approach from String Lake via Paintbrush Canyon.

South Face: {F} During the first descent, this author climbed the steep, broken southeast face, intending to ski that route. But huge piles of avalanche debris foiled that plan. In contrast, the south face was smooth neve at a continuous 40-degree pitch for nearly 2,700 feet to Holly Lake.

Traverse to the southwest end of the summit ridge and ski the exposed face to the south until you can make a short traverse between cliffs to the adjacent snow face on the west. If you miss this obscure traverse or it is melted out, you'll have to remove your skis and climb to avoid cliffs and rocks. The secondary slope narrows and steepens as it approaches Holly Lake.

(Early fixed-heel: Tom Turiano; May 20, 1991.)

Other potential routes: Countless other skiable couloirs and faces drape down this multifaceted peak. The only other route from the summit is the intricate southeast face, which begins on the south ridge and traverses northeast into a large bowl. Couloirs and faces lead the remaining 2,000 feet to Paintbrush Canyon. Very impressive couloirs drop to the north and south from the east ridge and Peak 10,919.

Point 10,880-plus (Paintbrush Peak): The northwest face of this elegant peak—just north of Paintbrush Divide—curves a moderate 2,200 feet into Leigh Canyon.

Rockchuck Peak (11,144 feet): This peak offers superb spring terrain, with a simple approach directly above String Lake trailhead.

East Face: {F} This classic descent actually is more like a draw than a face. From the summit, an exposed strip of snow traverses northeast above huge cliffs to the east ridge. Ski the east ridge until it looks good to drop onto the north-facing side of the east draw. Fantastic slopes as steep as 40 degrees lead all the way to String Lake. At one point, you'll encounter a maze of massive boulders; pass them by skiing through chutes, over drifts, and into moats.

The first attempt to ski this face apparently was made by Mike Quinn, John Carr, and Patti White in the late 1970s. Unclear about the summit's location, the team climbed too far north on the east face and thus skied from the northeast shoulder.

(Early fixed-heel: Mike Quinn, Victor Gerdin, and Frank Barrows; spring of 1979 or 1980. Early free-heel: Jim Duclos and Jon Schick; May, 1979.)

Other potential routes: Only one other route seems possible off this sharp summit. Instead of dropping north off the east ridge of Rockchuck, ski into Laurel Canyon via a couloir just west of the highest gendarme on the east ridge.

Laurel Swath: {D} This is the 300-yard-wide, treeless avalanche path that provides primary access to Laurel Canyon and the east face of Mount St. John. It makes a great short day ski from String Lake. In late spring, a climbers' trail leads up the swath, branching off from the Paintbrush Canyon Trail. Approach via String Lake trailhead-Laurel Swath.

Laurel Canyon: {F} This straight-sided hanging canyon between Mount St. John and Rockchuck Peak offers fantastic moderate terrain with all but west exposures. Allow more time to climb the canyon than you would expect to need. Skiing from the notch at the top of the canyon requires some interesting maneuvering. Approach via String Lake trailhead-Laurel Swath.

(Early free-heel, from notch: Tom Turiano and Russell Rainey; March 29, 1994.)

Mount St. John (11,430 feet): Viewed from the south, this peak's six couloirs, or ramps, captivate ski mountaineers. In the mid-1970s, several people attempted to ski from the summit. To their chagrin, however, they discovered that the couloirs, which looked straightforward from the valley, ended ominously in cliffs and ice funnels. They could locate no continuous routes from the summit.

After three reconnaissance trips—including aerial observation, a summer hike, and a spring 1991 attempt—this author discovered that no one south couloir could be skied continuously from the summit. I did, however, find that skiers could traverse inconspicuous ramps or ledges to connect adjacent couloirs. An outstanding snow year is necessary to cover the ramps completely with snow. Approach from Hanging or Laurel canyon.

East Face: {F} This is the most popular ski route on the mountain because of its short spring approach and continuous pitch. From the top of the face—the easternmost summit of Mount St. John—ski slightly northeast into the large snow face below. After about 800 feet, the face changes character and you must choose between one of two couloirs or the forested, cliffy ribs between the couloirs and on both sides of them. The couloir on the skier's right is longer, while the other is steeper and provides more continuous fall-line skiing. The southern edge of the face offers the best skiing of the ribs. The bottoms of the couloirs usually are strewn with avalanche debris. Approach from Laurel Lake.

(Early free-heel: Jon Schick; late 1970s or early 1980s. Early fixed-heel: Les Gibson, Paul Brabenac and Rob Woodson; May, 1985. Wade McKoy, Steve Curtis, Mark Wolling, and Walt Kirby; several times during mid- to late 1980s.)

Southeast Face of second summit: {F} The purest ski line on the south side of the mountain descends into Hanging Canyon off the second summit from the east.

(Early fixed-heel: Jorge Colón and Tom Raymer; mid-1970s.)

South Face Connection: {F} Short, exposed, dwarf-tree-covered ramps that make this route possible are difficult to find in good conditions. Not only is a good snow year required, but the ramps melt out quickly. From the true summit—the fifth peak from the east— ski south onto an exposed snowfield for several hundred vertical feet until you can traverse east into the adjacent snowfield. (Members of the first descent party had to remove their skis here to walk over 10 feet of talus.) Ski several hundred more feet to the lip of a large abyss, where a sloping ramp traverses east through a dwarf-tree forest. The final couloir or ramp takes skiers precipitously to the flats near Ramshead Lake. You'll encounter slopes as steep as 50 degrees, some of them above large cliffs. Approach from Hanging Canyon to Ramshead Lake, then climb straight north into the third couloir.

(Early fixed-heel: Tom Turiano; March 31, 1994. Early free-heel: John Fettig; March 31, 1994.)

Northeast Ramp: {F} This is the steep, exposed snow ramp/couloir leading northeast from the east summit of Mount St. John. Its first descent team climbed the route from Laurel Canyon. Brian Bradley fell in the deep slush but self-arrested before going over a huge cliff. Walt Kirby says attempting the route was a bad idea. Approach from Laurel Canyon.

(Early fixed-heel: Jim Duclos, Walt Kirby, and Brian Bradley; late May, 1979.)

The Jaw (11,400 feet): This sharp spire is the vortex of Hanging Canyon. One aspect is angled low enough to hold snow.

East Face: {F} With more than 4,500 feet of skiing to Jenny Lake, this route is a top-10 Teton classic. In March of 1982, Peter Koedt, Margot Snowdon and Larry and Janine Young made an early descent of the east face, with nordic equipment. They began skiing a little below the summit because of steep, exposed slopes and cliffs. Koedt remembered that another nordic party had made an attempt that ended the same way shortly after his. In spring of 1987, Tom Bennett, Dave Moore, and Ken Jern made an attempt on alpine gear but were stopped by rotten snow.

Moore and Bill Stanley finally made the first nordic descent from the top in the spring of 1990, picking their way through the summit cliffs on 45-degree slopes. At one point after picking through the rocky

---

Hanging Canyon culminates at The Jaw and is flanked on the north (right) by the numerous south couloirs of Mount St. John. All but two of the couloirs end at cliffs.

couloirs that constitute the crux, Moore's edges gave way on the hard surface and he slid 300 feet but didn't get hurt.

(Early fixed-heel: Tom Bennett, John Fettig, Tom Turiano, and Robert Iserbyt; April, 1990. Early free-heel, not from summit: Bob Graham; March 17, 1990. Early free-heel: Dave Moore and Bill Stanley; spring of 1990.)

Other potential routes: A steep ramp leads from the west ridge into the Jaw fork of Paintbrush Canyon.

Symmetry Spire: Though it is more famous for rock climbing, this peak offers at least two nice ski routes from the notch west of the summit. Approach from Jenny Lake or Hanging Canyon.

Symmetry Couloir: {F} Dropping south from the notch west of the summit, this classic 40-degree couloir turns east during its 3,500-foot drop into Cascade Canyon. Beware of moats in the lower snowfield; they have claimed the lives of several glissading climbers.

(Early figl descent: Roland Fleck, Manfred Effenhauser, Burkhard Hussl; May, 1983.)

Guide's Wall Couloir: {F} An exciting finish to the upper Symmetry Couloir drops west off the Ice Point/ Symmetry Spire Col into this 2,000-foot couloir, which leads into Cascade Canyon near Guide's Wall.

(Early free-heel: Jack McConnell; May 19, 1993.)

Other potential routes: The narrow north couloir plunges sharply north from the west notch, at angles of 50 degrees.

Jaw Fork: This scenic southern tributary to Paintbrush Canyon abounds with moderate ski terrain. Approach from Paintbrush Canyon.

Peak 11,097: Approached from Cascade or Paintbrush canyon, this yet-unskied peak is adorned with several good faces and couloirs on the north and south sides.

Peak 11,012: This elegant peak, nestled between Peak 11,270 and 11,097, sports an impressive unskied couloir between symmetrical rock buttresses when viewed from Paintbrush Canyon. The south and west sides offer interesting potential routes as well.

Peak 11,270: This peak is the highest summit in the interior range. It also features perhaps the nicest ski route of any minor peak. Approach from Cascade or Paintbrush canyon.

South Face: {F} In the course of this 3,100-foot route, ski terrain progresses from a narrow couloir to an exposed convex ridge to a wide gully to a moderate tree-covered spur. Slope angles fluctuate between 30 degrees and 45 degrees. The first descent was made in near-perfect corn conditions with Asolo Summits reinforced by Granite Gear cuffs and Rainey Super Loop tubing bindings. Climb directly north from the second bridge in the Cascade north fork trail.

(Early free-heel: Tom Turiano; May 25, 1993.)

Other potential routes: The primary attribute of the northeast face is a pair of extremely steep couloirs that extend 1,500 feet into Paintbrush Canyon. Two north-facing bowls on the north ridge run out onto Paintbrush Divide.

HIGH ROUTES

Holly Lake-Grizzly Bear Lake: {E} From Holly Lake, put on skins for the ski to the head of Paintbrush Canyon, to just below Paintbrush Divide. Drop north through a narrow gully to Grizzly Bear Lake.

Holly Lake-Mink Lake: {E} From Holly Lake, climb the avalanche-prone, cornice-capped Paintbrush Divide headwall. From the divide, ski northwest down a gully and headwall into the unnamed basin southeast of Mink Lake.

Paintbrush Divide-Littles Plateau: {D} This unlikely route follows a sharp ridge between these two plateaus. You'll encounter short climbs, descents, icy snow, and gaps between rocks during this long south-facing traverse, high above Cascade north fork.

Paintbrush Canyon-Cascade Canyon: {E} This classic summer hiking route makes a nice ski tour as well. But the Paintbrush Divide headwall is avalanche-prone and capped by a cornice.

Embracing the craggy peaks of Garnet Canyon and Glacier Gulch, this region represents the nucleus of the Teton Range and is one of the focal points of ski mountaineering in America. Since the mid-1960s, thousands have tested their skills on the couloirs and faces of these reverent peaks. Some return to the valley ecstatic about their fruitful adventures, while others return crestfallen about failed attempts but charged with new knowledge of their game. Others don't return at all.

For detailed reference to the High Peaks, use USGS maps for Grand Teton, Mount Moran, Moose and Jenny Lake.

APPROACHES

Teton Park Road: {K} Stretching from Moose

Try to pick out the Ford Couloir and Briggs' Route on this aerial photo of the Grand Teton's southeast face.

to Jackson Lake Junction, this road was the original valley highway until Route 89/191 was forged on the east side of the valley in the mid- to late 1950s. The only road between Moose and Yellowstone, it first was plowed to Moran in 1940. This gave skiers easy access to the canyons and peaks between 25 Short and Paintbrush Canyon.

Since 1959, however, the section of the road between Cottonwood Creek and Signal Mountain Lodge has been closed in winter. During a few years in the 1960s, the closure extended south to Beaver Creek. Many skiers and climbers approached the mountains via snowmobile during that time. When it widened and realigned the road in the early 1990s, the Park Service stretched the closure to the expanded Taggart Lake trailhead, a quarter mile south of Cottonwood Creek bridge.

In the spring of 1986, the Park Service began plowing the Jenny Lake Loop Road and the Teton Park Road between Cottonwood Creek and Signal Mountain Lodge for non-motorized use only during April of each year. This gives skiers early season bicycle access

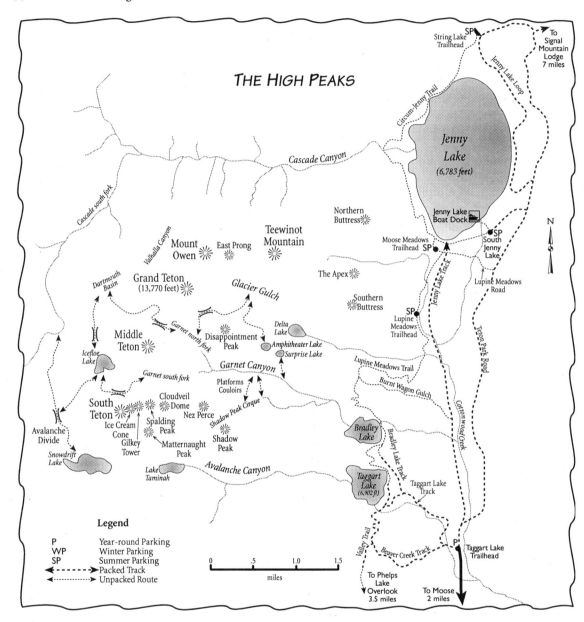

THE HIGH PEAKS

to the base of the mountains as far north as String Lake. This section closes about Nov. 1, depending upon weather. Plowing for non-motorized use begins in late March, and the road opens to vehicles about May 1.

Jenny Lake Loop Road: See Mount St. John Region.

Jenny Lake: See Mount St. John Region.
Circum-Jenny Trail: See Mount St. John Region.
Cascade Canyon: {C} In 1931 or 1932, Fred

Brown and Allyn Hanks made the earliest recorded ski tour into the mountains of Grand Teton National Park. They took a movie camera to film each other skiing in the south fork of Cascade. Inspired by this film, Bob Kranenberg became the first to ski to Lake Solitude, in 1933. When his beaver-skin climbers got caked with snow and ice, he wrapped a thin rope around his skis for climbing skins. On the descents, he grabbed trees to stop and turn.

Cascade since has become the most popular canyon in the range for overnight touring. This centralized canyon offers skiers perhaps a wider variety of terrain than any other. Intricate, exceptionally steep couloirs and faces on the massive north faces of Mount Owen and Teewinot Mountain form the south side of the canyon. Alternating couloirs and rock buttresses extend six miles along the north side of the canyon, from Baxter's Pinnacle to Paintbrush Divide. Peaks 11,270 and 11,097 boast long, steep south couloirs. The south fork is one of the most beautiful areas in the Tetons, with its rolling granite hummocks, rimmed by sedimentary plateaus and cliffs, and its breathtaking views of the high peaks. Moderate ski terrain abounds in places such as Dartmouth Basin, Icefloe Lake, Table Mountain, and Hurricane Pass. You'll find great camping and ski touring at Lake Solitude, which rests in the cirque at the head of the north fork.

Between the two main forks of the canyon, four major draws drain the spectacular peaks on the crest. Reach the southernmost, cliff-rimmed draw via a steep ski route on the north face of Table Mountain. Alpha and Omega Lakes basin offers skiers a sundry of terrain of all difficulties and exposures. Peak 10,650 and South Wigwam—both of which have fantastic south-facing bowls—are the area's primary skiable summits. Fryxell Lakes basin is capped by the craggy Wigwams and Peak 10,855, offering big verticals of moderate terrain. Mica Lake cirque includes bowls and couloirs of all exposures and late-season skiing on the Petersen Glacier.

In about 1936, the Civilian Conservation Corp built a barn and cabin near the forks for park personnel to use. In the 1960s, a massive avalanche from Fryxell Lakes destroyed the main cabin but left the barn standing. This barn since has been converted to a seemly cabin.

Lupine Meadows Road and Trail: {K} Branching left about four miles north of Taggart Lake trailhead, this unplowed, two-lane dirt road winds through Lupine Meadows to the Lupine Meadows trailhead. The road and trailhead usually open to automobile traffic between late April and mid-May.

The Lupine Meadows summer trail winds in a horseshoe shape around the Glacier Gulch end moraine and switchbacks up the fault scarp below Amphitheater Lake. It often is used to access Garnet Canyon, Amphitheater Lake, and Glacier Gulch in late spring and summer, or when Bradley Lake ice is unsafe to cross.

Jenny Lake Track: {A} Possibly the most popular cross-country tour in the range, ski mountaineers also use this route to approach Burnt Wagon Gulch, Teewinot, Cascade Canyon, Jenny Lake, and points north. From Taggart Lake trailhead, strike north along the west side of Cottonwood Creek through open meadows. After a mile and a half, cross Bradley Creek and continue another mile and a half north—across two large meadows and a creek—to Lupine Meadows. Yet another mile of open flats leads to the hilly, sparsely forested Jenny Lake moraine.

Glacier Gulch: {D} Sandwiched between the Disappointment and Teewinot massifs, this steep draw drains the enormous cirque that contains Delta Lake and the Teton Glacier. It's the primary approach to Mount Owen, the southwest side of Teewinot, and the north face of the Grand Teton.

Most early skiing in Glacier Gulch involved climbers attempting winter ascents on Mount Owen and the north and east sides of the Grand. In mid-December of 1965, two parties—one led by George Lowe—pioneered the route into Glacier Gulch en route to making the first winter ascents of Mount Owen.

Burdened with crevasses, seracs and rockfall exposure, Teton Glacier is not known for great skiing. In no other cirque, however, is the immense power and stature of the Tetons so evident. For this reason alone, it's worth the trip. Stephen Koch is the only person known to have skied from its apex; on June 13, 1991, he snowboarded from the upper northwest corner after a descent of the Koven Couloir. On March 31, 1994, *National Geographic* contributor José Azel photographed Koch snowboarding the bottom 100 feet of the Gunsight Couloir.

In winter, park at the Taggart Lake trailhead and follow Jenny Lake Track and Burned Wagon Gulch to the Valley Trail/Lupine Meadows trail junction. Do not follow the summer trail up the switchbacks toward Amphitheater Lake. Instead, traverse northwest a quarter mile across steep, densely forested slopes to Glacier Gulch.

In the gulch, switchback up the narrow, cliff-sided drainage or cross to the north side of the creek and wander up rolling hummocks to Delta Lake. Both routes make superb downhill runs.

Spring and summer options for accessing Glacier Gulch include traversing into Glacier Gulch from the fourth or sixth switchbacks above the Valley Trail/Lupine Meadows trail junction. Jeff Zell pioneered a route to Delta Lake that bypasses lower Glacier Gulch altogether. From Lupine Meadows trailhead, he climbed to treeline on the southeast shoulder of Teewinot, then dropped southwest to Delta Lake. Another interesting route follows a faint trail from Lupine Meadows trailhead to the top, west end of the lateral moraine on the north side of Glacier Gulch. Then traverse across the steep moraine and into the gulch. Skiers also may choose to hike the Lupine Meadows Trail to the first footbridge, then follow Glacier Creek all the way to Delta Lake. This author, along with Michael Keating and Sparky Colby, used that route on our approach to Disappointment Peak. Yet another option finds skiers climbing to Amphitheater Lake and making the delicate traverse under the north face of Disappointment Peak into Glacier Gulch. The ideal route depends entirely on snowpack conditions.

On Jan. 16, 1974, a 12-person National Outdoor Leadership School mountaineering expedition led by Teton skiing pioneer Tom Warren chose the latter route into the gulch. Seven members of the party were caught in a large, hard-slab avalanche on the seemingly safe secondary moraine of the Teton Glacier. Three people died. Contributing factors in the accident were subzero temperatures during the preceding week, followed by high winds and heavy precipitation. A National Park Service Board of Inquiry subsequently recommended that special-use permittees be under stricter regulation and that the park recruit qualified mountaineers for its ranger division on a year-round basis.

Burnt Wagon Gulch: {C} This shallow, steep draw leads between the Garnet Canyon and Glacier Gulch lateral moraines to the Amphitheater Lake Buttress and the Valley Trail/Lupine Meadows trails junction. Skiers often use the draw in winter to approach Glacier Gulch and Amphitheater Lake. Less commonly, this route has been used to approach Garnet Canyon when Bradley Lake is unsafe to cross and Lupine Meadows parking area still is snowbound. Follow Jenny Lake Track through the first large meadow, past a stand of trees and into the next meadow. Near the boarded-up Fabian Ranch cabins, branch northwest along the base of a moraine to another clearing—where you'll see a large boulder—at the mouth of Burnt Wagon Gulch.

Taggart Lake Track: See Buck Mountain Massif.

Bradley Lake Track: {C} From the Taggart Lake trailhead, ski west then north on a good track along the base of a moraine, pass the park horse stables, and cross the second footbridge. Follow the ski track up the creek for three quarters of a mile and bear right at the fork. (Go left for Taggart Lake.) The track leads up, over, down, and around moraines during its course to Bradley Lake.

Bradley Lake (7,016 feet): Skiers commonly cross the ice of this relatively benign lake en route to Garnet Canyon. Approach from Taggart Lake trailhead via Taggart and Bradley lakes' tracks. Use caution on the ice near the inlet and outlet.

Garnet Canyon: {E} Climbing nearly 5,000 feet from the valley floor, this canyon opens primary access to the South, Middle and Grand Tetons. In 1935, Fred Brown and Paul and Eldon Petzoldt skied to the caves of Garnet Canyon, thus becoming the earliest skiers in Garnet Canyon during their first-winter ascent of the Grand Teton. From their camp at the caves, they spent two days relaying loads to the lower saddle before making their ascent. In winter and early spring, the mouth of the canyon is best approached from Bradley Lake.

In the base of the canyon, the standard route follows the creek north until it bends west. It then crosses to the south side of the creek and ascends from the creek at the northern end of the large headwall at the base of the canyon. As you approach or descend from the Meadows, the easiest route and best snow usually is on the south side of the canyon. The north and south forks offer immense downhill skiing possibilities.

With vast expanses of snow clinging to the mountains thousands of feet above it, Garnet Canyon is a dangerous place when avalanche danger is high. During the extremely snowy winter of 1981-82, a massive powder avalanche burst from the upper east face of the Grand and flashed through Garnet Canyon to the valley floor. Climbers and skiers were in the area but none were hurt. Debris piles stacked 40 feet deep in The Meadows and didn't melt until late August.

Perhaps the safest camping spot in the canyon is at the Platforms, though steep snowfields linger above. Even the cave under the lower east buttress of the Middle Teton—long considered a safe bivouac—occasionally fills with avalanche debris.

Valley Trail: {C} From its junction with the Beaver Creek Track at the base of 25 Short, a good track climbs over a moraine to Taggart Lake. After skirting the east shore of the lake, it climbs over another moraine to Bradley Lake. From the outlet stream bridge, it switchbacks over another moraine and traverses north to the junction with Burnt Wagon Gulch and the Lupine Meadows Trail.

Taggart Lake: See Buck Mountain Massif.

Avalanche Canyon: See Buck Mountain Massif.

PEAKS AND BOWLS

Teewinot Mountain: Numerous severe ski routes with short spring approaches make this one of the most sought-after peaks in the range. Approach from Lupine Meadows, Glacier Gulch, or Cascade Canyon.

Northeast shoulder of Teewinot: {E} The northern 25 Short-like buttress of Teewinot offers two superb ridglets that arch between curving avalanche gullies nearly 3,000 feet to Lupine Meadows. But skiers beware: In the mid-1960s, a huge spring avalanche ripped a 100-yard-wide path through the trees.

The Apex: {E} This central forested triangular fault-scarp buttress offers a safe, consistent pitch as it drops nearly 3,000 feet to Lupine Meadows. A wandering summer climbers' trail joins the face near a cliff in the gully to the south.

Southern Apex: {E} Approached from Lupine Meadows, this forested buttress is the least enjoyable and most dangerous of Teewinot's lower faces. Skiers can, however, avoid the lower steep face by gaining the Glacier Gulch lateral moraine and following it to Lupine Meadows.

East Face: {F} or {G} From Lupine Meadows, this face serves up more vertical feet of spring skiing per approach foot than any other Teton ski route. The trouble is catching the face with snow all the way to the valley when the Lupine Meadow trailhead is open. If the parking lot is closed, skiers have to start from the ranger cabins on the east side of Lupine Meadows or at Taggart Lake trailhead.

Although the draw just south of the Apex is the standard approach and ski line, it's equally feasible to use the draw north of the Apex, as did the first descent party. From the Apex, most skiers climb straight up toward the Worshipper and Idol and pass them on the right. Steep snow leads through the Narrows to the summit or the notch, a good place to start a descent if the upper face isn't feasible.

From the summit, skiers negotiate a series of short, 50-degree chutes until just above the Narrows, which rarely is skiable. The first descent party was able to slip through this ski-width ice runnel. On May 5, 1985, Mark Stewart tried to jump through the Narrows and was killed in an ensuing 2,500-foot slide. Stewart tried to self-arrest with an ice axe but to no avail. His partners, Jeff Zell and Bill Bowen, had opted not to ski

the chute because of the severe conditions. On May 14, 1994, climber Arlo Morrill died in a similar "slide-for-life" during a 2,000-foot fall down the east face from near the summit notch. Morrill slipped on icy snow that was concealed by six inches of fresh powder.

Dean Moore finds good snow during the first descent of Teewinot via its east face, which offers more vertical feet of spring skiing per approach foot than any Teton ski route. The two towers are the Worshipper and Idol.

When the Narrows is melted out, many skiers traverse carefully to the south over a sharp snow ridglet to a narrow 50-degree face. In about 150 feet, this face leads back into the large bowl below the Narrows. A total of more than 5,500 feet of terrain leads to Lupine Meadows.

(Early fixed-heel: Dean Moore and Jim Bellamy; May, 1972. Early free-heel: Rick Wyatt, from the top, and Renny Jackson and Jeff Newsom, not from the top; early June, 1982. Wyatt returned in 1983 to ski it in firmer conditions. Early snowboard: Stephen Koch; April 23, 1991.)

Worshipper and Idol Couloir: {G} This hidden couloir passes those pinnacles on the south side.

(Early fixed-heel: Jorge Colón; mid-1970s.)

South Couloirs: {F} or {G} A series of steep, narrow, long couloirs drop southwest off the main south ridge of Teewinot. The first descent party split up. Steve Jones and Wilbur Pilkington skied the main couloir, while Dustin Varga explored a steeper, narrower adjacent line.

(Early fixed-heel: Steve Jones; May 23, 1993. Early snowboard: Dustin Varga and Wilbur Pilkington; May 23, 1993.)

Southwest Couloir: {F} Although this route is not skiable from the summit, it makes for an enjoyable ski from a camp in Glacier Gulch. The couloir actually faces southeast but is on the southwest side of the mountain. From the north end of the main Teton Glacier moraine, traverse into the large bowl below the couloir. At the top of the couloir, walk the large plateau east to the final steep couloir, which leads to a false summit along a southwest ridglet of the mountain. Slopes at the top of this couloir approach 55 degrees. Make some relaxing turns on the plateau before dropping into the 45-degree southwest couloir.

(Early fixed-heel: Tom Turiano; June 9, 1991. Early snowboard: Stephen Koch; June 9, 1991.)

Crooked Thumb Couloir: {F} This aesthetic, shaded couloir sometimes is skiable through the end of June. Pete Selkowitz and Tom Concannon descended on June 14, 1992. Rick Armstrong and Doug Coombs skied it in safe winter powder on Feb. 7, 1993.

Ascend the draw north of the Apex from Lupine Meadows into the steep bowl northeast of the east ridge of Teewinot. The couloir stretches above for more than 2,400 feet to the notch below the north ridge. It reaches 45 degrees and varies from 10 feet to 20 feet wide.

In May of 1993, Dustin Varga made the first descent of a variation of the Crooked Thumb, branching south to the base of the big yellow tower on the east ridge.

(Early fixed-heel: Jorge Colón and Andy Carson; April, 1975 or 1976. Early snowboard: Dustin Varga; June 6, 1994.)

Other potential routes: The northwest couloir might extend more than 4,000 feet into Cascade Canyon. The west couloir descends west from the notch south of the summit but is interrupted by a chockstone. Mark Newcomb and Hans Johnstone made an alpine descent from halfway up the east-southeast face in spring of 1993. The broad face continues to a point along the south ridge.

East Prong (12,000-plus feet): This sharp knoll just east of Koven Col has no clean ski routes from the top but offers a variety of couloirs and faces on the lower mountain. Approach from Glacier Gulch or Cascade Canyon.

Southeast Face: {E} From the lowest saddle between Mount Owen and Teewinot, this wide gully drops south to the Teton Glacier moraine.

(Early fixed-heel: Ty Vanderpool, Jeff Zell, Joe Larrow and Wade McKoy; May, 1990.)

South Chutes: {G} Several ice chutes drop south to the Teton Glacier from a narrow bench south of the summit. Stephen Koch's route finished in the lower Koven Couloir, while Ty Vanderpool ended near the southeast face.

(Early fixed-heel: Ty Vanderpool; May, 1990. Early snowboard: Stephen Koch; spring, 1990.)

North Side: {F} Joe Larrow slipped and stepped through tight rocks overhanging huge cliffs to force a descent from the summit. He then traversed east to ski the southeast face.

(Early fixed-heel: Joe Larrow; May, 1990.)

Mount Owen (12,928 feet): Long considered the most difficult Teton summit to reach, Mount Owen offers great challenges for ski mountaineers. After the Grand Teton was skied in 1971, Robin "Boomer" McClure wondered if a ski route off Mount Owen was possible. After bad snow foiled one attempt in late May of 1974, McClure approached Bill Briggs with the idea of another try. To McClure's surprise, Briggs already had set his sights on Owen as well. The rest is history.

Koven Couloir: {G} Rick Liu and Larry Bruce joined McClure on his first attempt to ski Mount Owen in the spring of 1974. Rotten snow stopped the trio above the Koven Col. This icy, narrow couloir reaches angles of more than 50 degrees, above large cliffs.

From the Teton Glacier, climbers have a choice about how to surmount the large cliff band below the couloir. Either climb directly up the fifth-class, icy, rocky lower Koven Couloir—which rarely holds enough snow to ski—or climb around the cliff to the west on the Teton Glacier and traverse on the 35-degree bench above to the base of the Koven. Stephen Koch has snowboarded both routes.

(Early fixed-heel: Robin "Boomer" McClure; May 31, 1974. Early snowboard: Stephen Koch; June 13, 1991.)

Direct Northeast Snowfields: {H} The second Mount Owen descent team reportedly used this extreme face, which plummets into the Teewinot/Owen cirque by way of hanging snowfields, exposed ramps, and narrow ice chutes at angles of 55 degrees to 60 degrees. Dan McKay, who had almost no climbing experience, followed experienced mountaineer Brian Bradley through numerous technical pitches, as rockfall and avalanches raked the face. After a steep fifth-class chimney near the top, McKay was so petrified that he swore never to climb again. But he did.

(Early fixed-heel: Brian Bradley and Dan McKay; spring, 1980.)

Briggs' and Boomer's Route: {G} Bill Briggs convinced a frustrated Boomer McClure that the way to ski the top was to climb the Koven and ski the northeast snowfields. To date, their 5,300-foot route is arguably the most intricate ski route yet completed in the range. They clicked into their boards on the 45-plus-degree slopes nearly 150 feet below the top. The only two parties that have skied from near the top since then had to put their skis on below the 40-foot, 70-degree, 5.7 rock slab that comprises the final climbing pitch before the top.

The direct approach is via Cascade Canyon to the large cirque below the north sides of Teewinot Mountain and Mount Owen. Pass the drainage confluence from this cirque on the canyon trail, then cross Cascade Creek on a log. You'll encounter intense bushwhacking on the steep hike to the pocket glacier below Mount Owen. West of the cascading creek, however, is a small talus field that helps minimize the nuisance. Good campsites are nonexistent in this cirque, so plan to bivouac on a sloping, rocky hillside.

Briggs' and Boomer's approach up the Koven Couloir and the east ridge, or Koven Route, from Glacier Gulch might be more practical, especially if skiers are attempting a one-day descent. This approach avoids bushwhacking on the north side but does not allow skiers to preview snow conditions on the lower, north-facing half of the route, where most of the questionable skiing is located.

From the point of highest snow, jump-turn down the spectacular exposed upper east ridge, then drop 100 feet north on a narrow, 50-plus-degree face to the top of the apron-shaped snowfield. When scouting the route from the valley, this face should be snow-covered for the descent to be worthwhile. Relax the adrenaline flow for 50 turns on the apron until the top of the east ridge chimney. This 10-foot-wide chimney loses about 300 feet to the Koven Col, with slopes of 55 degrees. A fall there could be tragic.

From the Koven Col, make an exposed traverse northeast to the top of the diagonal couloir, which descends to the east off a north/south running knife-edged spur. On the first descent, Bill Briggs' fused right hip made this steep traverse very difficult for him. But a belay from McClure ensured his safety. Briggs, in turn, belayed McClure across. Next, drop

east into the 45-degree diagonal couloir that leads 1,000 feet down to the main Teewinot/Owen gully. Another 3,600 feet of moderate skiing leads into Cascade Canyon.

(Early fixed-heel: Bill Briggs and Robin "Boomer" McClure; June 21, 1974.)

Other potential routes: The Gunsight Couloir into Valhalla Canyon would make a fun, 50-degree ski on hard snow.

Valhalla Canyon: Rimmed by the two highest peaks in the range, this steep canyon offers excellent terrain with no known descents. Approach from Cascade Canyon.

Disappointment Peak (11,618 feet): Cleaved on three sides by big rock walls, this mountain is more popular with rock climbers than with skiers. Approach from Garnet Canyon or Glacier Gulch.

East Face/Spoon Couloir: {F} In most years, the wind-scoured, unskiable upper east face impedes a descent from the summit. But heavy snow years might yield a skiable route from the notch just north of the craggy summit.

Despite the lack of a summit, this ski route remains a classic. The east face is moderate but exposed and the challenging Spoon Couloir is long, steep and narrow. From the bottom of the Spoon, several options will return you to Burnt Wagon Gulch. See Amphitheater Lake Buttress.

(Early free-heel: Glenn Vitucci; February, 1985. Early fixed-heel: Tom Bennett and Mark Smith; April 3, 1990.)

Southwest Couloir: {F} Though typically wind-scoured at the top, this long couloir makes a challenging descent to the Caves of Garnet Canyon.

(Early snowboard: Stephen Koch; May 22, 1989.)

Other potential routes: Just south of the Spoon Snowfield, two severe couloirs drop into Amphitheater Lake from the east face.

Amphitheater Lake Buttress: This is the large, forested fault scarp that culminates at Surprise and Amphitheater lakes. It offers three primary routes. Approach from Burnt Wagon or Glacier gulch.

East Face: {E} The Lupine Meadows summer trail switchbacks up this 3,000-foot gladed face, which makes a classic winter run.

(Early fixed-heel: Virginia Huidekoper, Mary Major and Fritz Weissner; 1940s.)

Surprise Pinnacle: {E} For an extra 600 feet of steep, wide-open skiing, climb this small summit just southwest of Surprise Lake.

(Early free-heel: Jim Olson; early 1990s.)

North Chutes: {E} and {F} Several chutes and faces drop to Delta Lake from Amphitheater and Surpise lakes.

(Early fixed-heel: Tom Turiano; late April, 1990. Early free-heel: Sparky Colby, Michael Keating and Greg Morgan; late April, 1990.)

Grand Teton (13,770 feet): The Grand Teton has always epitomized the development of mountaineering in America. Clinging to its ridges, walls, and gullies, thousands of climbers have learned the way of the alpine environment and trained for climbs of more committing mountains around the globe.

To ski mountaineers, the Grand represents America's ultimate test of endurance and skill. But it is not a place for skiers to become ski mountaineers. Being a masterful skier is only one of many requirements here. Only those with years of climbing and ski-mountaineering experience should attempt to ski the Grand. At publication of this book, fewer than 30 people had skied successfully from the summit.

Molar Tooth Couloir: {H} Disoriented in a whiteout, three Salt Lake City skiers pioneered this route, thinking it was the Stettner Couloir. This 1,000-foot chute leads from the north side of the Teepe Glacier to the east ridge of the Grand, just west of the Molar Tooth.

The Salt Lake trio stepped into skis just below the large chockstone at the top of the couloir. About half-way down, Andrew McLean belayed and lowered his partners through the 50-foot, 60-degree icy crux. He then sideslipped and stepped with an ice axe, self-belaying to safety.

(Early fixed-heel: Andrew McLean; June 15, 1991. Early free-heel: Scott Roach and Jordan Diamond; June 15, 1991.)

Briggs' Route: {H} After a successful descent of Mount Moran in June of 1968, mountain guide and ski instructor Bill Briggs wondered if there was a continuous snow route from the top of the Grand. He researched this question while guiding on the Grand that summer and studying *A Climber's Guide to the Teton Range*, by Leigh Ortenburger. Incidentally, Ortenburger told Briggs that the Grand would be impossible to ski.

Briggs decided that the most feasible route would involve skiing the Ford Couloir, then rappelling into the Stettner Couloir. In the spring of 1969, Briggs intended to try the descent but couldn't find any companions. Bad weather finally foiled his subsequent plans to attempt the descent alone. The winter of 1969-70 then brought very little snow and dangerous avalanche conditions, so Briggs didn't consider the descent that year.

The next winter, however, produced so much snow that by mid-January, Briggs had organized a team. Nonetheless, conflicting commitments eventually canceled that team's attempt. Determined not to waste the perfect conditions, Briggs quickly arranged another team made up of Jackson Hole Ski Club Coach Robbie Garrett, Jackson Hole ski patrolman and Exum guide Dean Moore, and national forest snow ranger Juris Krisjansons. The team made two attempts to ski Teewinot as a warm-up for the Grand, but foul weather stopped them.

Krisjansons and Moore dropped off the team and Briggs added John "Blackie" Bolton and Jorge Colón in their places. On June 15, 1971, the new team hiked to the Exum Mountain Guide's hut on the Lower Saddle. Garrett and Briggs made a short reconnaissance trip partway up the Stettner and found that it would work, though it would be difficult.

At 5 a.m. on June 16, the team started across the Black Dike Traverse toward the Stettner in above-freezing temperatures, the snow too soft for easy climbing. When they reached the steep, icy chimney leading to the Ford Couloir, it became apparent to Briggs that he would be unable to protect his partners across a difficult traverse. Plan B took the team to the top of the Stettner Couloir, where Briggs climbed the 5.7 overhanging chockstones and belayed Colón and Bolton to the Stettner Col at the top of the Underhill Ridge. Rockfall, rapidly softening snow, and intimidating climbing discouraged Briggs' partners, so he broke trail up the east face, through thigh-deep slush, alone.

Briggs began his descent at 2 p.m., after struggling to remove his right crampon, which had a broken strap. The snow on the upper east face was very soft and, at one point, Briggs' skis broke through, and he fell. He quickly rolled over and stood back up on his skis. Each turn on the lower east face cut off eight inches of slush, which avalanched into the abyss. Briggs smeared through the four-foot gap at the bottom of the east face and turned to a stop on the Stettner Col. He experienced excellent skiing down to the top of the rappel, where he rejoined his companions. Briggs left his skis on during the rappel and skied into space out of a cave, controlling his descent so that his skis barely touched the rock.

As they commonly do, avalanches splashed out of the Ford Couloir into the Stettner, so the team moved quickly to avoid getting caught. Briggs fell again when his ski tips augured into an avalanche runnel. He used his "emergency avalanche stopper" to avoid sliding into his partners below him. While rolling over, he turned one ski 90 degrees so it could be rammed to the boot in the soft snow. Briggs then used a fixed rope for safety as he sideslipped and stepped through the middle Stettner ice bulges.

At the bottom of the Stettner, Briggs turned east and climbed to Glencoe Col to reach the Teepe Glacier, while his partners headed west for the Lower Saddle to retrieve gear. On Glencoe Col, Briggs passed mountain guide and friend Vince Lee, who was so excited to see him that he forgot to take pictures. On Teepe Glacier, Briggs set off avalanches with every turn, transforming the slope into a blur. He fell a third time below the Teepe Glacier, then skied all the way to the 7,700-foot level.

In a good snow year, only one 165-foot rappel is required to ski Briggs' route. In lesser snow years, skiers may have to make as many as five rappels, making the descent barely worth the effort.

The east face produces a variety of snow conditions, including rime, powder, neve, slush and crust. The face graduates from 35 degrees at the top to 45 degrees at the bottom. The upper Stettner, though brief and tilted at nearly 50 degrees, usually serves up the best snow of the descent.

The crux of the climb undoubtedly surfaces in surmounting the double chockstone. Skiers usually endure the spooky mixed climbing in the dihedral right (east) of the lower chockstone. Once in the cave, a very difficult series of moves leads around the upper chockstone to the west. At least one skier has been able to crawl through a tunnel in the back of the cave under the upper chockstone to gain the upper Stettner. Several skiers with experience on vertical ice have climbed the 40-foot frozen waterfall left (west) of the double chockstone.

In 1978, Steve Shea and Dave Breashears surmounted the chockstones by spiraling behind the ice pillar, thus avoiding all difficulties. That year, they skied Briggs' route twice in powder, while filming *Fall Line*. In 1979, Shea arrived on the top of the Underhill Ridge just in time to avoid an avalanche that came off east-face snowfield and launched off the Stettner chockstone and Otterbody Snowfield. Confident that the route then was safe, he continued to the summit and made his third ski descent of the peak.

The east face fractured 10 feet deep in another massive avalanche during the spring of 1990. An old depth hoar layer and blistering spring heat were the culprits.

The Stettner usually supplies undulating neve and avalanche-polished snow at angles of 45 degrees to 50 degrees. The middle Stettner ice bulges usually pose easy fifth-class ice climbing for climbers and one 160-foot rappel for skiers. Rarely is there enough snow to bury the ice bulges enough to make this section of the couloir skiable. In low-to-average snow years, the

50-degree narrows near the bottom of the Stettner can provide the technical crux of the descent. Deep snow years can make these difficulties vanish.

From his perch at the saddle in 1983, Briggs recalls watching Sun Valley skier Kim Anderson slide head-first out of the Stettner after falling in this steep, narrow section. Anderson lost a ski, rolled over, then self-arrested before sliding over a 500-foot cliff.

East of Glencoe Col, skiers negotiate a short, exposed slope, often with rotten snow, to reach the Teepe Glacier. This author was tumbled 50 yards by an avalanche—toward certain death in the vertical Teepe Chimney—before self-arresting, gear scattered all over the slope.

Gain the Teepe Col via a descending traverse across this bowl. On the Teepe Glacier, snow conditions vary from powder to neve to slush. Loose-snow avalanches are the norm. Below the glacier, 2,000 feet of moderate slopes lead southeast to Garnet Canyon Meadows.

On June 19, 1993, Bill Iorio and Andy Booth made the first one-day Grand ski-descent attempt. They summitted at about 10 a.m. after an 11 p.m. start from Lupine Meadows. Exhausted from the long haul and postholing in dangerous slush, the pair descended the Owen-Spalding and skied from the Upper Saddle.

Approach from Garnet Canyon. Most parties camp at the base of the Teepe Glacier.

(Early fixed-heel: William Briggs, with support crew of Jorge Colón, John Bolton, and Robbie Garrett; June 16, 1971. Early snowboard: Stephen Koch, with skiers Tom Turiano and Andy Matz; June 9, 1989.)

Ford Couloir/Stettner Couloir: {H} The Ford couloir undoubtedly is the purest-looking ski line on the mountain. Nestled between the Exum and upper Petzoldt ridges, the couloir extends more than 1,000 feet and ranges from 35 degrees at the top to just more than 50 degrees about a third of the way down. The couloir ends abruptly for skiers, where it forks around the Petzoldt Ridge pinnacle. The right (west) fork is called the Beckey Couloir and is unskiable. The left (east) fork leads—via two double-rope rappels—to the Stettner Couloir, just above the middle Stettner ice bulges.

Pocatello student and mountaineer Jeff Rhoads read the *Teton Magazine* article about Bill Briggs' first ski descent of the Grand Teton and dreamed about

making the descent himself. After five years of planning and six attempts, the conditions finally were right in July of 1978. Not only did Rhoads and his friends plan to ski Briggs' route but they would attempt to ski a new route from the summit, the Ford Couloir.

After numerous attempts, Jeff Rhoads made the first descent of the Ford Couloir on the Grand Teton at age 21. He then continued to pluck new ski routes from the big Teton peaks.

On July 1, Rhoads and Chris Barnes climbed to their cache of gear on Glencoe Col and built an igloo/tarp combination for shelter. Friends Brad Peck and Diane Jerman planned to arrive on the evening of July 2. That morning saw Rhoads and Barnes cramponing up the firm snow of the Stettner Couloir. They climbed skillfully past the ice bulges and moved quickly up the east-face snowfield. When Rhoads began his descent of Briggs' route, the snow was suncupped and very firm. He downclimbed with his Scott boots through the narrow gap at the base of the east face and took a belay on the frozen snow of the upper Stettner Couloir.

After a frightening rappel over the chockstones, Rhoads skied carefully down the Stettner to the middle ice bulges, which were terribly runneled and unskiable. Arriving at camp exhausted, Rhoads and Barnes ate, relaxed, and waited for Peck and Jerman to arrive.

They spent July 3 resting, fixing ropes, and caching loads of gear higher on the mountain to ease the next day's work. Early on July 4, Peck and Rhoads quickly reclimbed the Stettner and the icy shaft to the base of the Ford. Clouds wafted about and snow began to fall as they cramponed hastily up the Ford to the summit. After a short break, they snapped into their bindings and skied the icy chute in a howling wind. Downclimbing and rappelling returned them to their camp triumphant. They celebrated with a bottle of Mateus. After packing up, they sent their backpacks tumbling down the Teepe Glacier and skied 3,000 feet to the Platforms.

On another stormy day in 1982, Rick Wyatt repeated Rhoads' and Peck's route—solo, ropeless, and on free-heel gear, a feat so pure in style that it has not been repeated. He used Asolo single, low-top leather boots without support cuffs and Fischer Expeditions with aluminum edges and Troll exploding bail pin bindings with Voilé plates for support. In the icy chute between the Stettner and Ford couloirs, Wyatt strapped his skis to his pack and downclimbed. He almost elected to jettison his pack because his ski tips were scraping continually on the rock and upsetting his balance. The

next day, he returned with photographer Chris Noble to film near the summit.

Inspired by the booming interest in skiing the Grand, Bill Briggs returned with companions Kim Anderson, Mike Rettig, Don Gronberg and Jack Levin in 1983 to attempt the first continuous ski descent. But Briggs got sick while on the saddle, while Anderson skied the Ford couloir with support from the others. Discontinuous snow thwarted their pioneering hopes. Rettig had hoped to ski the peak on free-heel gear.

Mike Collins made the first known attempt at snowboarding the Ford, with skier Tom Turiano, in June of 1988. Bad weather turned the pair back at the base of the Ford Couloir.

(Early fixed-heel: Jeff Rhoads and Brad Peck, with support from Diane Jerman and Chris Barnes; July 4, 1978. Early free-heel: Rick Wyatt; June 10, 1982.)

Owen-Spalding Route: {H} This is not an aesthetic ski route, and it requires at least two rappels for a descent from the summit. In certain exceptional snow years, skiers can take on two steep areas just below the summit on the west face. After a rappel in the Sargent Chimney, ski moderate but exposed, intricate slopes to the Emerson Chimney rappel, which ends at the Upper Saddle.

From this saddle, ski southwest to the couloir west of the Central Rib, which extends about 800 feet before ending at a large cliff next to a small pinnacle. At least two climbers died by sliding into the abyss here. Use extra caution. Either downclimb or ski the short, 60-foot chute east of the pinnacle and continue on 45- to 55-degree terrain to the Owen-Spalding water hole. From here, downclimb southwest to reach a long couloir that extends into Dartmouth Basin or downclimb wind-scoured rock to the drift just below the Black Dike. You can ski the drift to the Lower Saddle or to a wide southeast-facing couloir that leads into the Middle Teton Glacier moraine area.

The primary approach to the Grand Teton is via Garnet Canyon. Depending upon the time of year, park either at Lupine Meadows or Taggart Lake trailhead.

(Early fixed-heel: Mike Fischer; 1980s. Early

free-heel: Bill Iorio; June 19, 1993. Early snowboard: Stephen Koch; June 11, 1991.)

Enclosure Couloir: {G} or {H} On Sept. 10, 1993, Jim Zell and Rick Armstrong climbed the icy Enclosure Couloir intending to ski. Wisely declining to ski the ice-glazed neve, though, they rappelled the west face to safety.

Packing two 200-foot ropes and a pair of super-light Dynastar Altiplumes, Alex Lowe and Andrew McLean left the saddle at 6 a.m. and made their way gingerly around the Valhalla Traverse. Cold temperatures froze the neve solid, and the pair cramponed easily to the culmination of this 55-plus-degree couloir on the northwest ridge of the Grand.

After an hour-long wait on top, they skied about 300 feet, unbelayed, through a surprisingly soft slush that sloughed off with each turn. When they reached the shaded icy sections, they belayed several pitches to the Valhalla Traverse. Lowe called the route a bit contrived, with poor snow, but said it provided for an amazing adventure.

(Early fixed heel: Alex Lowe and Andrew McLean, randonnée; July 5, 1994.)

Black Ice Couloir: {I} After successful descents of numerous ice couloirs in the Tetons, Stephen Koch envisioned pushing the limits of ski and snowboard mountaineering to their fullest. On his first attempt to descend the Black Ice Couloir on July 17, 1992, he and Alex Lowe climbed the couloir with skis on their backs and discovered it was too icy. In August of 1993, Koch returned for a solo attempt. He rappelled into the couloir from the upper saddle and found a dangerous breakable crust on top of black ice.

Staring down from the Upper Saddle into the gloomy ice chute on his third attempt, Koch and his partner, Mark Newcomb, faced a choice. They could retreat to Dornan's and have a couple of beers or they could break new ground in American ski mountaineering and take it one step at a time.

Newcomb clicked into his bindings, looked Koch in the eye, and plunged into two turns on the 60-degree slope. The snow was several inches deep, with a breakable rain crust. Perceiving extreme danger, Koch insisted that the pair belay each other. A short distance from the saddle, Koch slung a horn and began paying out 10-foot stretches of rope for each of Newcomb's turns.

On his very next turn, Newcomb's edges broke through the three-inch rain crust and removed a plate of snow, revealing black ice. Though he lost his balance, he did not fall, and he jump-turned the challenging snow for a rope length. Newcomb then set up an anchor and belayed Koch on a top rope—anchored on the slung horn above—by tying an additional rope to the original rope. They belayed two such pitches. After making two rappels over the icy crux, they traversed northeast across the broad, 55-degree main icefield until they were below the west face.

A sustained falline of turns took Koch and Newcomb to the edge of the 1,000-foot cliff at bottom of the couloir, where they made two rappels (with one difficult pull) to the Valhalla Traverse ledge. The resplendent team then scrambled back to the Lower Saddle to retrieve their gear.

After reading about their descent in national backcountry skiing magazines, some claimed that Koch and Newcomb tamed the couloir in poor style, with belays and rappels. Newcomb responded by reminding that most unskied Teton routes would require rappels to connect patches of snow. Besides, he said, dying wasn't part of his plan.

(Early fixed-heel: Mark Newcomb; June 5, 1994. Early snowboard: Stephen Koch; June 5, 1994.)

Dike Snowfield: {F} This wonderful ski run drops 1,400 feet into Glacier Gulch from the notch between Disappointment Peak and the east ridge of the Grand. Start from the col at the lower northeast corner of Teepe Glacier.

(Early fixed-heel: "Palmy" Bob; 1971. Early snowboard: Stephen Koch; June 11, 1991.)

Other potential routes: In June of 1979, Steve Shea made an attempt on the Otterbody Snowfield and Chimneys, as did Tom Turiano and Andy Matz in June of 1989. But huge avalanches raking the east face kept both parties away. During the exceptionally wintery spring and summer of 1993, a massive slide raked the face on a hot day in late July!

It's possible that Dan McKay had this same east-face route in mind during his second attempt on the Grand on July 11, 1982. He traversed to Teepe Glacier on the Black Dike, searching for a continuous snow route. Tragically, he fell while soloing fifth-class slabs 100 feet above the glacier. For months before his fateful attempt, McKay dreamed of making the first nordic descent of the mountain.

During this author's third attempt to ski the northeast Hossack-MacGowen Couloir on June 10-11, 1991, Stephen Koch and I climbed over 20 pitches of ice and rock to the Second Tower notch. Realizing that a ski descent over the ice would have been tantamount to suicide, we started toward the summit to attempt a descent of the Ford Couloir. Waist-deep wallowing in slush on the east ridge turned us back to the notch, where we were forced to bivouac at 10:30 a.m. in perfect weather. At 2 a.m. on June 11, intense shivering drove us to make another attempt for the summit.

Jeff Rhoads also was the first to ski this southeast side of the Middle Teton via the classic Ellingwood Couloir, which descends nearly 1,500 feet at angles of 50 degrees from the Dike Col to Garnet south fork.

Only a one-inch crust formed on the surface of the previous day's slush, making the climb horrifying and exhausting. We watched the northern lights as we arrived at the summit at 4 a.m. in a frigid west wind. Due to biting cold, we agreed to forego a descent of the Ford, and skied the Owen-Spalding from the Upper Saddle.

Three other extreme routes, the Vision Quest Couloir, the east face of the Grandstand, and the east ridge also have been identified as ski lines. Two climbers were killed in a wet-snow avalanche on the east ridge in April of 1979. The Dartmouth Couloir, skied by Mark Newcomb on June 1, 1995, is a very aesthetic route. It leads 1,400 feet to Dartmouth Basin from just north of The Lower Saddle. This couloir reaches angles near 45 degrees.

Dartmouth Basin: This steep side canyon branches southeast toward the Middle and Grand Tetons, a mile south of the Cascade Canyon forks. *Bonney's Guide to Wyoming Mountains and Wilderness Areas* notes that Dartmouth Basin offers magnificent ski terrain. What makes this draw extra special is its proximity to the big Teton peaks.

There are several ways to approach the draw, all of which require considerable effort. Climb directly from Cascade Canyon or descend from the Lower Saddle via the Dartmouth Couloir (see Grand Teton). The most enjoyable approach follows the Avalanche Divide-Icefloe Lake-Dartmouth Basin route.

Middle Teton (12,804 feet): This peak offers moderate to severe ski routes of all aspects. Skiers have skied more routes from its summit than from any other major Teton peak. Approach from Garnet Canyon.

Cave Couloir: {E} This moderate, accessible classic is one of the most popular couloirs in the range; moguls were observed there in late July of 1993. Begin the descent on a bench in Garnet south fork, just below the southeast couloir. Ski east down this wide, 38-degree gully between two huge rock islands.

Southeast Couloir: {G} This is the relatively short chimney that empties into Garnet south fork, just west of the top of the Cave Couloir. John Griber believes this route is key to a continuous descent of the Dike Pinnacle.

(Early fixed-heel: Wade McKoy and Nils Bane; June, 1993. Early snowboard: John Griber; June, 1993.)

Ellingwood Couloir: {G} This classic line descends nearly 1,500 feet at angles of 50 degrees from the Dike Col to Garnet south fork. Combined with the upper east face of the Middle, this route is one of the most challenging in the range. A chockstone some two thirds of the way up forces skiers to the side in a narrow runnel. Jeff Rhoads skied the chute in late afternoon and cut off avalanches with every turn.

(Early fixed-heel: Jeff Rhoads; June, 1979. Mike Fischer and Dan McKay; spring, early 1980s. Early free-heel: Tim Quinn; spring of 1984 or 1985.)

Chouinard Couloir: {G} This is the narrow, exposed chute just west of the Ellingwood Couloir. The main buttress of the Buckingham Ridge separates the two ski routes. A large overhanging chimney caps the top of the couloir, making it unskiable from the summit.

With sufficient energy remaining after a successful first snowboard descent of the north face of Spalding Peak, John Griber climbed and snowboarded this couloir in the wet snow of early afternoon. He returned the following year to catch it in better conditions.

(Early snowboard: John Griber, from near top; May 17, 1992.)

Southwest Couloir: {F} The snow in this couloir often is frozen and chunky, yet provides the easiest route from the summit. In some years, late winter descents offer the best snow. Slope angles range from 30 degrees at the bottom to near 45 degrees at the narrows in the middle. Approach from Garnet south fork to the saddle between the Middle and South Tetons. Sixteen boy scouts made the first sledding descent with plastic bags in the late 1980s! Amazingly, they all survived.

During a 1983 figl descent, Roland Fleck and Brents Hawks watched in fright as renowned mountaineer Yvon Chouinard fell and began cartwheeling down the couloir. He was able to self-arrest, but scratched any plans for marketing figls.

(Early fixed-heel: Bill Briggs, with the support crew of Julie Briggs, Dick Person and Fletcher Manley; early June 1967. Early free-heel: Rick Wyatt; mid- to late 1970s. Jay and Sue Moody; May 1983. Early snowboard: John Griber; June 11 or 12, 1993.)

Northwest Hanging Snowfield: {G} Reaching angles of nearly 50 degrees, this platter of snow in the sky ends abruptly at a 1,000-foot cliff. Conditions range from wind pack to powder. On the first and only descent, Steve Shea climbed back up the face after skiing it. Approach from the southwest or northwest couloir.

(Early fixed-heel: Steve Shea; spring, 1979.)

Northwest Ice Couloir (Frishman Couloir): {G} or {H} Many had dreamed of skiing this spectacular snow and ice chute, but Stephen Koch made the dream a reality on a day meant for chipping ice from the Exum Hut platform. A cold west wind kept the couloir firm on that mid-June afternoon.

In January of 1981, Teton skier and guide Harry Frishman died in a fall while solo climbing in this couloir, which ends abruptly in a steep, icy chimney.

From the Lower Saddle, scramble between Pinocchio and Bonney's pinnacles, then out of a notch to the north ridge of the Middle. Make an exposed ascending traverse on boulders and an icy ledge into the northwest couloir. Expect angles of 55 degrees on the descent.

(Early snowboard: Stephen Koch; June 15, 1991. Early fixed-heel: Alex Lowe, with Stephen Koch on snowboard; July 17, 1992.)

Pinnochio Couloir: {G} Tilted at more than 55 degrees and less than 10 feet wide at the top, this chute descends onto the Middle Teton Glacier from the notch between Bonney's and Pinnochio pinnacles.

(Early fixed-heel: Steve Shea; spring of 1978 or 79.)

Glacier Route: {G} This difficult descent is a Teton classic. During the 1,800-foot course into Garnet north fork, you'll find a wide variety of terrain and snow conditions. From the summit, make an extremely exposed traverse to the notch between the south and north peaks. Depending on snow depth, you may have to make a short jump. The pitch below the notch is one of the steepest skiable slopes in the Tetons. In summer, climbers find 5.7 rock there. The slope angle ranges from 55 degrees to 65 degrees, depending on the snow depth. Just above the Dike Col, pass a cliff band by skiing one of three extremely steep passages. Stephen Koch took the southern couloir during the first snowboard descent, scraping over 60-degree water ice to reach the col. Tim Quinn went north toward the main northeast-facing runnel during the first nordic descent and broke through crust, causing a terrifying slide for life. The center route seems to be the safest, though it reaches angles of 55 degrees.

From the Dike Col, the Dike Couloir descends north at grades of 40 degrees to 50 degrees. Skiers may find powder near their right edge. On skiers' left and center, expect avalanche-polished runnels and neve. Use caution at the bottom of the couloir, where a large crevasse crosses the falline. The glacier itself extends for 1,000 feet below the crevasse into Garnet north fork.

(Early fixed-heel: Steve Shea; late May or early June, 1978. Mike Fischer and Dan McKay; spring, early 1980s. Early free-heel: Rick Wyatt, from Dike col; early 1980s. Tim Quinn, from just below notch; May 23, 1989. Early snowboard: Stephen Koch, from notch; May 23, 1989. John Griber, from south summit; June 9, 1989.)

Koch's Couloir: {G} This couloir is either a variation of the Glacier Route or an endeavor in itself. The couloir extends more than 1,000 feet and is just east of the Middle Teton Glacier. Entering the couloir from above might require a jump or downclimb. The crux, however, is at the bottom, where you'll have to tackle a short, 60-degree ice bulge.

Steve Shea skied the couloir while making the National Geographic movie, *Fall Line*. His film crew wanted him to ski it again, so he climbed around on the glacier for a second run. Still unsatisfied with the footage and eager to take advantage of the prime terrain, the crew asked him to ski it a third time! Unfortunately, Shea agreed and, just a few turns below the top, he fell. Without a doubt, it was one of the most horrifying falls ever captured on film and seriously bated Steve's future enthusiasm for pushing his limits in ski mountaineering.

(Early fixed-heel: Steve Shea; spring, 1979. Early snowboard: Stephen Koch; May 23, 1989.)

Other potential routes: The final prize descent on the Middle Teton leads from the summit of the Dike Pinnacle. The highly exposed east ridge leads to a bench; drop north onto the glacier or south toward the southeast couloir.

Shadow Peak (10,725 feet): This seldom-visited, relatively insignificant peak has neither a known descent party nor an obvious ski route from its summit. Overshadowed by Nez Perce to the northwest, the cliffy summit spire of Shadow Peak is barely visible from Jackson Hole. Its east-facing lower, forested slopes, however, stand out clearly as alluring powder skiing terrain culminating at the east shoulder.

To approach, follow the Bradley Lake Track to the top of the primary moraine between Taggart and Bradley lakes. Skin up the steep morainal ridge and gain the east slopes of Shadow Peak at 8,400 feet. To reach Shadow Peak cirque, climb the Platforms Couloir from Garnet Canyon.

East Slopes: {D} and {E} Dropping toward Jackson Hole from the rocky east shoulder (Point 10,160-plus), three excellent ski routes are possible. The terrain is quite rocky, however, and typically requires a deeper snow cover than do 25 Short and Maverick before it is safe to ski. One route drops northeast from the top and should be attempted only when avalanche conditions are very stable. Ski northeast from the top on a 30-degree slope through a sparse dwarf-tree forest (avalanche path) for 1,400 feet to the creek that drains Shadow Peak cirque. At 8,800 feet, traverse southeast onto the lower east face for another 2,000 feet of skiing to the valley.

The other two routes begin a short distance east of the east shoulder, at 9,600 feet. Ski east through a spectacular sparse white-pine forest to the inconspicuous top of a draw that splits the face. The face on the south side of the draw offers rocky southeast-facing terrain and ends near the mouth of Avalanche Canyon. The face to the north sports steeper terrain, intermittent cliffs, and both northeast and southeast exposures en route to Bradley Lake. The large moraine between the two lakes also splits the face into two routes.

(Early free-heel: Bob Graham; Jan. 3, 1988.)

Nez Perce (11,901 feet): Though most ski mountaineers never even considered Nez Perce to be skiable, two of Jackson Hole's most skilled—Stephen Koch and Mark Newcomb—wondered about the discontinuous system of couloirs and faces on the northeast side. They dubbed the route "Spooky Face" because rocks near the summit form a visage of anger and forlorn.

Spooky Face: {H} On April 30, 1994, Koch and Newcomb made a bold attempt on this route, which had never even been climbed. With a 2 a.m. start at Taggart Lake trailhead, they bicycled to the Climbers' Ranch bridge, hiked up Burnt Wagon Gulch, and traversed into Garnet Canyon. From The Meadows, they climbed into the eastern Hourglass Couloir and endured three hours of thigh-deep postholing in newly fallen powder. They passed a chockstone with 5.7 difficulties on the right and searched for a feasible route up a 250-foot overhang, which guards the bottom of Spooky Face. No such luck. They continued up the couloir and arrived at the East Peak Sliver notch.

From the notch, it seemed impossible to traverse into Spooky Face, so Mark led upward—on snow-covered, nearly vertical, 5.9 rock with insecure holds—to a sloping ledge system. It was getting late and the duo still was a long way from the summit. They wisely decided to retreat. But before they rappelled, Koch wanted to determine whether the route ultimately would lead to the summit. He inched across the precarious sloping ledge for one and a half pitches to get a view. The ledge ended hopelessly at a sheer cliff. No go.

Koch and Newcomb returned the following year with Hans Johnstone and resolved to climb the standard route to the summit before skiing the Spooky Face.

With one double-rope rappel into the East Hourglass, the trio was successful in an amazing 15-hour push.

(Early fixed-heel: Mark Newcomb and Hans Johnstone; April 21, 1995. Early snowboard: Stephen Koch; April 21, 1995.)

East Peak Sliver: {G} This narrow couloir extends nearly 1,500 feet from the notch southwest of the East Peak to Shadow Peak Cirque. On the first descent, a 10-foot cornice jump was required to enter the couloir from the notch. Couloir angles average close to 50 degrees.

(Early fixed-heel: Doug Coombs, Rick Armstrong, et al; early February, 1994.)

West Ridge Couloir: {G} This obscure strip of snow drops northwest off the west ridge near the highest gendarme into Garnet south fork.

(Early fixed-heel: Kevin Brazell and Josh Daigel; late May, 1991. Early snowboard: Dustin Varga; late May, 1991.)

Hourglass Couloir: {G} Although there actually are two hourglass couloirs on the north face of Nez Perce, the western one is *the* Hourglass Couloir. Skiers may climb as high as they like in this straightforward, popular Teton classic. Expect angles of nearly 45 degrees in a fairly narrow space. Approach from the Garnet Canyon Meadows.

(Early fixed-heel: Les Gibson et al; April, 1978. Early free-heel: Les Gibson, et al; April, 1979.)

East Hourglass Couloir: {H} This is the lower half of the Spooky Face route described above and first was alpine skied from below the chockstone.

(Early fixed-heel: Mike Fischer and Dan McKay; spring, early 1980s.)

Cloudveil Dome (12,026 feet): With no recorded descents from the summit, this Garnet Canyon peak remains one of the Teton's last ski-mountaineering challenges. Approach from Garnet south fork.

Northeast Snowfield: {E} In 1972, Bert Redmayne, Davey Agnew, and Ian Wade teamed up for a winter ascent of the north face of Cloudveil Dome. Redmayne and Wade successfully climbed the face while Agnew decided that skiing this moderate snowfield was more in his cards for the day. This classic route plummets north from the saddle between Nez Perce and Cloudveil Dome.

(Early fixed-heel: Davey Agnew; March 9, 1972.)

Other potential routes: The only feasible route drops to the northwest side on an exposed hanging snowfield. After a short traverse to the col west of the summit, plunge north onto the Zorro Snowfield. The crux of the route is the exit from the bottom of this Z-shaped apron. Rappels and/or fifth-class downclimbing might be required to reach easy snow in Garnet Canyon south fork.

Spalding Peak (12,040-plus-feet): This insignificant peak along the complex Nez Perce-South Teton ridge offers one ski route. Approach from Garnet south fork.

North Face: {G} From the summit, the first descent party skied 50-plus-degree slopes through a short cliff band onto a wide-open, 40-degree powder face. One nordic skier from the party crossed his tips and slid 400 feet on firm under-powder crust before self-arresting unshaken.

(Early fixed-heel: Tom Turiano and Andy Booth; May 17, 1992. Early free-heel: Steve McCormick, from top, and David Bowers, not from top; May 17, 1992. Early snowboard: John Griber; May 17, 1992.)

Gilkey Tower (12,320-plus feet): Conspicuously protruding from the South Teton/Nez Perce ridge, this peak often is mistaken from Garnet Canyon for the South Teton. Approach from Garnet south fork.

Northwest Couloir: {G} Reaching the ridge west of the summit in good snow years, this often wind-scoured couloir drops about 300 feet onto the north glacier.

(Early fixed-heel: Dave Hagen; May 24, 1992.)

Other potential routes: In excellent snow years, the east ridge might be skiable.

South Teton (12,514 feet): Though dwarfed by its neighbors on the Garnet Canyon side, the South Teton is the monarch of Avalanche Canyon north fork. Approach from Garnet south fork or Avalanche north fork.

East Ridge: {G} or {H} This extremely steep, 200-foot ridge is skiable from the summit to the Ice Cream

Cone notch only during excellent snow years. From the notch, ski the north glacier or the Ice Cream Couloir. During the only known attempt on this ridge, Christoph Schork stepped into his alpine touring bindings about halfway up the ridge, at the base of a 60-degree snow pitch.

(Early fixed-heel, not from summit: Christoph Schork; May 4, 1992.)

Ice Cream Couloir: {H} This 55-plus-degree ramp drops south from the notch between the South Teton and Ice Cream Cone. The only skier of this route downclimbed a long, steep ice chimney to connect steep couloirs and hanging snowfields during his harrowing descent into Avalanche Canyon.

(Early fixed-heel: Jim Zell; May 24, 1993.)

Southeast Couloir: {H} Larry Detrick and Jim Duclos made a reconnaissance climb of this striking couloir and determined that it was too steep to ski. Stephen Koch and this author made an attempt in June of 1989 but were thwarted by deep runnels and extreme steepness.

Koch spent the winter of 1990-91 in Chamonix pushing his limits as a snowboard mountaineer, all the while keeping the southeast couloir in mind. That spring—with incredible efficiency and skill—Stephen returned alone to set a new standard by snowboarding this 60-plus-degree couloir. Approach the same as the southeast face.

(Early snowboard: Stephen Koch; May 29, 1991.)

Southeast Face: {G} This classic route offers almost 3,500 feet of skiing into the Avalanche north fork. Mike Fischer approached from a camp at Lake Taminah because he wasn't sure there was a route from the bottom of the upper face into the canyon below. Doug Doyle and Ian Campbell approached from Garnet south fork during the second descent of the route in the spring of 1984.

From the point of highest snow on the southeast face, ski the narrow southeast ridge through a 50-plus-degree upper headwall. Below the headwall, ski a 1,000-foot vast hanging snowface until you can traverse northeast on steep slopes into the deep, wide gully between the South Teton and Matternaught Peak. The gully curls to skiers' right and ends abruptly at a 100-foot cliff. A 10-foot-wide couloir provides the only passage to the slopes above Lake Taminah.

(Early fixed-heel: Mike Fischer; spring, 1983. Early snowboard: Stephen Koch, with skier Tom Turiano; June 23, 1989. Early free-heel: Jack McConnell; May, 1991.)

Northwest Couloir: {F} This standard ascent route usually is wind-scoured and thus rarely in shape for skiing. A descent from the summit via this route would require a very healthy snow year with little wind. Most skiers start this descent from the bottom of the couloir proper and ski the vast north snowfield into the south fork of Garnet Canyon.

At age 8, David Berkenfield became the youngest skier to ski a Teton Peak. He skied this route with his father—a climbing ranger—on May 19, 1988.

(Early fixed-heel: Jorge Colón; late 1960s or early 70s. Early free-heel: Jim Roscoe and Sherm Wilson; June, 1974.)

North Glacier: {E} This moderate "glacier" spans the north side of the ridge between the South Teton and Gilkey Tower. You can find good snow here into late June. Start from a notch on either side of Ice Cream Cone.

(Early free-heel: Les Gibson; April, 1980.)

Other potential routes: Numerous couloirs stripe the south and southwest sides of the mountain, but none go from the summit. One striking couloir begins at the 11,600-foot contour line and ends at Snowdrift Lake. What is known as the northeast couloir would make a challenging descent, beginning 100 yards west of the summit.

HIGH ROUTES

Garnet Canyon-Glacier Gulch: {F} There are two ways to connect these chasms. At the 8,720-foot level on the Garnet Canyon Trail, climb the Surprise Lake outlet gully to Surprise Lake. Climb to Amphitheater Lake, then traverse into the gulch on a ledge. A higher route climbs the Teepe Glacier moraine from Spalding Falls to the amphitheatre west of Disappointment Peak. From the col between the east ridge of the Grand and Fairshare Tower, drop down the Dike Snowfield into the gulch.

Garnet Canyon north fork-Dartmouth Basin: {F} One couloir leads from near the Black Dike into Dartmouth to make this high loop possible. (See Grand Teton, other potential routes.)

The southeast side of the South Teton offers challenging descents with big vertical relief. The South Teton is the monarch of Avalanche Canyon north fork, though it is dwarfed by its neighbors on the Garnet Canyon side.

Platforms Couloirs: {F} These two steep, avalanche-prone chutes connect the Platforms of Garnet Canyon with Shadow Peak drainage. Climb the longer western gully to access Shadow Peak cirque, and use the narrow eastern couloir to drop into Garnet Canyon from Shadow Peak drainage below the middle headwall.

Icefloe Lake-Dartmouth Basin: {F} or {G} Surprisingly, this is the only route known to have been used to access the basin during winter or spring. In June of 1991, Dave Moore and Hope Sneller climbed to Icefloe Lake from a camp in Cascade south fork. From the lake, they climbed the western, more obvious of two couloirs that gain the lower west ridge of the Middle Teton. From the notch, they skied a steep snow face leading into Dartmouth Basin.

On May 9, 1993, this author, Matthew Goewert, Gail Jensen, and Dave Coon joined Dave Moore when he returned to the area on a tour from Avalanche Divide. This time, he chose the more easterly couloir, which involved exciting, 50-degree postholing up a five-foot-wide chute. When we arrived at the col, the difficult descent into Dartmouth was revealed. We skied one at a time near the top, then reunited for the 3,000-foot, shin-deep powder run to the Cascade forks.

Icefloe Lake-Garnet Canyon South Fork: {G} During a solo climb of the South Teton in April of 1985, Peter Koedt followed coyote tracks all the way up the Garnet south fork. To his surprise, the tracks led to a steep couloir that drops 500 feet through the escarpment above Icefloe Lake. Koedt resolved to return, postulating that if a coyote could do it, so could he.

In June of that year, Koedt started up Stewart Draw, circled around Buck Mountain into Alaska Basin, crossed beneath The Wall of Avalanche Canyon, traversed to Icefloe Lake, and began his climb on foot up to the saddle between the Middle and South Tetons. He found only short sections of easy rock climbing in the couloir.

In the spring of 1992, Scott McGee used this couloir to descend into Cascade Canyon after ascending the South Teton from Avalanche Divide.

In March of 1995, Mark Limage and Tom Wuthritch used a couloir closer to the Middle Teton to make the passage.

Avalanche Divide-Icefloe Lake: {C} This magnificent, scenic route traverses and gently climbs under the west side of the South Teton, across the top of Cascade south fork.

Cascade south fork-Avalanche north fork: {D} Fred Brown and Betty Woolsey pioneered this classic, easy connection in April of 1940. Manage a small cornice on the south side of the pass, known as Avalanche Divide, making a circum-Grand Teton tour possible.

Some say the Buck Mountain Massif offers the best skiing in the Teton Range, based on volume and variety of terrain. Albright Peak, Maverick Buttress and 25 Short afford enormous acreages of moderate powder and corn-skiing terrain, while areas such as Stewart Draw, No Wood Basin and upper Avalanche Canyon offer fantastic high routes. For more challenging chutes and faces, check out Buck Mountain and Mount Wister.

For detailed reference to the Buck Mountain Massif, use USGS maps for Grand Teton and Moose.

APPROACHES

Taggart Lake Track: {C} From the Taggart Lake trailhead, ski west then north on a good track along the

---

Like a miniature K2, Buck Mountain dominates the south fork of Avalanche Canyon. This monarch of the region offers challenges for budding and expert ski mountaineers alike.

base of the moraine. Go past the park horse stables, and cross the second footbridge. Follow the ski track up the creek for three quarters of a mile. Bear left at the fork for another half mile to the lake; bear right for Bradley Lake.

Taggart Lake: {D} Cross this relatively benign lake to reach Avalanche Canyon, but use caution on the ice near the inlet and outlet. Approach from the Taggart Lake trailhead via the Taggart Lake Track. On Aug. 30, 1985, lightning sparked a forest fire that encompassed the entire Taggart Lake moraine. Today, the area remains an enchanted forest of what appear to be giant toothpicks.

Avalanche Canyon: {D} No trail is maintained here, so this spectacular canyon seldom is visited in summer, but skiers use it often. In April of 1940, Fred Brown and Betty Woolsey made the first descent of the north fork, skillfully maneuvering their metal-edged skis on the steep, icy headwall below Snowdrift Lake. In the early 1980s, Theo Meiners, Brian Bradley, Whitney Thurlow and Jim Duclos pioneered skiing in the south fork. They laid in a

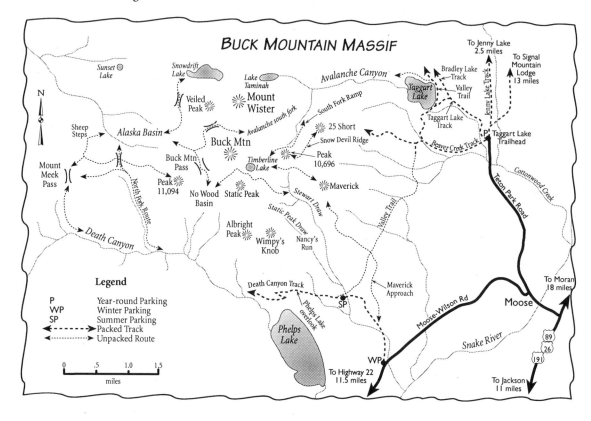

BUCK MOUNTAIN MASSIF

gear cache and made several trips to ski in the area.

Approach from Taggart Lake. If the lake ice is not safe, follow the Valley Trail north along the east shore until a faint climbers' trail forks to the left. This trail traverses the dry south face of a moraine and leads to the canyon mouth. In the canyon, either side of the creek is easy to follow to the fork. Access the south fork by climbing straight up the creek bottom. To reach Lake Taminah in the north fork, switchback up the large treeless south-facing avalanche path and traverse steep slopes above cliffs to get to the lake from the northeast {E}. To reach the upper north-fork basin and Snowdrift Lake, cross Lake Taminah and climb a steep gully through the headwall above {F}.

Teton Park Road: See The High Peaks.

Beaver Creek Track: {B} From the Taggart Lake trailhead, strike southwest across the flats toward the southeast side of the Taggart Lake moraine. Follow a good ski track, skirting the base of the moraine for nearly a mile, to the junction with the Valley Trail.

Valley Trail: {D} The section of the Valley Trail in this region stretches from the mouth of Open Canyon to the junction with the Beaver Creek Track. From Open Canyon mouth, drop slightly north and make a descending traverse across a moraine face to the Phelps Lake inlet. Climb three switchbacks to Phelps Lake overlook and ski down the well-packed track to a fork in the trail near the Death Canyon summer trailhead. Bear left at the fork and follow the summer trail swath through the forest on the 6,800-foot contour for three miles to the Beaver Creek Track. Sections of this route may not have packed ski tracks.

Moose-Wilson Road: See Open Canyon Region.

Death Canyon Track: {B} Branching northwest from the Moose-Wilson Road, about four miles south of Moose, the Death Canyon Road leads almost two miles to the summer trailhead. This road used to be plowed to White Grass Ranch in winter but now is closed at its junction with the Moose-Wilson Road. It usually opens to vehicle travel in early to mid-May. In winter and spring, park at the junction or in the large lot to the north. (That lot is, however, plowed mainly for local residents.) Ski up the well-traveled summer road, bearing left at the White Grass Ranch entrance. The summer trailhead is about a mile away, after a 90-degree bend in the road.

A popular scenic track continues west; it follows the summer trail on a good track as it climbs gently westward through thick forest, over several footbridges and past some meadows, to the Phelps Lake overlook. To continue up Death Canyon, drop into the basin to the south. Follow the canyon bottom at first, then stick to the switchbacking summer trail on the north canyon flank.

Maverick Approach: {C} The most popular approach to Maverick Buttress, here you'll often find a well-used ski track. Follow the Death Canyon Road for almost a mile from your vehicle, then branch northwest at the White Grass Ranch gate. Follow a road swath through the forest, along the foot of a short moraine and into a spectacular vast meadow. Flat-track to the northwest end of the meadow and enter the forest near some old cabins. After 100 yards, turn right on the Valley Trail and follow it for about a third of a mile. Turn uphill through thick forest and gain a drainage and avalanche runout clearing at the foot of the slopes of Maverick.

Stewart Draw: {D} For the most efficient access to the east face of Buck Mountain and the southeast face of Peak 10,696, use this steep canyon. Peak 10,552, Static Peak and Maverick Buttress also are easily accessed via this approach. Like the Open Canyon mouth, however, you'll find thick-forested moraines and gullies near the mouth of Stewart Draw.

For the quickest access into the draw, follow the Death Canyon Road and Trail to the third footbridge and turn north through the woods. In spring, look for a faint trail. You'll soon reach the huge meadow below Peak 10,552. A long ascending traverse to the north, across low-angle open slopes, leads to a shallow gully between the Static Peak Draw terminal moraine (Nancy's Run) and the Stewart Draw lateral moraine. This diagonal passage channels skiers to a short traverse across a steep east-facing moraine. Continue an ascending traverse north through a jumble of forested moraines and gullies to the clearings near the canyon mouth. Slither into the draw just beneath the cliffs that form its south side.

Be careful with route-finding in this area. In April of 1992, Harry Valiente lost his sense of direction in the thick forest and followed the Valley Trail to the north. After two miles, he realized he was headed the wrong way. But instead of following the snow-covered Valley Trail easily to Beaver Creek, he turned east and set himself up for three more hours of intense bushwhacking to the road near the park entrance.

Static Peak Draw: {D} This short drainage lies between Stewart Draw and Peak 10,552 and provides the primary access to Static Peak. Follow the Stewart Draw approach to the shallow gully between the Static Peak Draw end moraine and the thick-forested Stewart Draw lateral moraine. Just past some boulders, a creek, and a narrow rib of trees, climb the end moraine (see Nancy's Run) and follow the creek to the top of the draw, which is V-shaped at times. To access the large cirque below the north face of Peak 10,552 and the southeast face of Static Peak, follow a low-angle, treeless gully on the south side of the top of the draw.

Phelps Lake: See Open Canyon Region.
Death Canyon: See Open Canyon Region.

PEAKS AND BOWLS

Mount Wister (11,490 feet): This multifaceted mountain lies between the north and south forks of Avalanche Canyon, from which it is approached. Because of the mountain's relative remoteness, only a few have attempted to ski its flanks, including only one descent from the summit.

Southeast Couloir: {F} From the east-ridge col, 2,000 feet of narrow skiing are available on 40- to 45-degree slopes into Avalanche south fork. When searching for this couloir from Avalanche south fork, several skiers have been fooled by the couloirs on the southeast side of Point 10,960-plus, Mount Wister's east summit. They did not climb up the south fork long enough to see the east ridge and this obvious deep couloir leading to the east col. On Feb. 3, 1985, climber Bruce Melliger mistook one of these initial couloirs for the southeast couloir. The couloir avalanched, carrying Melliger some 1,300 feet to his death.

(Early fixed-heel: Theo Meiners, Brian Bradley, Whitney Thurlow and Jim Duclos; spring, 1982.)

East Ridge: {G} This intricate ridge is the only possible ski route from the summit of the mountain. Along the ridge, this author encountered short cliff bands that seem to be covered only in good snow years. I found pitches approaching 55 degrees and ski-width-wide couloirs near the top. Exposed traverses between eastern, southern and northeastern exposures connected discontinuous aprons and chutes. From the col, ski south into the southeast couloir or north into the northeast snowfield.

(Early fixed-heel: Tom Turiano, with Steve Stenger on foot; May 12, 1990.)

Northeast Snowfield: {F} Reaching angles of 40 degrees to 45 degrees at the top, this avalanche-prone route is comparable in aesthetics and difficulty to the southeast couloir. Some 2,000 feet of skiing leads into Avalanche north fork.

Other potential routes: The northwest couloir is choked in the middle by a large chockstone that would require a rappel to pass. A series of extreme northeast-facing couloirs plunge from Point 10,960-plus to the forks of Avalanche.

Veiled Peak (11,330 feet): This insignificant and remote spire along Mount Wister's west ridge affords no feasible ski routes from the summit but offers fantastic bowls on its north and south flanks. Approach from Avalanche Canyon.

South Bowl: {E} From the Wister/Veiled saddle, ski south nearly 1,000 feet into Avalanche south fork.

(Early fixed-heel: Jorge Colón; 1970s.)

Northeast Bowl: {E} This 1,000-foot glacial scoop is a favorite spring powder run. Steep spring corn runs are found on the east faces of Veiled Peak's two subsidiary north summits. Both faces lead into the northeast bowl.

(Early free-heel: Whitney Thurlow and Greg Miles; early 1980s. Matt Herman; June 19, 1990.)

Other potential routes: The large cirque on the northwest side offers copious cornice-capped powder bowls that last into July.

25 Short (9,975 feet): Known to a few local skiers in the 1960s and early 1970s as "The Ski Hill," this 3,000-foot forested shoulder has become the most popular winter day trip in Grand Teton National Park. Between 1974 and 1986, park research biologist Bill Barmore lived at Beaver Creek and skied this backyard mountain often. He used seven-and-a-half-foot wooden lap skis with Tempo bindings, which had a typical toe plate but a rigid heel stem and loop. Robert Hammer, Dean Millsap and Joe Gale skied often with Barmore and dubbed the mountain "Bill's Hill" in the mid 1970s. That name stuck with locals until 1980, when the next wave of skiers began calling it 25 Short.

Approach from Taggart Lake trailhead via Beaver Creek Track. Do not park at Beaver Creek. After nearly a mile and a half on the Beaver Creek Track, turn south across a footbridge onto the Valley Trail and begin the arduous climb through a clearing of burned forest.

Northeast Ridge: {D} This classic, broad ridge of 25 Short is sparsely forested and has a consistent, moderate pitch. Although these 15- to 25-degree slopes aren't immune to avalanches, they provide a relatively safe place to ski when conditions are questionable elsewhere. In the late 1970s, rangers Pete Hart and Jim Olson began visiting these slopes regularly to study the snowpack.

(Early fixed-heel: NPS residents of Beaver Creek; 1950s. Barry Corbet; 1960s. Dean Millsap, Joe Gale,

Robert Hammer, and Bill, Woody and Jim Barmore; 1974-1977.)

North Couloir: {G} This Apocalypse-like couloir drops north toward the forks of Avalanche Canyon from the bench at the top of the northeast ridge. The first descent trio negotiated steep, narrow shafts and some third-class downclimbing.

(Early free-heel: Ed Bice, Chris Charters and Jeremy Silcox; spring, 1994.)

Turkey Chute: {E} This superb, curving gully plunges into Avalanche south fork from the notch just south of the summit.

(Early free-heel: Doug Doyle, et al; spring, mid-1980s.)

Uller's Run: {E} This vast avalanche path, directly east of the subtle summit, makes for a wonderful spring ski through sparse dwarf trees. Merge with the Valley Trail to return to Taggart Lake trailhead.

(Early fixed-heel: Les Gibson; spring, 1979. Early free-heel: Jim Day; spring, 1979.)

Peak 10,696: Though insignificant in size next to Buck, Static and Mount Wister, this fine mountain offers novice ski mountaineers wonderful moderate skiing with surprising exposure. Approach from Stewart Draw via forested chutes on the south side of Maverick Buttress, or from 25 Short.

Chute-the-Moon: {E} This classic, moderate couloir drops north 700 feet to the South Fork Ramp from a small col on the east ridge. Some 100 yards northeast, a narrower couloir known as "Moon Walk" {F} connects to the South Fork Ramp as well.

(Early free-heel: Dave Moore, Hope Sneller, Bob Wagner; March, 1995.)

Southeast Face: {E} This large hanging snowfield stands out rather prominently from the south, though untrained eyes often mistake it for part of the Grand Teton. This descent most commonly is made as an extended 25 Short excursion, as it was by the first descent party. From the bottom of the face, that party skied northeast into a large bowl that funneled them into a prominent avalanche path. This naturally carved ski run channels to the bottom of Uller's Run on 25 Short. The day after their descent, Bill Barmore looked up to see that an avalanche in the gully had erased their tracks!

From the bottom of the upper face, skiers subsequently have descended steep couloirs into Stewart Draw or accessed the top of Maverick with a short ridge traverse east.

(Early fixed-heel: Bill Barmore, Dean Millsap, Joe Gale and Robert Hammer; late 1970s.)

Other potential routes: The east couloir drops nearly 1,000 feet from the top of the rocky east buttress of Peak 10,696 into the small basin north of Maverick Buttress.

Barry Corbet and Ann LaFarge relax after the first ski descent of Buck Mountain (behind) in 1961. The convex upper East Face that they skied approaches 45 degrees, with an 800-foot cliff below.

Maverick Buttress (9,680-plus feet): Like 25 Short, this is one of the classic day ski trips in the range. Many skiers prefer Maverick because it offers more terrain and variety, and longer fall-lines. Approach via Maverick Approach, Taggart Lake trailhead via Beaver Creek Track and Valley Trail, or Stewart Draw.

East Face: {D} or {E} This favorite mile-wide face has moderate gladed and open terrain, split into at least five different shots. The southernmost face is the most open and offers the most sustained fall-line.

North Face: {C} or {D} This 500-foot face offers easy gladed terrain but funnels skiers into a large avalanche gully.

Buck Mountain (11,938 feet): The monarch of this region provides challenges for budding and expert ski mountaineers alike. Approach from Stewart Draw or Avalanche Canyon.

During the second assault to ski Buck—in April of 1966—Bill Briggs, Peter Koedt, Chuck Quinn, John "Blackie" Bolton, Rod Newcomb, and Robbie Fuller left Jackson at about 10 p.m. and arrived at Timberline Lake at dawn. With the snow still frozen solid, they decided to nap at the lake but overslept. Meanwhile, Chuck Satterfield and Keith and Denny Becker also were on their way up Stewart Draw to ski Buck. When Briggs' party awoke, the snow had softened considerably. Hastily, Newcomb and Bolton broke trail to the summit for the others. During their descent, they ran into Satterfield's party, still struggling through the deep snow, and even belaying pitches near the top. Concerned about that party's safety, Briggs' party waited at Timberline Lake. Upon the Satterfield party's safe return, all nine skiers skied back to Jackson Hole together.

East Face: {F} This Teton classic has a relatively short approach and exposed, but not death-defying, skiing off a sharp granite peak.

Although Barry Corbet skied confidently with his leather boots unbuckled during the first descent, this route should not be taken lightly. The convex upper face approaches 45 degrees, with an 800-foot cliff below. During an April, 1992 nordic descent attempt, Matthew Goewert fell after his second turn from the top and tumbled 1,000 feet. One ski popped off, and he kicked in his boot to make a miraculous self-arrest, 50 feet short of the cliff. His ski-pole self-arrest grips did little to slow his slide. Several other skiers share this experience with Goewert. In the late 1980s, for example, nordic skier Judd Stewart was carried more than 1,000 feet down the face by a loose snow avalanche. He also stopped just short of the huge cliff.

From the bottom of the steep upper face, ski an exposed 25-degree ramp, or bench, above the cliff. Continuous fall-line skiing runs from the base of the upper face to the lower couloir at the far northern end of the face. Only a few actual traverses are needed.

On May 10, 1993, blistering sun released a four-foot slab with a 200-yard crown from the top of this ramp. For the two weeks before the slide, snow constantly was deposited on an older suncrust.

In the lower couloir, skiers encounter 20-foot-wide, 45-degree slopes during the 400-foot descent to the bench below. Because of its sheltered position, snow in the couloir can be powder but more often is firm neve.

In spring of 1982, Skeeter and Lenny Cattabriga made a nordic descent of the east face. A week later, they heard that Dan McKay skied the peak with Bob Comey and Steve Dollmeyer, claiming a first nordic descent and writing a story for *Powder Magazine*. None of them knew of Jim Roscoe's descent almost 10 years earlier.

(Early fixed-heel: Barry Corbet, Ann LaFarge and Eliot Goss; May 29, 1961. Callum Mackay and Jorge Colón; winter, 1972. Early free-heel: Jim Roscoe, with Jerry Balint on Silvrettas; May, 1973. Early snowboard; John Griber; May, 1989.)

Northeast Couloirs: {G} From the central bench of the east face of Buck, traverse and climb across a steep slope to the northeast ridge. Below, to the northeast, a 45- to 50-degree couloir descends 450 feet before the angle lessens. At this point, you can traverse east back into Stewart Draw or continue down a steep couloir for more than 2,000 feet into Avalanche Canyon.

(Early free-heel: Tim Quinn, upper couloir; May, 1985. Jay Moody and Whitney Thurlow, lower couloir; May, 1981. Bob Graham, lower couloir; December, 1985.)

Northwest Snowfield: {E} In August of 1981, Theo Meiners retrieved his skis—which he cached in Avalanche south fork that spring—and skied this permanent snowfield, which drops east from the northwest shoulder of Buck Mountain.

North Couloir Right: {G} or {H} The first descent trio negotiated slopes near 60 degrees in this extremely narrow and exposed route.

(Early fixed-heel: Mark Newcomb and Rob Haggart; April 18, 1995. Early free-heel: Halsey Hewson; April 18, 1995.)

Bubble Fun Couloir (North Couloir Left): {H} During the first descent of this extreme route, Stephen Koch stretched the limits of technical surf mountaineering. With a pre-dawn start, he climbed swiftly up the firm spring snow of Stewart Draw and the east face of Buck Mountain. Skeeter Cattabriga also was on the mountain that day and was astounded to hear of Koch's plans. Koch started down the 45- to 50-degree couloir, thoroughly enjoying the soft powder with his wide snowboard. After more than 1,000 feet, Koch reached the large cliff at the bottom of the couloir, which had always discouraged ski mountaineers from attempting the route. In horror, Koch discovered that the cliff was almost three times the size he had expected; he had only 100 feet of rope! Reluctantly, he searched for anchors for what would have been the first of at least four frightening 50-foot rappels. But the smooth rock yielded no cracks for pitons, so Koch was forced to make another plan.

He spotted a snow ramp-and-ledge system that traversed around the central north rib of Buck into the north couloir right. Koch's sense of adventure kicked in, and he climbed partway back up the Bubble Fun Couloir and began a perilous and tedious traverse across downsloping, crackless slabs covered with sugar snow. He tried to protect himself by doubling the rope through a manky piton and feeding the rope through his figure-eight as he moved across. Suddenly, the ledge system ended at a 100-foot cliff, which dropped off vertically into the north couloir right. Koch found the best anchor he could, attached his 100-foot rope, and rappelled to safety on a single strand. Leaving his rope behind, he clicked into his snowboard and descended the steep south slope of Avalanche south fork.

During the second descent, Mark Newcomb skied an icy base with a thin cover of rimed, crusty powder in the upper couloir. At the bottom, he made four rappels down the west end of the cliff with his 80-foot rope. To get to piton cracks that were just out of reach, he lengthened his rappels with slings tied onto the end of his rappel rope. Mark also left his rope behind on the final 80-foot rappel.

(Early snowboard: Stephen Koch; May 3, 1992. Early fixed-heel: Mark Newcomb; May 22, 1994.)

Other potential routes: Several highly technical lines on this mountain have not yet been skied. Two of them drop into No Wood Basin and one drops into Avalanche south fork.

Nancy's Run: {C} This 400- to 500-foot east-facing slope makes an excellent training area for those who wish to ski the similarly angled, but longer, slopes of 25 Short. Approach as for Static Peak Draw.

Static Peak (11,303 feet): Viewed from the valley, the wide-open snowbowls of this mountain stand out to tourists as the only skiable terrain in a sea of rock spires. A relatively short approach and moderate ski terrain make Static Peak one of the most frequently skied Teton peaks. But Static is closed to skiing from Nov. 1 to April 30 each year to protect bighorn sheep winter range. Approach from Static Peak Draw.

Southeast Face: {E} Especially popular as a nordic descent, this is one of the classic moderate ski routes in the range, with grades ranging from 15 degrees to 35 degrees. In June of 1993, Bridger Productions filmed skier Dave Ellingson playing here in thick spring snow.

(Early free-heel: Brian Bradley, Greg Miles, Jim Duclos, Richard Collins and Jon Schick; 1979-1983.)

East Face: {E} Here's another classic line with a

consistent grade of more than 35 degrees. It rarely is used by skiers because the wind-scoured east ridge hampers easy access from the summit.

(Early fixed-heel: Jorge Colón and Tom Raymer; spring, mid-1970s.)

North Face: {G} This route drops off of the east ridge about 50 yards east of the summit. While climb-

ing the southeast face, Brian Bradley and Theo Meiners saw two bighorn sheep disappear over the edge of the north face. They looked over to see if the animals had survived and discovered a steep ramp and powder face leading to Timberline Lake. They tackled a 15-foot cornice jump onto the ramp and skied the exposed face

---

This northeast aerial view of seldom-skied Mount Wister shows the exposed east ridge and the wide northeast snowfield. Wister lies between the north and south forks of Avalanche Canyon.

below. On May 8, 1990, John Scott, Scott Harris and this author skied the route in a whiteout and found no cornice. Nonetheless, slopes approaching 55 degrees above large cliffs triggered plenty of adrenaline.

(Early fixed-heel: Brian Bradley and Theo Meiners; spring, 1983.)

Wimpy's Knob (10,080-plus feet): Dave Moore and friends so named this northeast summit of Peak 10,552 because they felt wimpy, amid high-avalanche danger, when they didn't go for the main summit. But that is how you stay alive in the mountains. Approach as for Stewart Draw, but begin climbing the steep forested ridge immediately south of Nancy's Run.

East Face: {E} This multifaceted mountainside is one of the longest-sustained fault scarps on the east side of the Tetons. Skiers beware: The probability of avalanches is considerably higher here than on lower-angled slopes, such as 25 Short or Maverick. Most skiers yoyo the top bowl several times before ending their day on the southernmost of three ridges. Nearly 3,500 feet of skiing leads to White Grass Ranch.

(Early free-heel: Dave Moore, Mike Whitehead and Kent McBride; Jan. 4, 1989.)

Northwest Couloirs: {E} and {F} Several steep couloirs drop from the summit ridge into upper Static Peak Draw. Mark Limage and this author climbed one narrow, cornice-capped chute on Dec. 20, 1994 during a tour from 25 Short.

Other potential routes: Several steep couloirs lead into Static Peak Draw from the north side of Wimpy's Knob.

Peak 10,552 (Albright Peak): With 4,000 feet of skiing and a relatively short approach, this peak has become one of the most popular spring descents in the range. Approach from Death Canyon Track. At the first big meadow, climb gently up a wide, gladed slope to the base of the peak.

East Face: {F} In mid-January, 1992, accomplished nordic skier Doug Marden triggered an avalanche that carried him 2,000 feet down this oft-skied classic. Marden traversed onto the summit nipple's steep east-facing slope while his partner, Dave Ellingson, watched the slope collapse and Marden desperately attempt to remain afloat. The avalanche path since has been called "Doug's Ditch," to acknowledge his frantic—but successful—fight for survival. Historically, the top 150 feet of the east face is a sensitive starting zone because of perfect positioning for wind-loading. The bottom slopes of the face offer some of the nicest {C} terrain in the range.

(Early fixed-heel: Steve Lundy, Dave Fox and Ed Lowton; March 1974 or 1975. First fixed-heel descent probably was made in the late 1960s. Early free-heel: Jay Moody and Dan McKay; April, 1981. Larry Detrick and Richard Collins; early 1980s. First free-heel descent probably was made in the early 1970s. Early snowboard: John Griber et al; spring, 1988.)

North Face: {F} and {G} This short, steep face has several couloirs, or ramps, leading into Static Peak Draw. An easier route drops into the draw from the northeast shoulder of the peak.

(Early free-heel: Dave Ellingson; June, 1993.)

Other potential routes: The south side of the mountain has a 4,000-foot avalanche path, which rarely offers safe, enjoyable conditions.

No Wood Basin: {E} This high, treeless cirque is bound by Static Peak on the east, Buck Mountain on the north, and Peak 11,094 on the west. To the south, four gully systems, each with more than 2,500 feet of relief, provide fantastic skiing from the upper basin to the floor of Death Canyon, near the patrol cabin. This area is sensitive bighorn-sheep winter range. Approach directly from Death Canyon, Alaska Basin, or Stewart Draw.

(Early free-heel: Whitney Thurlow; early 1980s.)

Peak 11,094: This massive sedimentary mountain shares the guard of No Wood Basin with Static and Buck and is sensitive bighorn-sheep winter range. Approach from No Wood Basin, Alaska Basin or Death Canyon north fork.

West Face: {F} This wide-open face is striped with a cliff band about halfway down, offering only a couple of ways through. Peter Koedt and party trended west from the summit and downclimbed a steep, narrow hourglass couloir near the northwest ridge of Peak 11,094.

(Early free-heel: Peter Koedt, Bill and Kip Wallace; May or June, 1986.)

East Face: {F} You can ski almost 1,000 feet from the summit through any one of numerous couloirs above No Wood Basin. During a 1986 spring tour, Peter Koedt and Bill and Kip Wallace climbed the northernmost gap in the large cliff. During an early descent of the face, this author set off sloughs with each turn and jump-turned through a six-foot-wide, 45-degree chute, south of Koedt's route.

(Early free-heel: Tom Turiano; May 2, 1994.)

Other potential routes: Several north couloirs spike from upper Alaska Basin toward the summit plateau. On May 2, 1994, this author reached the summit via a two-foot-wide, 50-degree, 500-foot snow chimney on the east end of the north face.

HIGH ROUTES

Snow Devil Ridge: {E} Although committing to this traverse often means foregoing fantastic skiing on 25 Short, a little extra effort affords equally rewarding terrain and at least 700 feet more skiing. Downclimb from the summit of 25 Short and follow the long, undulating, strenuous, sometimes-exposed ridge south and up to the northeast shoulder of Peak 10,696. Continue up the sharp east ridge or face to the summit of Peak 10,696.

South Fork Ramp: {D} In February of 1979, Peter Koedt and Jara Popelkova pioneered this high route between Stewart Draw and Avalanche Canyon. With randonnée gear, they followed a broad, sloping ramp from the Buck/10,696 saddle two miles to the Avalanche Canyon forks. Few canyon-to-canyon loops can match the beautiful views, fantastic positions, and great snow of this classic. Beware of avalanche danger.

Alaska Basin-Avalanche Canyon south fork: {D} Whitney Thurlow and Theo Meiners used this high divide between Buck Mountain and Veiled Peak during a traverse from Grand Targhee in 1980. It often is wind-scoured on the west side and avalanche-prone on the east.

Alaska Basin-Snowdrift Lake: {E} These two paradisiacal basins are connected by this classic touring route, which slithers between the Veiled Peak massif and The Wall of Avalanche Canyon via "the old Wall Trail Pass." In spring of 1966, Peter Koedt, Rod Dornan, Jane Waters, Art Gran and Suzie Chaplin pioneered this route during a tour from the tram to Avalanche north fork.

Timberline Lake-Maverick Buttress: {E} After a long traverse from the tram to Timberline Lake in January of 1991, Tom Bennett, Mark Smith and this author used this route to get from upper Stewart Draw to the Taggart Lake trailhead. From Timberline Lake, we made a descending traverse east under the south-facing cliffs of Peak 10,696 until we saw an obvious snow ramp leading diagonally up to the northeast. At the top of the ramp, we climbed steep couloirs to their top at the Maverick/10,696 plateau.

Stewart Draw-No Wood Basin: {E} Peter Koedt repeatedly used this aesthetic avalanche-prone crossing during his thorough explorations of the Buck Mountain Massif in the early to mid-1980s. Margot Snowdon joined him on his first tour of the passage. They started in Death Canyon and came out Stewart Draw in June of 1983.

No Wood Basin-Alaska Basin: {C} In the early 1980s, Whitney Thurlow made an early traverse from Teton Canyon to Death Canyon using this 10,480-plus-foot pass—known as Buck Mountain Pass—between Peak 11,094 and Buck Mountain.

Mount Meek Pass-Peak 11,094: {E} Terry Brattain and Mike and Linda Merigliano skied this route during their tour up Darby, out Teton, looking for bighorn sheep. They followed the long west/northwest ridge through a hourglass couloir, just south of the ridge, to the summit.

Sheep Steps: See Teton Canyon Region.

Death Canyon north fork-Alaska Basin: {E} A popular width traverse climbs sharply to a pair of passes at the head of this remote fork of Death Canyon. Either drop to Mount Meet Pass and Sheep Steps or climb directly north over a corniced ridge into Alaska Basin.

Death Canyon-Mount Meek Pass: See Open Canyon Region.

OPEN CANYON REGION

Bordered by Granite Canyon on the south and Death Canyon on the north and west, the Open Canyon Region is distinguished by 3,000-foot ski runs on the southeast faces of Mount Hunt and Prospectors Mountain. In addition to long and steep descents, scenic high touring abounds on vast plateaus and basins near Fox Creek Pass and Indian and Coyote lakes. You'll also find little-known powder reserves on Olive Oil and near Forget-Me-Not Lakes.

Though approaches into the region are not particularly long, they often weave through avalanche terrain and thick forest. Skiers with the patience and stamina to handle the approach and the knowledge and experience to foresee avalanche dangers will be rewarded accordingly.

For detailed reference to the Open Canyon

Stephen Koch picks his way through the icy crux of the Apocalypse Couloir of Prospectors Mountain during the first descent. Prospectors is one of the range's most challenging mountains to access for skiing.

Region, use USGS maps for Grand Teton, Teton Village, and Rendezvous Peak.

APPROACHES

Moose-Wilson Road: The southern end of this road (the Teton Village Road), from Highway 22 to the R Lazy S Ranch, has been plowed in winter since the late 1940s and allows skiers access to Peak 10,450 and Granite and Open canyons. The National Park Service has plowed the northern end of the road, from Moose to the JY Ranch, since 1956, opening winter access to Death Canyon. The two-and-a-half mile middle section of the road, from the JY to the R Lazy S, is closed to automobile traffic in winter, from about Nov. 1 each year. It is, however, open to snowmobiles.

When approaching from the north end of the Teton Village Road, try to park as far north as possible to shorten your ski to the mountains. Parking-area locations vary from year to year. In the best case, you'll be able to park at the Granite Cañon Ranch gate. If you're unlucky, you'll be parking at the R Lazy S turn. In any

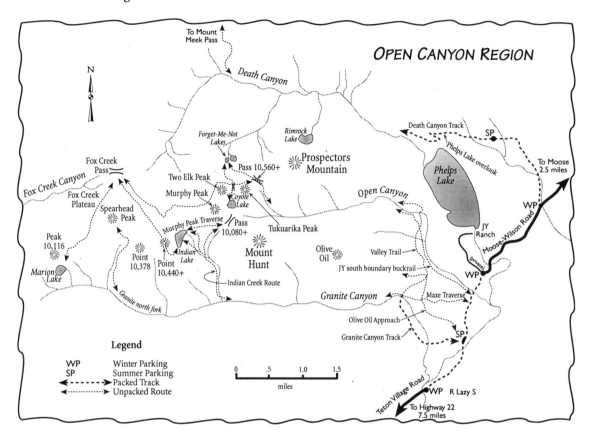

OPEN CANYON REGION

Legend

WP	Winter Parking
SP	Summer Parking
◄- - - -►	Packed Track
◄- - - -►	Unpacked Route

0   .5   1.0   1.5

miles

case, do not block access to private property, and try not to clutter the locals' small plowed parking areas.

Death Canyon Track: See Buck Mountain Massif.

Death Canyon: {D} Although better known for rock climbing than skiing, Death Canyon is an important part of Teton ski mountaineering because one of the most popular Teton traverses passes between Death and Teton canyons. Excellent, scenic ski terrain is found near Fox Creek Pass and in tributary basins such as No Wood Basin, north fork, and Forget-Me-Not Lakes.

Approach from the Death Canyon Track.

Phelps Lake (6,615 feet): Phelps usually is the second lake to become unsafe for travel in spring because of its position in southern Jackson Hole, where temperatures are warmer, there is less winter snowfall,

and spring rain is more abundant. Unless special arrangements are made with JY Ranch managers, accessing Phelps Lake via the ranch property is forbidden. Most skiers access Death Canyon via Phelps Lake overlook on the Death Canyon Track.

Motorboats and hand-propelled craft are permitted on this lake, but there is no public road access to the lake.

JY Ranch south boundary buckrail: {C} After years of reconnaissance, this straight buckrail fence delineates the best winter route to the mouth of Open Canyon. Almost two miles north of the north end of the Teton Village Road or less than a half mile south of the JY Ranch entrance, leave the Moose-Wilson Road and follow this fence west toward the mountains. The fence slices through forest and meadows, passes an outhouse and hut platform, and crosses a creek and avalanche path that curves down from Olive Oil. Do not follow the fence all the way to its crossing of Open Creek. Instead, ski west up a shallow morainal gully into the mouth of Open Canyon.

With special permission from JY Ranch managers, you can follow a two-track Jeep road—just north of the fenceline—that ends at the outhouse and platform.

In late spring, hike a horse trail that follows the fence on its south side. It is faint at first, and there are several junctions. It leads west on a low moraine, crosses a creek, and meets with the Valley Trail, which you then can follow to Open Canyon mouth.

Valley Trail: {B} From the mouth of Granite Canyon, break trail during a gradual ascending traverse through thick forest, crossing several gullies, to the mouth of Open Canyon.

Open Canyon: {D} Access to this canyon is not straightforward. Extensive forest and jumbled moraines create obstacles to the canyon mouth, on a trip that takes two hours in the best conditions. Skiers have investigated numerous routes—both from the north and south ends of the Moose-Wilson Road. Both parking areas share the JY Ranch south boundary buckrail as the fastest, most apparent approach. When exiting the canyon, a more enjoyable route follows the Valley Trail and Olive Oil Approach back to the north end of the Teton Village Road.

Travel in the canyon is surprisingly safe and easy. In a few places, though, the V-shaped bottom is exposed to potentially massive avalanches.

During an attempt to ski Banana Couloir in February of 1993, Jim Olson and Greg Marin were carried 100 yards in a large avalanche on the lower east face of Tukuarika Peak at the head of Open north fork. They had chosen what seemed to be the safest route and were traveling far apart, but not far enough. Olson lost a ski and a pole and Marin lost both poles.

Maze Traverse: See Rendezvous Mountain.

Olive Oil Approach: {C} From the Granite Canyon trailhead, climb gently northwest through meadows and forest to the Valley Trail and the base of Olive Oil.

Granite Canyon Track: See Rendezvous Mountain.

Granite Canyon: See Rendezvous Mountain.

PEAKS AND BOWLS

Prospectors Mountain (11,241 feet): Surprisingly, this is one of the range's most challenging mountains to access for skiing. This author attempted to ski it five times before succeeding. The standard approach is via Open Canyon, though fun routes lead from Death and Granite canyons and Fox Creek Pass. Unless the snow is very firm, you know the route, move very quickly, and get an extra-early start, you'll probably want to set aside two days for spring descents of this peak.

Banana Couloir: {E} This actually is more a face or gully than a couloir, though it undoubtedly acquired its name from its long, relatively narrow, banana shape. A steepening 3,200-foot pitch—ranging from 20 degrees near the bottom to 35 degrees at the top—make this a classic descent. It extends southeast into Open Canyon from the northeast end of Prospectors' summit plateau. In late season and in low snow years, the 40-degree, water-eroded headwall at the bottom of the Banana is bare. Cliffs in this area also make the upper Banana seem inaccessible. But it's possible to bypass these obstacles by continuing up Open Canyon to the first treeless, east-facing headwall. Ascend this and the series of faces above until you can traverse northeast back to the Banana.

(Early free-heel: Davey Agnew, Todd Stearns, Carson Hubbard and Wes Fox; 1974. Early fixed-heel: Jorge Colón, Davey Agnew, Donny Black and Mark Wolling; mid- to late 1970s. Winter free-heel: Mike Best, in waist-deep powder; Jan. 17, 1990.)

Southeast Face: {E} One of the largest faces in the range, you'll find plenty of skiing possibilities here. The best route, however, heads directly down the face southeast from the summit, just southwest of a small basin and rock buttress. Expect continuous 30- to 40-degree treeless slopes for about 3,000 feet.

(Early fixed-heel: John Carr, Jim Bellamy and Maggie Filmore; April, 1976.)

West Ridge and Bowl: This is probably the safest, easiest route from the summit, though it often is wind-scoured. Once you reach Pass 10,560-plus, you can drop to Forget-Me-Not Lakes and traverse to Fox Creek Pass, or ski this large wind-loaded bowl south into Open Canyon. During the first descent of this route, Margot Snowdon fell and slid nearly 500 feet on hard snow.

(Early free-heel: Peter Koedt, Margot Snowdon, Bill Wallace and Charlie Otto; May, 1983.)

Rimrock Lake Route: {F} During their spring, 1983 tour, Koedt and friends climbed Prospectors via this steep and complex route. The best way around the icy slabs below the lake is to follow a pair of couloirs west of the main draw. Expect to encounter avalanche terrain and conditions during the 3,400-foot descent to the meadows of Death Canyon.

(Early free-heel: Tom Turiano and Dave Moore; April 21, 1995.)

Apocalypse Couloir: {G} With a 5 a.m. start from the parking area at the junction of the Death Canyon and Moose-Wilson roads, the first descent party of Mark Newcomb and Stephen Koch raced to the base of this perilous sliver of snow in two hours. Temperatures had barely dropped below freezing during the night, so they knew they had to move fast. Just as they started up the tunnel of the 500-foot sheer walls above the chute, an ice-chunk avalanche crashed through. The team split up and dove to opposite sides of the couloir to avoid certain mutilation. With unprecedented postholing speed, they reached the large snowfield above the narrows in less than an hour.

The day before, Newcomb had climbed the Snaz, a rock-climbing route on the opposite side of the canyon. From there, he noticed a couloir that isn't visible from Jackson Hole. This 900-foot chute branches southeast from the upper snowfield, some 400 feet above the narrows. It almost reaches the northeast ridge of Prospectors Mountain before narrowing to an ice chimney.

To avoid the steep, wet snow of upper Apocalypse,

Newcomb and Koch climbed this previously unknown, northwest-facing, 45-degree cleft. It was powder!

They started down the 20- to 80-foot-wide funnel, ecstatic about their discovery. After reaching the main couloir, they continued through the 10-foot-wide, icy, 50-plus degree crux. A total of 3,300 feet of skiing returned them to Death Canyon.

Koch emphatically discouraged attempting this objectively hazardous route.

(Early fixed-heel: Mark Newcomb; April 17, 1994. Early snowboard: Stephen Koch; April 17, 1994.)

Other potential routes: A very steep, technical descent drops off the northeast end of the summit plateau via what has been dubbed the "V Couloir." This couloir has sections angled at more than 55 degrees and should be attempted only in heavy snow years so that short cliffs are buried. It leads into the small basin just east of the summit massif. This basin boasts terrific moderate ski terrain all the way to the mouth of Open Canyon.

East of the Apocalypse Couloir lies a 2,400-foot straight couloir that extends from a point along the northeast ridge into Death Canyon.

Peak 10,988 (Tukuarika Peak): This handsome pyramid stands at the head of Open Canyon, just west of Prospectors Mountain.

East Face: {E} Some 2,200 feet of moderate slopes lead to the floor of Open Canyon.

(Early free-heel: Christoph Schork; February, 1990.)

South Face: {E} or {F} A steep chute widens to a vast bowl above Coyote Lake.

(Early free-heel: Tom Turiano; Feb. 7, 1995.)

Peak 10,116: This peak is obscure, though comely, from the east. It rises northwest of Marion Lake and could be considered the northeast peak of Housetop Mountain. Approach from Granite Canyon shelf.

North Couloir: {G} This couloir drops at 40 degrees from the summit plateau, a little west of the summit to upper Fox Creek Canyon.

(Early free-heel: Forrest McCarthy; March 8, 1994. Early fixed-heel: Wes Bunch; March 8, 1994.)

Peak 10,905 (Murphy Peak): Viewed from the top of the tram run, the large Rendezvous Bowl-like southeast face of this peak stands out. Approach from Open Canyon or Indian Creek Route.

Southeast Ridge: {E} This fun 600-foot ridge leads to the pass west of Mount Hunt.

(Early free-heel: Tom Turiano; March 22, 1993.)

Other potential routes: The southeast face is a classic corn bowl. The cliffy west side blocks an easy traverse from the summit to Fox Creek Pass. The northeast face to Coyote Lake has steep skiing potential, especially in spring.

Point 9,877 (Olive Oil): This point is the culmination of the massive lower east ridge of Mount Hunt. Robbie Fuller found virgin snow when he skied here in the mid-1980s. In fact, he said, it was "extra virgin." Approach from the north end of the Teton Village Road via Olive Oil Approach.

East Side: {E} At least three major avalanche gullies swoop east from the large upper northeast face; these gullies provide the primary ski routes below the upper face. The ridges between the gullies are thickly forested and thus offer limited skiing potential. The first descent party made a nice tour from Open Canyon and Mount Hunt Divide. On the lower slopes, you'll find excellent {C} terrain through aspen glades.

(Early fixed-heel: Peter Koedt, Jack Lewis and Ehmann Bernhard (randonnée); February, 1979.)

Mount Hunt (10,783 feet): Every ride on Apres Vous chairlift at the Jackson Hole Ski Area provides an excellent view of this classic ski mountain. In fact, Doug Coombs was filmed from Apres Vous on Jan 3, 1995. From the tram, he reached the summit in two and a half hours and skied the entire southeast face non-stop! Mount Hunt is a sensitive bighorn-sheep winter range. Approach from the aerial tram or Granite or Open canyon.

South and East sides: {E} and {F} The 3,000-foot south and east bowls and faces of this peak were made for skiing. The easternmost bowl has been called "Grunt," and the southeast bowl, which drops directly off the summit, has been dubbed "Gum's Gulch." High visibility has made these routes quite popular since the early 1970s. Jorge Colón skied here on alpine touring

equipment three times in the mid- to late 1970s. Jim Duclos made three nordic descents of the three main south faces during the early 1980s.

(Early fixed-heel: Callum Mackay and Jorge Colón; January, 1972. Davey Agnew and Callum Mackay; skied "Grunt" in 1972 or 1973. Early free-heel: Jim Roscoe and Mike Fitzpatrick; skied "Grunt" in May, 1972. Early snowboard: Joe Larrow; April 10, 1988.)

Northwestern Cwm: {E} This glacially carved

Open Canyon scores steeply across the bottom of the Banana Couloir and broad southeast face of Prospector Mountain. Travel in Open Canyon is surprisingly safe and easy. In a few places, though, the V-shaped bottom is exposed to potentially massive avalanches.

bowl often is wind-hammered but does get good powder.

(Early free-heel: Gregg Martell and Lyle Shultz; May, 1988.)

North Face: {F} Confronted by two hourglass cruxes, the first descent party tackled this 1,500-foot complex face in stable spring powder.

(Early free-heel: Tom Turiano and Mark Limage; March 30, 1995.)

HIGH ROUTES

Death Canyon bend-Mount Meek Pass: {D} Climb a steep hillside out of Death Canyon on southeast-facing slopes below Mount Meek Pass during width traverses between Death and Teton canyons.

Open Canyon-Forget-Me-Not Lakes: {E} At more than 10,560 feet, this scenic passage allows an arduous loop between Open and Death canyons.

Spearhead Peak-Granite Canyon north fork: {E} On Jan. 12, 1991, Ron Matous, Renny Jackson, Jake Elkins and Dean Moore toured up Granite to Marion Lake, then climbed toward Spearhead Peak. To return into Granite, they skied this steep drainage from the saddle between points 10,043 and 10,378.

Coyote Lake-Forget-Me-Not Lakes: {F} This precipitous passage between Two Elk and Tukuarika peaks often involves shallow sugar snow over rocks.

Pass 10,560-plus-Fox Creek Pass: {D} This interesting route offers—from east to west—nearly continuous downhill traversing, straight running and turning. Some tricky route-finding and avalanche danger will be involved as you round the northwest ridge of Two Elk Peak and during the last quarter mile to Fox Creek Pass. From west to east, this route is mostly an uphill traverse.

This route probably was used first when Tom Bennett, Ken Jern and Roger Millward exited the range via Fox Creek Canyon after ascending the southeast face of Prospectors Mountain during the spring of 1987.

Murphy Peak Traverse: {D} Slogging through the shallow November TG snow of 1980 or 81, Peter Koedt and Dan McKay used this route to traverse from Pass 10,080-plus, at the head of Open Canyon, to Indian Lake. The exciting route stays above huge cliffs but doesn't encroach on the avalanche bowl on the southeast side of Murphy Peak.

Indian Lake-Fox Creek Pass: {E} During their November, 1980 or 81 tour between Open and Teton canyons, Peter Koedt and Dan McKay climbed the moderate south ridge of Point 10,440-plus, a small summit west of Indian Lake, to access the Fox Creek plateau. The ridge is equally useful in the other direction.

Indian Creek Route: {E} Rising steeply north out of Granite Canyon, about three miles up, this avalanche-prone draw accesses both Indian Lake and Pass 10,080-plus between Mount Hunt and Murphy Peak. A 50-foot waterfall about 280 feet above the floor of Granite Canyon prohibits skiers from following the draw itself. Slopes to the west are the best.

Marion Lake-Fox Creek Pass: {D} Climb steeply north above Marion Lake and traverse across a vast plateau to the pass.

RENDEZVOUS MOUNTAIN

The Jackson Hole Ski Resort and Aerial Tram has lured skiers to explore every bowl, glade, cliff, couloir, and avalanche path of this region. This chapter will provide a general history of the notable skiing done here, as well as information about its approaches, peaks, and major high routes. The Rendezvous Mountain region includes areas north of Phillips Pass, south of Granite Canyon, and east of the Teton crest.

For detailed reference to Rendezvous Mountain, use USGS maps for Rendezvous Peak, Teton Village, and Grand Teton.

APPROACHES

Moose-Wilson Road: See Open Canyon.
Maze Traverse: {A} Use this oft-packed track to

access Granite Canyon from the north. Just more than half a mile south of the JY Ranch entrance, a large flat boulder marks the trail as it turns west. Follow a maze of summer trail swaths west through small meadows, short moraines, and thick forest to the canyon mouth.

Granite Canyon Track: {A} A mile north of the north end of Teton Village Road, this trail turns west from a summer parking area, on a good track. Climb a short hill, then wander west through the woods, crossing Granite Creek twice en route to the mouth of Granite Canyon.

Teton Village-Granite Canyon Mouth: {C} Whereas skiers commonly use the Saratoga Traverse to return to Teton Village from Granite Canyon, this route is recommended for skiers traveling in the other direction. Skin up Teewinot run under the chair lift a quarter mile, then turn right on the Valley Trail. Follow this ski track to the shallow gully between lower Saratoga Bowl and the Granite Canyon lateral moraine. Follow the gully or the moraine north to the top of the

Tom Bennett has a ball in the powder on Goldmine Bowl. This broad, hidden southwest face of Peak 10,277 is perfect for beginner powder skiers, but the bottom of the slope is at least 5 miles from any trailhead.

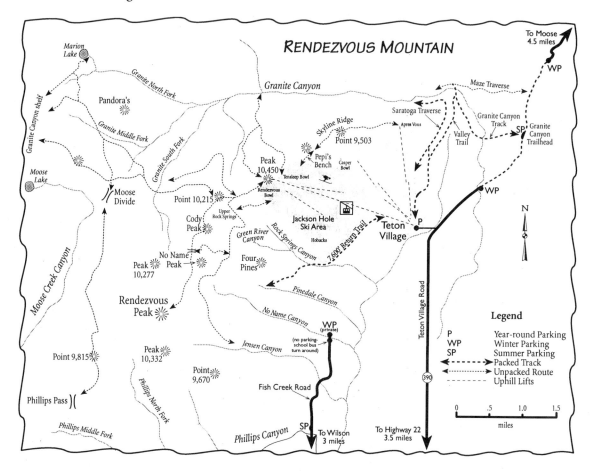

moraine. Drop slightly and traverse to the mouth of Granite Canyon.

Saratoga Traverse: {E} Using a small, rocky bench on the steep, narrow lower northeast ridge of Apres Vous Mountain, this route connects lower Granite Canyon with Teton Village. From a point where the forest thickens near Granite Creek, traverse on the steep, avalanche-prone south wall of the canyon toward that bench. From the bench, take a slight descending traverse to the south, beneath some cliffs and trees. A packed ski track typical here climbs 100 feet before contouring at 7,000 feet to the ski area. In the right conditions, you can contour from the bench on the northeast ridge more than two miles to the Village without climbing.

Granite Canyon: {C} Throughout the 1960s and 70s, Jackson Hole resort skiers explored the out-of-bounds terrain south and north of the ski area thoroughly. When Theo Meiners arrived in 1978, he set his sights on the unexplored treasures in the three forks of Granite. During his many adventures into these remote, steep areas, Meiners was extremely cautious, venturing out only on days when avalanche potential was low.

This southernmost major Teton canyon accesses Pandora's, Mount Hunt, Indian Lake, and the Teton Crest. Combined with the Saratoga Traverse, it's the primary exit from the mountains for out-of-bounds resort skiers heading north or west. East of the canyon meadows, travel is easiest on the north side. But you'll often find an out-of-bounds return track on the south side.

To approach, you have several options. From Teton Village, use the Teton Village-Granite Canyon mouth route. From the north end of the Village Road, flat-track to Granite Canyon trailhead on the Moose-Wilson Road and follow the Granite Canyon Track to the mouth. From the JY Ranch gate, use Maze Traverse.

Jackson Hole Nordic Center: Established in 1982, this cross-country skiing area offers a full-service shop and rentals. Its extensive terrain winds along the base of the Tetons, both south and north of Teton Village.

Fish Creek Road: See Mount Glory Region.

Phillips Canyon: See Mount Glory Region.

PEAKS AND BOWLS

Peak 9,814 (Pandora's Mountain): This island mountain sits between the middle and north forks of Granite Canyon.

The Arch: {G} Theo Meiners and Whitney Thurlow were skiing in a storm to Jackson Hole from a Professional Ski Instructors of America certification exam at Grand Targhee. There was tension between the two because Meiners passed the exam and Thurlow did not. In the middle of an argument, the pair looked up at the north side of Point 9,814 and noticed a camouflaged limestone arch with a stunning couloir passing through it. Their quarrel ended instantly. Since that day, Meiners has returned numerous times to ski The Arch and nearby shots. He even cached rescue and survival equipment so he could share this remote paradise with friends and clients more safely.

(Early fixed-heel: Theo Meiners and David Stump; April 1, 1979.)

Other potential routes: You can find at least eight other powder couloirs adjacent to The Arch. The southwest face offers almost 1,000 feet of moderate slopes into Granite middle fork.

Peak 10,450 (Jackson Hole Ski Area): With 4,139 feet of Teton east-front terrain, this mountain ranks among the best ski areas in the world. (Get a ski area map from the resort for in-bounds terrain descriptions.) The resort offers accommodations, eating establishments, and a full-service ski school and guide program.

Opening of out-of-bounds skiing at the Jackson Hole Ski Area is governed by the U.S. Forest Service and administered by the ski patrol. Under stable spring-like conditions, some areas are opened to the public.

In an effort to manage the growing out-of-bounds skiing crowd more efficiently, the ski patrol and Forest Service put up gates and warning signs at all standard backcountry entrances, including Upper and lower Rock Springs Canyon, Granite Canyon-summit and Headwall entrances, Pepi's Bench and Saratoga Bowl. Instead of signing out, skiers simply enter the backcountry through the gates posted by the ski patrol as "open" or "closed." Check with the ski patrol for up-to-date out-of-bounds openings and snow conditions. Sign boards with current out-of-bounds skiing status are placed strategically throughout the ski area.

Ski patrollers have gone to great lengths to make skiing on Rendezvous Mountain as safe as possible. When the Jackson Hole Ski Area opened in the mid-1960s, the ski patrol faced the overwhelming job of continually monitoring and controlling huge areas of prime avalanche terrain. People pooled skills and knowledge to safeguard each other and the public from danger. Bridger-Teton National Forest avalanche forecaster Juris Krisjansons developed an unprecedented snow-control system that allowed patrolmen to bomb the slopes efficiently without endangering one another. Cannons were situated at different sites on the mountain and in Teton Village to bomb areas like Casper Bowl and Headwall. Krisjansons' successor, Gary Poulson, built a computer from a kit to record storm and snow stratigraphy data for statistical forecasting. Patrolmen Jim Kanzler and Larry Livingood put in long hours modernizing and continuing Poulson's work. In the late 1960s, patrolman John Simms founded Snow Research Associates, which produced instruments for snow-data collection. This equipment was used in

Jackson Hole and other American ski areas and was sold to snow researchers worldwide. In 1978, Simms cofounded Life-Link International to manufacture backcountry skiing accessories such as backpacks, shovels, and probe poles.

Despite these Herculean efforts, many a painful lesson would be learned the hard way. In December of 1966, ski patrolman Dick Porter was buried in an avalanche for 55 minutes in "Dick's Ditch." Some patrolmen were dispatched from the base to tram tower two, carrying probe poles down the Thunder run while other patrolmen traversed from Apres Vous. After frustrating probing in the debris below South Pass Traverse, Peter Lev left the probe line and set his probe in the snow near the last seen point and, amazingly, struck Porter's ski! Porter survived but suffered complications from suffocation.

In April of 1967, a late-season storm dumped three feet of snow in S&S Couloir. For a bit of closing-day fun, ski patrolmen made two runs, entering the chute by sidestepping in from the east. On their second run, the couloir avalanched, knocking six patrolmen over and partially burying all of them. The surprise avalanche left a three-foot crown all the way across Corbet's Couloir!

In 1971, Gary Poulson tossed a hand charge out of the tram but it stuck momentarily to the friction tape on his glove; it landed on top of the tram car, rolled to the other side, and fell off, just before the 60-second fuse was consumed. In yet another close call, a shot from a control gun near tram tower three was misdirected and exploded a tree near Casper Bowl—on a slope open to skiers.

In early December of 1985, patrolman Paul Driscoll died in an avalanche on Dean's Slide while he and several others were setting up fencing. Frustrated by the extreme danger and capriciousness of avalanches that year, patrolman Richard Francis and crew detonated a string of 50-pound charges—dubbed the "big bomb"—on Rendezvous Bowl, thus releasing the largest slide ever seen there. On Feb. 17, 1986, avid ski mountaineer and patrolman Tom Raymer died in another unpredictable avalanche on Moran Face.

Though not all accidents were so tragic, the fact remains that much of this mountain is avalanche terrain, and the potential for human injury and/or death is incessant. Most accidents stem from overconfidence in stabilization methods or from a disregard for obvious signs of danger, ski-patrol recommendations, and closed-area signs.

Following is a selection of out-of-bounds runs that are part of Peak 10,450:

Why Not: {E} This enjoyable route culminates at Ship's Prow (Point 9,400-plus) on the south boundary of the ski area. It faces southeast at first, then turns to face directly south during its 1,600-foot descent into Rock Springs Canyon. In the spring of 1994, a skier who entered the area illegally broke his femur in the soft snow. He was rescued by helicopter and was billed for those expenses.

Space Walk: {G} This narrow classic drops at 45 degrees from the top of Rendezvous Bowl, just outside the ski-area boundary. Halfway down, you'll have to negotiate a four-foot-wide chute. Most skiers do the "space walk"—10 feet of downward sidestepping, the rocky walls of the narrow couloir supporting ski tips and tails. Instead, some skiers might schuss the 60-degree chute and attempt to slow down on an awkward snowdrift in the dogleg below.

(Early fixed-heel: Mike Quinn, et al; May, 1975.)

Zero G: {G} Some 200 yards from the ski-area boundary—on the southwest ridge of Peak 10,450—drop southeast into this harrowing classic testpiece. Negotiate the 60-degree entrance with dynamic skiing maneuvers. Scout the route first to find out exactly where and how to enter. In the early 1990s, a skier fell in this entrance and slid uncontrollably on firm 50-degree slopes, slamming into a rock pillar in the middle of the couloir. He was rescued but suffered severe head injuries.

(Early fixed-heel: Mike Quinn et al; May, 1975.)

West Face: {E} Carry skis west across wind-scoured rocks from the top of the tram. Ski the broad, gladed face below for 1,200 feet to a small drainage. Follow the drainage north through a narrow, steep gap to a rocky moraine where you can meet the Tensleep Bowl-Granite Canyon route.

Bird Brain Boulevard: {H} This unique run begins with a four-foot-wide slot that drops off the west end of the large cliff north of Peak 10,450. Renny Jackson, Jim Roscoe and Gregg Martell skied through the slot into the main couloir, which ended at a 60-foot cliff. Rappelling with stoppers for their anchor, they landed on a ski-width snow ramp that led to the moraine below. They then climbed to Tensleep Bowl.

(Early fixed-heel: Renny Jackson, Jim Roscoe and Gregg Martell; February, 1991.)

Horseshoe Couloir: {F} or {G} Visible from the tram dock, this 600-foot couloir drops off the east end of the large cliff north of Peak 10,450. Slopes angled at more than 50 degrees at the top end at a 25-foot cliff in low snow years. In most years, however, the cliff presents a challenging 10-foot leap. The first descent trio tried to use snow bollards to anchor their 60-foot, 7mm rappel rope, but the TG snow just broke away. Eventually, they used a rock horn as an anchor. Climb east along the base of the cliff to reach Tensleep Bowl.

(Early fixed-heel: Renny Jackson, Jim Roscoe and Gregg Martell; February, 1991.)

North Ridge: {F} This is the steep, exposed ridge between Hourglass and Horseshoe couloirs.

Hourglass Couloir: {G} Wide at the top, this couloir funnels skiers through a near-60-degree slot, which requires dynamic ski maneuvering. Here, you might find ice and/or rock. Drop into this 500-foot couloir northeast of the tram top station and you'll end up in Tensleep Bowl. First skied in the late 1960s, the Hourglass remains a technical testpiece.

Shot 10: {F} This short-but-sweet Howitzer target drops southeast from Point 9,815 to Pepi's Bench. Approach from Tensleep Bowl up the low-angle southwest face of Point 9,815.

Headwall: {E} This classic face plummets more than 1,500 feet from the ridge north of Point 9,815 to Gros Ventre at the ski area. Approach via Pepi's Bench.

The Headwall historically has been a difficult avalanche-control area. In February of 1986, a 12-day storm dumped eight and a half feet of snow on the Tetons. Toward the end of the storm, temperatures remained above freezing and snow turned to rain. On Feb. 24, the ski patrol triggered a massive wet avalanche, which plunged 3,300 feet—to within 100 feet of a house in Teton Village! Groves of trees were toppled like match sticks, and a 25-foot wall of snow destroyed the Halfway House at the base of Thunder. Damage at the ski area was estimated at $60,000.

On Super Bowl Sunday in 1990, a massive blizzard loaded the Headwall with enough snow to release naturally and avalanche into the ski area during operating hours. Ski Corp employees were summoned to an

The annual Powder Eights competition in Cody Bowl—begun in March, 1970—draws thousands of skiers from throughout the world. Gene Downer is the event's founder.

extensive probe search in the debris. Thankfully, nobody was buried.

Casper Bowl: {E} and {F} Once controlled for avalanches with a Howitzer from near what now is the Teton Village gas station, this craggy basin can offer powder and corn on the same day. And you'll find a variety of lines representing all difficulties. Approach as for Headwall, but continue north a short distance.

The Crags: {F} A popular out-of-bounds run approached from Apres Vous in the mid-1960s, this multifaceted face of cliffs and chutes is on the southeast side of Point 9,503. Approach as for Casper Bowl, but continue on Skyline Ridge to Point 9,503.

Triple Direct and ABC Chutes, or Triple-A Chutes: {F} These four Granite Canyon chutes are west of Endless Couloir and a massive granite buttress but east of Point 8,545. Follow Skyline Ridge to the top of Casper Bowl, then drop northwest. Use Saratoga Traverse to return to Teton Village for this and the following six routes.

Endless Couloir: {F} or {G} This classic gully drops more than 2,000 feet from Point 9,503 to the 7,300-foot level of Granite Canyon. Follow Skyline Ridge toward Point 9,503, then drop north, just west of a large granite buttress. A jump might be required in low snow years. (Probably first skied in the late 1960s.)

Mile Long Couloir: {F} This classic gully and face drops more than 2,000 feet from Point 9,503 into Granite Canyon, passing just east of the granite buttress mentioned under Endless Couloir. Approach as for Endless Couloir or climb from Casper chair lift. (Probably first skied in the late 1960s.)

Double Chutes: {F} Double Dare, Double Dog Dare, and Double Direct are among several chutes between Air Force Couloir and Mile Long. Approach from Casper chair lift or follow Skyline Ridge past Point 9,503 and drop north from a flat bench.

Air Force Couloir: {F} In 1984, Benny Wilson and Dave "the Wave" Muccino started the "Jackson Hole Air Force," for which this aesthetic couloir is named. Wilson and Muccino institutionalized a tradition of out-of-bounds skiing and big-air prowess that was born in the late 1960s. The few who exemplify the aggressive style of the air force are issued embroidered patches that read "Swift, Silent, Deep: First Tracks OB."

From near the top of Moran Face, drop north and ski the couloir that marks the east end of the vast Granite Canyon avalanche path. Approach as for Double Chutes.

Spock Chutes: {F} Popular for spring runs in the 1960s, numerous chutes through forest and cliffs drop into Granite Canyon from Apres Vous Mountain. Approach from Apres Vous chair lift.

Saratoga Bowl: {E} From the top of Apres Vous chair lift, ski northeast along the undulating ridge until marvelous 1,500-foot gladed bowls unfold below.

Sheridan Bowl: {E} This aesthetic but often avalanche-prone bowl is the east face of Point 9,503. Ski a wide gap through cliffs to a basin, below which you'll find easy gladed skiing to Moran Traverse at the ski area.

Rock Springs Canyon: {E} Approach this classic canyon descent of Rendezvous Mountain from the upper entrance, which leaves the ski area from the top of Rendezvous Bowl. Or use the lower entrance, which leaves the ski area at the bottom of the bowl. You'll find a variety of bowls and chutes to explore here. Ross's Slide to Rock Garden is a standard south-facing route combination. Use 7,600 Return Trail to return to Teton Village.

On April 1, 1994, Minnesota youths Tom and Mike Halberson slipped on firm snow above cliffs near Zero G and Space Walk. Mike, 17, was able to self-arrest but watched Tom, 13, slide helplessly over the cliff. Tom's body struck the cliff several times in the course of his 500-foot fall. Stricken with fear, Mike downclimbed the cliff to reach his brother, much to the dismay of rescuers already on the scene. Tom was flown by helicopter to a hospital in Salt Lake City, where he died.

Green River Canyon: {E} On April 3, 1992, Jackson Hole ski instructors Robert "Drew" Dunlap and Hank List were caught in a massive wet-slab avalanche on the northeast side of Point 9,840-plus, near the head of Green River Canyon. List tumbled over a cliff band and stopped, buried to his waist. Dunlap was carried 900 feet over two cliff bands and was entombed beneath four feet of debris for more than 90 minutes. Fighting against impending suffocation, Dunlap clawed an air space for himself with one free hand. Searchers and rescue dogs were dispatched from the ski area by helicopter. Dunlap finally was located by audible cries for help, with assistance from a Jackson Hole Ski Patrol search dog named "Coup." The rescue marked the first time in North America that avalanche dogs found a skier alive.

Conditions were unseasonably warm that day, critically weakening the snowpack by 9:30 a.m.; the avalanche occurred at about 10 a.m. In safe conditions, you'll find terrific undulating terrain through sparse forest, chutes and boulders in the course of the 2,000-foot run between Peak 10,450-Jensen Canyon and 7,600 Return Trail.

Four Pines (9,600-plus feet): {E} This large dome-shaped mountain, with four pine trees near its top, appears to stand alone but actually is the lower east ridge of Cody Peak. Approach from Peak 10,450-Jensen Canyon by dropping slightly into Pinedale Canyon and contouring the south side of Point 9,840-plus.

East Face: {E} This Teton classic leads 2,000 feet through sparse trees and short gullies to 7,600 Return Trail. The final 1,000 feet above the valley is especially enjoyable, featuring wide-open spring snow terrain. But you then have to ski north along Fish Creek for a mile and a half of flat to return to Teton Village.

Broken Branch Couloir: {F} On the southeast side of Four Pines, ski this exciting chute into Pinedale Canyon. Expect angles near 40 degrees and narrows just 10 feet wide.

North Face: {E} In late March of 1970, experienced ski mountaineer Richard Ream was carried 1,500 feet by an avalanche on the north side of Four Pines. Ream wasn't buried but was raked over rocks and through trees. Despite severe lacerations and multiple fractures of both arms and legs, Ream was praised for his courage and stamina in the face of pain and blood loss. The ski area sponsored a "Richard Ream Weekend" and raised $2,725 to help him pay medical bills. This nice powder run leads into Green River Canyon.

Cody Peak (10,753 feet): Its close proximity to

the ski area and its concentration of steep couloirs and faces helped transform this peak into a symbol of extreme skiing in the Jackson Hole area. Approach via Peak 10,450-Rendezvous Peak. If the tram is closed, the quickest route follows the ski-area cat tracks to the bottom of Rendezvous Bowl, then follow Upper Rock Springs Canyon-Rendezvous Bowl.

Southeast Face: {D} Approach by climbing Cody Bowl from upper Rock Springs Canyon. This nice face has a southwest exposure that drops into upper Pinedale Canyon from the east shoulder of Cody Peak. You can ski this face to access Upper Pinedale Canyon-Granite Canyon south fork quickly.

Twice Is Nice: {G} Although skiers consider this one easier than Once Is Enough, a dogleg at the bottom of this couloir makes it more dangerous. Amazingly, Tom Raymer and Russ Scotty slid the length of this couloir with only minor injuries.

Twice Is Nice drops from near the summit southeast into the upper basin of Pinedale Canyon.

(Early fixed-heel: Glen Jaques, Bob Barrows and Mike Quinn; June 1974. Tom Raymer and Bob Sealander; mid-1970s.)

Once Is Enough: {G} This accessible couloir splits the large cliffy southeast face 100 yards southwest of the summit. With slopes at the top reaching near vertical, this is one of the steepest the Teton Range has to offer. Nordic skiers Brian Rudder and Forrest McCarthy slid the entire length of the couloir. Luckily, they survived. The crux is getting off the cornice at the top.

(Early fixed-heel: Tom Raymer, Victor Gerdin, Frank Barrows, Lon Kelly and Mike Quinn; early to mid-1970s.)

Pucker Face: {F} North of No Shadows, a large east face approaching 50 degrees leads into Rock Springs canyon.

No Shadows: {F} This gully is northwest of Four Shadows.

Four Shadows: {F} This is the large gully system west of Cody's north-face cliffs. The cornices at the top are the crux. On June 3, 1979, Tom Bjornsen was skiing fast at the bottom of Four Shadows when he went over a rise to confront rocks that were concealed from above. Tom jumped, landing 10 feet short of snow on the other side of the 30-foot band of rocks. He suffered a compound fracture in his leg and had to be rescued by helicopter.

(Early free-heel: Mike Fitzpatrick; spring, 1972. Early monoski: Davey Agnew and Jerry Balint; spring, 1972.)

Central Chute: {H} This testpiece drops north from the summit ridge into upper Rock Springs Canyon. The massive cornice at the top, the narrows in the middle, and the cliff at the bottom are its main obstacles. Dur-

ing some years, you can pass east of the cornice. To avoid unexpected downclimbing on ice or rock, be sure the narrows has plenty of snow cover. Over the cliff at the bottom, expect a jump of 20 feet to 50 feet. As John Fettig discovered, however, you can traverse west on a narrow, awkward and exposed ledge to avoid the lower cliff band in some years.

(Early fixed-heel: Larry Detrick and Steve Lundy; June, 1974. Early snowboard: John Recchio; 1993. Early free-heel: Mike Collins; March 9, 1995.)

Koch Route (Talk is Cheap): {H} Possibly the most

The south flank of Granite Canyon offers big vertical powder skiing. Access couloirs such as Mile Long and Endless from Jackson Hole Ski Area only when Pepi's Bench and Granite Canyon Headwall entrances are open.

technical route ever descended in the southern Tetons, this harrowing line follows the north ridge, which steepens until it ends abruptly at a 350-foot cliff. Koch made a 30-foot diagonal rappel near the bottom of the snow into Central Chute below its crux.

(Early snowboard: Stephen Koch; March 1, 1995. Early fixed-heel: Mark Newcomb; March 29, 1995.)

Shirley's Snowfield: {H} From the summit, John Griber struck northeast on a convex, hanging snowfield until he was forced to downclimb over some fourth-class rock. He was caught in a small wet-slab avalanche in a couloir below this cliff band. He named the route after his mother, Shirley Jones, who recently had died of cancer.

(Early snowboard: John Griber; April 2, 1992. Early fixed-heel: Rob Haggart; early March, 1995.)

Cody Bowl: {E} This classic bowl on the north side of Cody's east shoulder has been immortalized by the annual Jackson Hole and National Powder Eights Competition, organized by Gene Downer and first run in March of 1970.

Pinedale Canyon: {E} You'll encounter wonderful terrain in this steep canyon, which more commonly is used for ski descents than ascents. Approach via Peak 10,450-Jensen Canyon. To return to Teton Village, follow the 7,600 Return Trail.

Peak 10,706 (No Name Peak): This unnamed but popular peak is situated elegantly between Cody and Rendezvous peaks. Approach from the Jackson Hole Aerial Tram.

South Face Hanging Snowfield: {F} or {G} This snowfield hangs above 400-foot cliffs. During good snow years, it might be possible to exit the face near the east end of the cliff by way of a steep, narrow ledge-and-apron system.

North Face Hanging Snowfield: {E} This classic hanging snowfield begins 100 feet below the summit and boasts 500 feet of 35-degree slopes.

No Name Canyon: {E} Approached by way of

Peak 10,450-Jensen Canyon, this steep draw drains east from the cirque between Rendezvous and No Name peaks. Nice bowls and chutes in the upper canyon dissipate into cluttered forested gullies and large cliffs in the middle canyon. At about 7,600 feet, traverse north or south to the adjacent fault scarps to avoid the thickly forested, narrow lower canyon.

Park at the end of the Fish Creek Road but be respectful of private land in the area.

Jensen Canyon: {E} Approached via Peak 10,450-Jensen Canyon, this steep draw offers excellent skiing and serves as the primary exit from steep descents on Rendezvous Peak, predominately in spring. It is standard to shuttle a car to Fish Creek Road to simplify the return to the ski area. (Warning: Cars often are towed here. See Fish Creek Road under Mount Glory Region for more details.)

The lower portion of this draw is steep-sided, V-shaped, and choked with thick brush. Skiers typically traverse northeast across steep, obstacle-congested south slopes to the Rendezvous Peak lower east ridge fault scarp, which they ski to the valley floor. Most of the property at the base of this draw is private.

Point 9,670: The lower southeast ridge of Rendezvous Peak is the highest fault scarp in the southern Tetons. If your goal is to climb the largest east-facing avalanche chute or adjacent faces, shovel out a spot for your car along the straight stretch of the Fish Creek Road, where it crosses a meadow about three miles north of Wilson—just before Moose Creek Ranch.

South Face: {E} Wonderful bowls near the summit funnel into scary avalanche gullies for a 3,000-foot ride into Phillips Canyon.

(Early free-heel: Jim Olson and John Collins; 1992.)

North Avalanche Chutes: {F} Several steep, dangerous chutes through trees plunge north nearly 2,000 feet into Jensen Canyon. Short cliffs stripe across the couloirs, forcing skiers to jump in places.

(Early free-heel: Mike Whitehead et al; spring, early 1990s.)

Peak 10,332: This is the small, craggy, wind-scoured summit south of Rendezvous Peak. Approach from Phillips north fork or Jensen Canyon.

During the winter of 1991, Tom Bennett, Pat Clark, John Fettig and this author ascended Point 9,670 to the summit of Rendezvous Peak. We experienced exposed third- and fourth-class scrambling and loose rock on the east ridge of Peak 10,332.

Southwest Drift: {E} This wind-packed pillow fills a wide depression between talus fields for a 1,500-foot run into Phillips north fork.

(Early free-heel: Stephen Sullivan; spring, 1994.)

Other potential routes: The cliffy north face has been proposed for extreme skiing exhibitions and competitions.

Rendezvous Peak (10,927 feet): This majestic peak is the highest in the southern Tetons. The easiest approach is from the Jackson Hole Aerial Tram—or from Teton Pass, the first descent party's route.

East Ridge: {E} Skiers encounter two or three sections of steep, third-class rock below summit. The lower forested fault scarp makes an excellent ski run. Park at the end of Fish Creek Road to approach. Andrew Adolphsen and this author made an early winter ascent of this ridge in 1987.

(Early free-heel: Whitney Thurlow, Craig Tanner and Jay Moody; March 1981 or 1982.)

Southeast Couloir: {G} You can ski a 50-degree couloir directly from the summit to a bench above a large cliff. From the valley, a short cliff band in the couloir indicates snow depth. The first descent party had to make a short jump. From the bench, traverse south above the cliff to the Jensen Headwall couloirs to access Jensen Canyon.

You can find other routes southeast off the summit ridge, but they all end on the large bench above the cliff. Two hourglass couloirs pass through the northeastern end of this large cliff.

(Early fixed-heel: Mark Wolling, Victor Gerdin, Andy Norman, Mike Quinn and Glen Jaques; spring, 1979.)

Jensen Headwall: {F} and {G} You can ski several exciting couloirs from the saddle south of Rendezvous Peak east into Jensen Canyon.

Southwest Face: {E} This spectacular 1,800-foot bowl leads off the west ridge into Phillips north fork. In winter, windblown conditions often persist. In spring, few runs can match this one.

(Early fixed-heel: Rod Newcomb and Frank Ewing; Jan. 25, 1961.)

Southwest Ridge: {E} This tedious ridge is the standard ascent route from Phillips Pass. Steep couloirs, deep postholing in sugar snow, and rock-hard snow all are common here. When avalanche danger is high, it may be prudent to descend this ridge to avoid the southwest face.

St. Patrick's Day Couloir: This steep, wind-loaded couloir drops northeast into No Name Canyon from steep scree near The Wave. For a 1994 Jackson Hole promotional ad for Japan, John Griber and Adam McCool were filmed from helicopter while snowboarding and skiing this couloir.

(Early free-heel: Gregg Martell and Mary Schwind; early 1990s. Early snowboard: John Griber; spring, 1994.)

Peak 10,277: The two-mile-long northwest ridge of this insignificant peak forms the west border of the Granite south fork. Approach via Phillips Pass-Moose Divide, Granite Canyon or from the Jackson Hole Aerial Tram.

Goldmine Bowl: {C} This hidden southwest face of Peak 10,277 is a broad 2,000-foot slope, perfect for beginner powder skiers. The only drawback is that the bottom of the slope is at the head of Moose Creek, at least 5 miles from any trailhead. This was a popular High Mountain Heli-Skiing run before it officially became wilderness in 1984.

Northeast Face: {F} and {G} This long face offers seldom-skied but extremely avalanche-prone chutes topped with cornices.

(Early fixed-heel: Theo Meiners; late 1970s.)

Point 9,815: This is the first summit north of Phillips Pass. Approach from Phillips middle fork.

Southwest Face: {C} A wonderful, though often wind-affected, 900-foot gladed bowl leads back to Phillips Pass.

HIGH ROUTES

Skyline Ridge: {D} This scenic ridge tour accesses all routes off the sides of the Rendezvous Mountain ridge, between Point 9,815 and Apres Vous Mountain.

Pepi's Bench: {C} This classic passage between two cliff bands makes an ascending traverse from the ski area, at The Cirque, to the ridge northeast of Point 9,815. Use it to access the Headwall and points north.

Tensleep Bowl-Granite Canyon: {D} This route is an enjoyable way to begin a Granite Canyon tour. From Tensleep Bowl, contour around the upper Gros Ventre basin to the col on the north ridge of Peak 10,450. Ski west off the col under the large cliff containing Horseshoe Couloir and cross north over the moraine to low-angle bowls and forest that lead into Granite Canyon just below the forks.

7,600-foot Return Trail: {E} Follow this route to return to Teton Village from tours as far south as Pinedale Canyon. From the 7,600-foot level in Pinedale Canyon, this long traverse leads under the east face of Four Pines and over a short moraine into lower Rock Springs Canyon. From the treeless flats at the canyon's 7,520-foot level, enter the forest and follow a shallow creek bed 100 yards. Begin a descending traverse through moguls and forest to the gully at the south boundary of the ski area on the South Hoback. Use the Union Pass Traverse and surface lift to return to Teton Village.

Upper Rock Springs Canyon-Rendezvous Bowl: {C} This short route traverses under Zero G and Space Walk, from the flat upper basin of Rock Springs Canyon to the base of Rendezvous Bowl at the lower entrance to Rock Springs Canyon.

Peak 10,450-Jensen Canyon: {D} This classic high route traverses between cliffs, over saddles, around cirques, and across basins along its four-mile course. During spring and sometimes in winter, a ski track is broken most of the way. From the tram, ski southwest along the ridge to the first saddle. Drop southeast into upper Rock Springs Canyon and make an undulating traverse—under the north-facing cliffs of the flying buttress northeast of Cody Bowl—to its east ridge. Contour high around the symmetrical upper Green River basin and climb slightly to the flat east ridge of Cody Peak.

Next, skate south across the flats of upper Pinedale Canyon and climb slightly to the east ridge of No Name Peak (Peak 10,706). Drop into upper No Name Canyon, then cross the basin and climb to the east ridge of Rendezvous Peak. Jensen Canyon lies below to the south. Use the pertinent segment of this route to access the aforementioned canyons and ridges.

Upper Pinedale Canyon-Granite Canyon south fork: {E} This unlikely route is a spur of the Peak 10,450-Jensen Canyon route, which is used most often in spring for three reasons. First, it is the easiest way to reach No Name Peak for a descent of its north face. Second, in bypassing the wind-scoured cliffs and loose rock on the south ridge of Cody Peak (Peak 10,450-Rendezvous Peak), it provides the easiest and most efficient route from the tram to the summit of Rendezvous Peak. Third, it allows skiers to "bag" a steep chute on Cody Peak en route to points farther south.

From the east ridge of Cody Peak on the Peak 10,450-Jensen Canyon route, make an ascending traverse southwest into the basin of upper Pinedale Canyon. Climb steeply to the col between Cody and No Name peaks. Sugar or wind-hammered snow are the norm on the west side of this col.

Peak 10,450-Rendezvous Peak: {F} This long, classic ski-mountaineering ridge tour involves more walking and scrambling than it does skiing. You'll encounter difficulties on the knife edge summit ridge of Rendezvous Peak, on the rocky north ridge of No Name Peak, and on the rubble, sugar snow, gullies and short cliffs of Cody Peak's south ridge.

The most commonly used stretch of this route is between the tram and Cody Peak. Ski carefully south from the tram, down the wind-scoured ridge to the first saddle. Remove your skis and climb third-class rock on the northeast ridge of Point 10,215 until you can traverse exposed, loose terrain to the ridge connecting to Cody Peak. Follow Cody Peak's wind-scoured north ridge to the summit.

Peak 10,450-Granite Canyon shelf: {D} This high route is part of the classic traverse between the tram and Housetop. From the top of the tram, you'll find many ways to ski into Granite Canyon for a Teton traverse. The safest and most efficient course employs the Peak 10,450-Rendezvous Peak route to reach Point 10,215. From just south of its summit, ski northwest down wind-scoured snow and rocks. Pass a short cliff to the north and ski a line of trees to a bench that the summer trail follows. Ski along the edge of the south fork valley and make an ascending traverse to the spur between the south and middle forks of Granite.

From here, choose one of two routes to the shelf. The higher, more strenuous route climbs almost to Pass 9,085 (Moose Divide) and ascends the avalanche-prone headwall to the west near a rib of trees. Continuing west, go around the south sides of three summits to the Granite Canyon shelf. The lower route ascends the middle fork through its upper headwall to gain the shelf.

Phillips Pass-Moose Divide: {D} Though most travel in the Tetons seems to be in canyons or couloirs or on ridges, bowls, and shelves, this route calls for a long traverse across forested slopes. For skiers who have to break trail with heavy packs, it is undoubtedly one of the tougher and least-enjoyable parts of the Teton Crest trip. On the positive side, the views into the headwaters of Moose Creek are spectacular.

From Phillips Pass, make a descending traverse until you reach a small promontory. Drop into the basin to the north, using extreme caution in high-avalanche conditions. Next, begin a long traverse through the forest and beneath the Madison Limestone Moose Creek cliffs. Then make a gradually ascending traverse for two miles to Moose Divide. If you're traveling south from Moose Divide, be sure to make a descending traverse to the west end of the Moose Creek cliffs. In 1940, tired and hungry Fred Brown, Betty Woolsey, and Katie Starratt added hours of unnecessary climbing when they traversed too high and ended up above the cliffs.

MOUNT GLORY REGION

With easy access from the Teton Pass Highway and close proximity to Jackson and Wilson, WY and Victor and Driggs, Idaho, the Mount Glory Region undoubtedly receives more attention from backcountry skiers than any other region of the range. A fair share of credit for this popularity should go to the fantastic terrain and snow here. Main attractions are the big vertical runs on Glory and Taylor, the elegant ridges and numerous cirques of the Phillips Canyon headwaters, and the sea of bowls south of Highway 22. This region is bordered by Teton Pass Highway on the south and Moose and Phillips canyons on the north.

For detailed reference to the Mount Glory Region, use USGS maps for Teton Pass, Rendezvous Peak, Victor, Idaho and Teton Village, WY.

American Avalanche Institute founder Rod Newcomb shows excellent form during this Teton Pass tour in 1962. The Mount Glory Region receives more attention from backcountry skiers than any other region in the range.

APPROACHES

Fish Creek Road: Almost completely surrounded by private property, this road allows skiers access to Phillips Canyon and Rendezvous Mountain. Parking is prohibited along the road; to reduce the chances of having your car towed, shovel out a parking spot at the Phillips Canyon summer trailhead, about three miles north of Wilson. Or park in a small plowed area at the north end of the road, where it splits into several driveways.

Phillips Canyon: This surprisingly large watershed drains at least seven cirques between Sugar Bowl and the southeast ridge of Rendezvous Peak. To access the mouth of Phillips Canyon, park at an unplowed pullout three miles north of Wilson on Fish Creek Road. In the lower canyon, expect moderate bushwhacking, creek crossings, and a confusion of trails near the mouth.

On Feb. 11, 1991, Michael Kulik got disoriented while alone on a day ski tour in lower Phillips Canyon. Hypothermic and frostbitten after falling into the creek

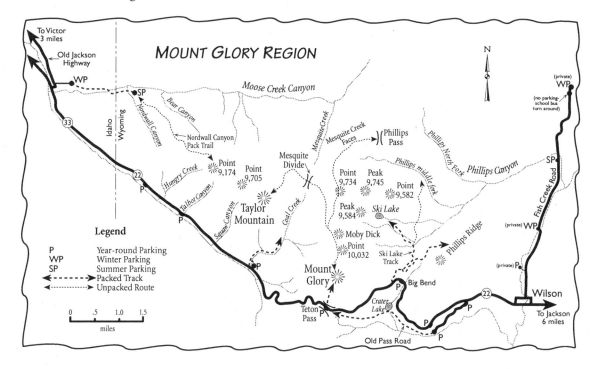

twice and spending two cold nights on pine boughs, Kulik was rescued by a 12-person team during his third day out.

A drawback to ski travel in the north and middle forks is that they are severely V-shaped, especially above the forks. Travel is not recommended in the creek beds because of waterfalls and deadfall. The easiest routes follow the north sides of the canyons above the creek beds.

The head of the north fork boasts one of the largest bowls in the southern Tetons—the southwest face of Rendezvous Peak. This is approached best from the Jackson Hole Aerial Tram. Endless gladed and open skiing leads into the middle fork from all directions. Try the east face of dome-shaped Point 9,582, the northeast couloir of Peak 9,745, or the wide-open south face of the long ridge east of Phillips Pass. These areas are best approached from Teton Pass via the Mount Glory-Phillips Pass route or via Ski Lake Track and Big Bend parking area-Phillips Canyon middle fork.

The main fork of Phillips Canyon drains such classic ski runs as Sugar Bowl, Moby Dick, Whale's Tail, Peak 9,584, and the south side of Point 9,582. To honor the area's high-quality terrain, Betty Woolsey named Lake 8,650 "Ski Lake." Approach these areas from Teton Pass via the Mount Glory-Phillips Pass route or via Ski Lake Track.

Big Bend parking area-Phillips Ridge: {C} From the parking area, walk up the highway 200 yards and ski up the Phillips Canyon Jeep Road. After a third of a mile, bear right and follow this curving road through clearcuts and past power lines for two miles to the top of Phillips Ridge. You also can break a direct trail to the ridge from the junction of the highway and Trail Creek north fork.

Big Bend parking area-Phillips Canyon middle fork: {B} This route represents one of three ways to begin or end a Teton Crest traverse. From the parking area, walk up the highway 200 yards and ski up the Phillips Canyon Jeep Road. After a third of a mile, bear left on the Ski Lake Track and left again at the next junction. After a mile and a quarter, you'll reach a large flat meadow. Strike off north, aiming just left of the Rendezvous Peak summit. Don't waste effort trying to traverse high because you'll come upon steep, thickly forested avalanche terrain. Instead, contour from the meadow through the forest, then cross an avalanche runout zone and stay below steep terrain until you reach the middle fork.

From the middle fork, look for the first low-angle exit on the south side and make an ascending traverse until the terrain above flattens. Then contour to the big meadow and the Ski Lake Track.

Ski Lake Track: {C} This scenic, short and easy tour is a Teton classic. From the parking area, walk up the highway 200 yards and ski up the Phillips Canyon Jeep Road. After a third of a mile, bear left on the Ski Lake Track, then left again at the next junction. Follow the track two miles to the lake. Jackson Hole Mountain Guides operated a quonset ski hut near the lake during the 1980s and early 90s, but porcupines destroyed the premises.

Old Jackson Highway (1080S): Before construction of the current Teton Pass Highway, this was the primary route between Victor and the mouth of Trail Creek Canyon. From there, the road spiraled up mountainsides to Teton Pass and Jackson Hole. This road now merges with the Teton Pass Highway near the mouth of Moose Creek and provides access to Moose and Game creeks.

Moose Creek Canyon (Targhee National Forest Road No. 276): {K} This long, straight, flat canyon has little to offer skiers except an interminable, often skier-packed track into and out of the mountains. Skiers in areas such as Mount Wow, Goldmine Bowl, and the north side of Taylor Mountain commonly use Moose Creek during their tours. Try to follow the summer trail in the canyon.

Four miles southeast of Victor, Idaho—on Idaho Route 33, near the mouth of Trail Creek Canyon—the Old Jackson Highway turns east toward the Tetons. It then turns 90 degrees immediately and heads to Victor.

About 100 yards down the road, turn right (east) onto the Moose Creek Road, which is plowed in winter for nearly a mile to a small parking area that's near a ranch entrance. Avoid the south-facing slopes of the canyon because they are sensitive wildlife winter range.

Nordwall Canyon Pack Trail: {D} This moderate route ascends the mellow ridge between Nordwall and Bear canyons for travel between Point 9,174 and Moose Creek.

Bear Canyon: {D} This beautiful, exciting draw leads northwest into Moose Creek Canyon from a headwater on the west ridge of Taylor Mountain. It is used primarily as an exit from the fantastic bowls at its head and Powder Reserve to the east. During your descent, you'll find excellent gladed terrain on the northeast flanks of the draw.

Hungry Creek: {E} This draw provides one of the quickest, more moderate routes between Wyoming Route 22 and the long west ridge of Taylor Mountain. Gain the ridge northwest of Point 9,174. Look for the entrance to the draw about three miles west of Coal Creek on Wyoming Route 22. Park in the nearest plowed area.

Talbot Canyon: {E} Though the lower portion of this draw is very steep and narrow, Talbot Canyon provides convenient access to the west ridge of Taylor Mountain and the bowls of upper Bear Canyon. Many skiers zigzag up the ridge west of the drainage instead of struggling in the canyon bottom. Look for the concrete drain at the entrance to the draw, about two miles west of Coal Creek on Wyoming Route 22. Park in the nearest plowed area.

Coal Creek Canyon: {C} This is the primary route to and from Wyoming Route 22 for skiers on the west side of Mount Glory or the east side of Taylor Mountain. A steep ski track west of the creek will keep your adrenaline pumping all the way to the road. Avoid the east side of the creek. Coal Creek also is used as a starting point for Teton Crest traverses, especially in marginal weather.

Teton Pass Highway (Wyoming Route 22/Idaho Route 33): Tracing the southern boundary of the Teton

Range, this highway follows long, broad Trail Creek Canyon from Victor, Idaho southeast to Teton Pass, then down the north flank of Trail Creek Canyon—on the east side of the range—to Wilson, WY.

Avalanches always have posed a major threat to travelers on this route over Teton Pass. One the earliest attempts to control avalanche danger with explosives was in late February of 1917. Some 50 pounds of dynamite was detonated in Glory Bowl after a wet snow blizzard, but the temperature already had dropped enough that the snow was solid, and no avalanche occurred.

On Jan. 15, 1970, a massive avalanche mangled a bridge that was under construction at the Glory slide path and carried remains of the bridge to Crater Lake. Frustrated road crews filled the gully with earth and built the road across the avalanche path, planning more bombing to reduce the size of avalanches. Regardless, accidents continued.

In February of 1986, so much snow fell that the highway department couldn't keep up. It had no choice but to block the road for what turned out to be the longest closure in recent history—nearly three weeks. A 300-foot pile of debris, some 25 feet deep, had to be cleared from the road at the base of Glory Slide.

Since then, numerous solutions—including snow sheds, fences, and tunnels—have been proposed to keep avalanches from hitting the highway. In 1992-93, the Wyoming Transportation Department installed a weather station near Glory summit and placed several Gaz-Ex remote propane exploders on Twin and Glory slides. The Transportation Department detonates the exploders only after closing the pass highway.

Old Pass Road: {C} The first recorded use of this natural passage dates to the early 1800s. The first Indians in Jackson Hole certainly used Teton Pass for years before that. In 1901, a rugged trail over Teton Pass was improved into this crude road, designed for horse-drawn wagons. In the late 1800s, the primary winter users of the road were the mail carriers who skied and drove gandy wagons back and forth between Victor and Wilson. By 1905, however, Teton Pass was used enough by horse-drawn freight sleds carrying huge loads of groceries, hardware, mail, clothing and machinery, that snow on the road stayed packed throughout winter. In October of 1939, the Civilian Conservation Corps cleared ski trails between the road's switchbacks off both sides of the pass. In the late 1960s, the wide two-lane Teton Pass Highway of today was constructed.

Today, a good ski track follows the Old Pass Road on the Jackson Hole side, offering an excellent tour and 5.5-mile return route from Teton Pass to Jackson Hole. At the Heidlberg House, a mile and a quarter west of Wilson on Wyoming Route 22, turn left toward Trail Creek Ranch and park at the end of the road.

PEAKS AND BOWLS

Phillips Ridge (8,442 feet): This seven-mile-long, low massif is isolated by Trail Creek north fork on the south, Phillips main fork on the north, and private property on the Jackson Hole side.

Wilson Faces: {D} and {E} In good snow years, take incredible runs covering as much as 2,100 feet through a variety of terrain on these vast southeast faces. A 30-foot cliff band extends nearly the length of the face and provides an interesting challenge about halfway down. The best ski routes seem to be the large, open faces near the northern end of the escarpment. The light snowcover on these faces usually is TG, slush, or crust due to elevation and distance from the range crest.

To ski on the northern end of the escarpment, park on the west side of the Fish Creek bridge, two miles north of Wilson, or at the Phillips Canyon trailhead pullout. For southern routes, park across from the Heidlberg House, near the junction of Wyoming Highway 22 and the road to Trail Creek Ranch, or park at the Big Bend parking area on Wyoming Route 22 and use the Big Bend parking area-Phillips Ridge route or a pullout near the first big bend in the highway as it heads up the pass. For all other approaches, get special permission from landowners to park and ski on private property.

Ridge Tour: {D} This popular six-mile traverse follows either the ridgetop or power-line swath between Big Bend parking area and Fish Creek Road.

Point 9,582: This is the large treeless dome-shaped mountain visible from Teton Village Road. Approach from Ski Lake or Big Bend parking area-Phillips Canyon middle fork.

East Avalanche Path: {E} This popular powder run drops as far as 2,000 feet into Phillips lower middle fork. Only attempt this one when avalanche danger is low.

South Face: {D} This large, convex face offers 1,000 feet of fantastic spring skiing.

Peak 9,745: You'll find two enjoyable ski routes from this sharp summit. Both lead into Phillips middle fork. Approach from Ski Lake.

Northwest Face: {C} This gentle, gladed bowl makes a nice tour from Ski Lake.

Northeast Couloir: {F} This 400-foot, 50-degree chute is excellent training for the steeps and narrows.

Point 9,734: This insignificant horn stands two miles north of Mount Glory, along the crest at the head of Phillips middle fork. Approach via Mount Glory-Phillips Pass.

Southeast Bowl: {E} This extremely avalanche-prone, half-mile-wide, 400-foot bowl rims the head of Phillips Canyon above Ski Lake.

West Side: {C} This mile-wide beginner run angles gently through thick forest, with several open shots, 1,000 feet into Coal Creek.

Mesquite Creek Faces: {E} and {F} Less than a mile along the crest southwest of Phillips Pass are points 9,375 and 9,250. Northwest off this rocky ridge sprawls a mile-wide forested face of chutes and bowls that undulates 1,600 feet to Moose Meadows. Approach from Phillips or Teton pass.

Peak 9,584: This nunatak rises sharply above Ski Lake. Approach from Ski Lake, or from Mount Glory via Moby Dick or Whale's Tail.

North Side: {F} Several steep chutes through trees and rocks adorn this north face.

Point 10,000-plus (Moby Dick): This is the whale-like hump a mile north of the Mount Glory summit. Approach via Mount Glory-Phillips Pass.

East Face: {E} A fabulous ski descent on slopes approaching 40 degrees continues east down a small canyon. One way to exit the canyon is to follow the creek through a steep draw and thick brush for a flat mile to the big meadow in the Ski Lake Track. You also can ski a steep spur that drops east from the bench just south of the creek. Pass a large cliff en route to the low-angle, gladed face above Point 8,376. Or continue south along this bench and you'll reach the base of Little Tuckerman's Bowl.

Neil Rafferty stands proudly on the deck of his Teton Pass rope tow, which was powered by this 1941 Army weapons carrier truck. The rope tow provided early season lift-served skiing on Telemark Bowl.

Southwest Face: {D} From the west, Moby Dick is the monarch of the Mount Glory massif. The upper west side of Moby Dick is quite rocky, wind-scoured, and not recommended for skiing. A short distance northwest of the summit, however, this nearly 2,000-foot gladed gully flank is a classic moderate run of the Mount Glory Region. Aspen glades at the bottom make this a special one.

West Ridge: {C} or {D} From the bench northwest of Moby Dick, follow this beginner run all the way into Coal Creek, or fork southwest at 9,400 feet for a steeper shot above the aspen glades of the southwest face.

Northeast Face: {E} This shaded, wind-loaded bowl often is avalanche-prone but, in safe conditions, offers excellent powder for more than 600 feet into a short side canyon above Ski Lake.

Whale's Tail: {D} and {F} This is the northeast ridge of Moby Dick. Both the north and south sides sport excellent chutes and faces. Use caution on the steep, avalanche-prone north side.

Point 10,032: This is the minor bump half a mile north of Mount Glory. Approach from Teton Pass.

Sugar Bowl: {F} or {G} This is the small, cliffy cirque just north of Little Tuckerman's. Safer from avalanches during spring, circuitous lines of all exposures lure only expert backcountry skiers. Exit to Ski Lake Track or traverse south to Little Tuckerman's creek.

South Face: {E} See Little Tuckerman's.

West Ridge: {E} This steep, gladed ridge drops into Coal Creek. For a great run, catch it in deep-powder conditions in late season.

Northeast Ridge: {E} and {F} Several powder chutes drop north off this ridge into the small canyon east of Moby Dick.

Mount Glory (10,086 feet): This is the most easily accessed and frequented summit in the range. Approach from Teton Pass parking area via the south ridge of Mount Glory; you usually can find a boot track there. The large billboard-like telecommunications repeater near the summit was installed in the mid-1960s.

Glory Bowl: {E} This east-facing bowl is one of the classic Teton descents, with a 30-degree pitch for more than 2,200 feet to Wyoming Route 22. Before the current pass highway was constructed in the late 1960s, skiers enjoyed an unobstructed 3,000-foot ski run to Crater Lake! Then they would meet the Old Pass Road there for a quick ride back to the top of the pass.

Teton skiers always have shown great respect for avalanche dangers in this bowl. But people still forget or misjudge. On April 10, 1977—Easter morning—a massive Glory slide cut loose amidst a steady flow of corn skiers. Remarkably, no one was caught. Don't let yourself develop a false sense of security from your knowledge that the highway department blasts the avalanche paths below the summit during and after storms.

Southeast Ridge (Rocky Gulch and Shovel Slide): {E} Skiers often ski the top half of Glory Bowl, then traverse under cliffs south onto this broad ridge for another 1,000 feet of forested terrain.

Twin Slides (Upper and Lower): {E} This popular duo of avalanche gullies drops south to Teton Pass from the telecommunications repeater. Twin Slides' avalanches have carried several vehicles off the highway in their day. In January of 1913, an avalanche crippled a gandy wagon and its 12-horse team as well.

Southwest Ridge (Snowslide Gulch): {E} This popular run follows the southwest ridge of Mount Glory from near the summit. At about 9,000 feet, three options present themselves for the remaining 700-foot descent to Wyoming Route 22, just west of the pass. Either continue straight down, or traverse east or west into adjacent clearings.

Snowshoe Bowl: {D} This alluring bowl drops southwest from the west ridge a third of a mile from the summit. On Jan. 20, 1991, Ray Shriver and his son, Matt, were carried 1,200 feet and buried in an avalanche in this alluring bowl. Jay Pistono and Zach Shriver acted quickly to rescue them. Numerous slides have been observed in this bowl, particularly after infrequent northerly weather flows. At the bottom of the bowl, follow a gully and power-line swath through the trees to Wyoming Route 22, near Coal Creek parking area.

Southwest Bowl: {D} From Point 9,100 on the west ridge, drop south for 1,500 feet of open bowls and thick-forested gullies. At the bottom, follow a gully and power-line swath through the trees to Wyoming Route 22, near the mouth of Coal Creek.

West Ridge: {C} Combined with Lord Calvert's or the southwest bowl, this long, broad ridge of Mount Glory leads 2,800 feet to Coal Creek parking area.

(Early fixed-heel: Wallace Cherry; 1930s.)

Lord Calvert's: {E} From the west end of a level, corniced section of the west ridge—near Point 9,100— a wonderful northeast-facing shot drops north into Coal Creek. When the trees become denser, turn west over the ridge for another 800 feet of some of the best medium-growth tree skiing in the Tetons.

Northwest Face: {E} From the top of the west ridge, ski northwest through a stand of rime-encrusted trees into these gladed steeps. Follow a steep draw into Coal Creek or climb back to Mount Glory for another run.

Little Tuckerman's: {E} and {F} Resembling a larger New Hampshire basin, this bowl offers steep faces and chutes of all but western exposures.

Directly below the summit of Mount Glory are excellent steep ski runs. The slopes get easier as you traverse farther north along the fragile corniced ridge between Mount Glory and Point 10,032. Wind slab conditions are common on all aspects of this bowl.

To exit the cirque, traverse southeast to Glory Bowl under the northeast chutes of Mount Glory. Or follow the creek all the way to Wyoming Route 22 via a steep break in a long cliff band and the Surprise avalanche path.

Chicken Scratch Couloirs: {F} You'll find several steep chutes through cliffs off the lower northeast ridge.

Point 9,705: This bump lies a half mile west of Taylor Mountain. Approach from Hungry Creek or Bear or Talbot canyon.

Squaw Canyon: {E} Combine this uncelebrated bowl and gully with the west face of Taylor Mountain

for a 3,000-foot spring run to Wyoming Route 22. Interesting cliffs rim the canyon, and you'll encounter short, avoidable cliffs during the descent.

West Slope: {B} Ski this beautiful meadow in shallow powder.

Powder Reserve: {D} and {E} This classic, mile-wide, 400-foot face drops off the east side of the north ridge of Point 9,705. Yoyo it when everything else is tracked up.

Taylor Mountain (10,352 feet): Bordered by Moose Creek in the north, Mesquite and Coal creeks in the east, and Trail Creek in the south, Taylor Mountain is one of the largest massifs in the range. Approach via Mount Glory-Taylor Mountain; from Coal Creek via the south face, south ridge, or southeast ridge; from Moose Creek via Bear Canyon or Nordwall Canyon Pack Trail; or from Wyoming Route 22 via Hungry Creek or Talbot Canyon.

East Face: {F} This classic Teton descent is safest when skied early on spring mornings. Large cornices are the norm at the top of the face.

(Early free-heel: Davey Agnew, Gary Beebe and Todd Stearns; early 1970s.)

South Face (Poop Chute): {F} With its short approach, direct line, consistent 35-degree pitch, and 2,800-foot relief, this is one of the classic descents of the range. Spring is the safest time of year to ski it but it has become a frequent winter descent for both skiers and avalanches.

On April 19, 1995, snowboarder Kevin Marriott was killed after the cornice on which he was standing collapsed. He slid 700 feet off the south ridge and was buried for four hours in a V-shaped gully. An intense rescue effort couldn't save him.

(Early fixed-heel: Chuck Satterfield; early 1970s.)

West Face: {D} to {E} Although this convex face commonly is wind-hammered and broken by cliff bands, you must ski it to reach the more suitable ski terrain west of the summit. A cliff-band-free route and better snow usually are available slightly south of the summit.

Taylor Basin: {E} Almost completely ringed by

cliffs above, this glacial scoop makes a prime yoyoing area. You may ski a route directly north off the summit into the basin, but it is extremely avalanche-prone. To exit the basin, traverse to Bear Canyon or climb to the top of Squaw or Talbot canyon. The draw that drains Taylor Basin is blocked by cliffs. Mike Whitehead discovered this the hard way and had to throw his skis off and jump!

West Face of North Ridge: {D} This mile-wide convex face offers moderate, sparsely forested slopes into Taylor Basin. But a cliff near the bottom of the face forces skiers north.

North Couloir: {E} This 1,500-foot avalanche gully drops north from Taylor's summit ridge to Moose Meadows.

(Early free-heel: Skeeter Cattabriga and Mark Dawson. February, 1995; John Collins and Mike Best followed moments later.)

HIGH ROUTES

Mount Glory-Phillips Pass: {D} This is the most popular high-ridge traverse in the range. Follow the undulating, curving ridge about four miles between these points. You'll encounter tricky sections of rocks or steep side-hilling near Moby Dick and points 9,375 and 9,250.

Mount Glory-Taylor Mountain: {E} This popular high route is an enjoyable way to reach the summit of Taylor Mountain for descents of its east and south faces or tours to points west. Traverse the north ridge of Mount Glory to Point 10,032. Continue north, contouring just below steep areas on the west side of Moby Dick and through sparse forest—for a total of two miles—to Pass 9,197 (Mesquite Divide). To reach the Taylor Mountain summit, climb the steep east ridge of Point 10,068 and follow the mile-long north ridge.

RAMMEL MOUNTAIN MASSIF

Contained by South Bitch Creek Canyon on the north and east and South Badger Creek on the south, this vast forested highland contains just two major peaks, Rammel and Dry Ridge. The long, monotonous approaches into the region compel many skiers to use snowmobiles or four-wheel drive vehicles on rugged roads below treeline. Although clearcuts and logging roads riddle the countryside, a treasure trove of relatively untainted bowls awaits hardy skiers in the enormous headwaters of South Bitch Creek.

For detailed reference to the Rammel Mountain Massif, use USGS maps for Rammel Mountain, Clawson, McRenolds Reservoir, Ranger Peak, Mount Moran, Granite Basin, and Lamont.

Dry Ridge Mountain's 2,100-foot west side is a vast avalanche path that offers good skiing in safe conditions. In 1992, however, a mile-wide avalanche claimed the life of snowmobiler Dan Schwendiman.

APPROACHES

Coyote Meadows Road (Ashton Ranger District Road No. 265): See Northern Range.

Bitch Creek Canyon: {D} Stretching more than 25 miles between Teton Valley and Dead Horse Pass and draining more than 15 miles of the Teton Crest, this canyon is, by far, the most extensive in the range. The headwaters are surrounded by some of the most elegant bowls and the highest peaks on and near the Teton Crest, including Glacier and Doubtful peaks and Dry Ridge and Rammel mountains.

Because the lower canyon is relatively uninteresting, most skiers approach the headwaters directly. From the west, use Badger Creek High Route to Dead Horse Pass. From the east, cross over Pass 10,160-plus from the north branch of Snowshoe south fork.

Approach from Coyote Meadows to access lower Bitch Creek. Climb a draw southeast of Coyote Meadows and gain a ridge. Then contour east into the next drainage south and gain another ridge farther south.

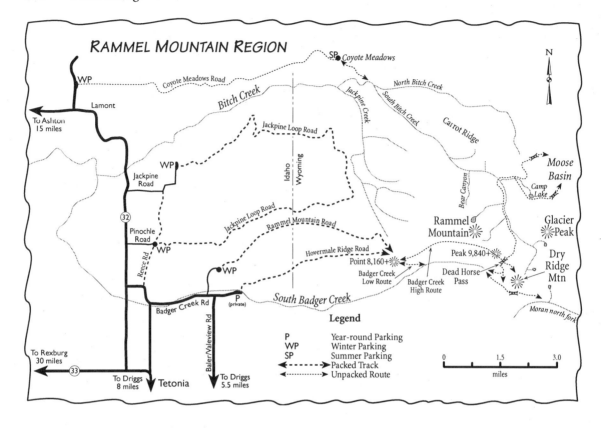

From there, drop into Bitch Creek Canyon above the narrows. This circuitous route bypasses a very narrow section of the canyon south of Coyote Meadows, above which the canyon forks immediately; be sure to bear right. Higher in the canyon, Bitch Creek Narrows is best negotiated on the northeast side of the creek.

Jackpine-Pinochle Loop Road (Teton Basin Ranger District road No. 266): {A} It might be possible to use the northern member of this loop as an alternate approach to Bitch Creek Canyon. Follow Idaho Route 32 for nine miles north of Tetonia, Idaho. Turn right on Jackpine Road, and drive 2.5 miles to a parking area.

Rammel Mountain Road: {B} Two advantages to using this road instead of the Hovermale Ridge Road are its superior parking facilities and its straightforward course. Skiers can get out of their cars, get on this road, put down their heads, and follow the main snowmobile track

nearly 11 miles to Point 8,160-plus. But the road begins dreadfully far from the mountains and makes a huge bend north during its indirect route into them.

Follow the Badger Creek approach to the T intersection. Turn left and drive a third of a mile. Turn right on Rammel Mountain Road, which crosses a flat and climbs a shallow draw to the north.

Hovermale Ridge Road (Targhee National Forest Road No. 398): {B} Pronounced 'Hoovermail,' this is the easiest, most efficient access to Point 8,160-plus, the culmination of the huge, gentle plateau bordered on the west by Teton Valley, on the north by Bitch Creek, on the east by Jackpine Creek, and on the south by Badger Creek south fork. Travel on the ridge is easy—mostly across large clearcuts—and views are abundant.

Follow the same access as for South Badger Creek, then cross the creek and ascend a shallow draw just north of the residences at the end of the road to gain Hovermale Ridge.

The east end of Hovermale Ridge Road joins the Rammel Mountain Road just north of Point 8,160-plus. Although they aren't as plentiful here as they are on the Rammel Mountain Road, snowmobile tracks help with route-finding and trail-breaking. Still, route-finding at the west end of Hovermale Ridge is tricky because snowmobile tracks and roadcuts shoot in all directions. In firm conditions, Hovermale Ridge can be one of the quickest western exits from the Tetons. It heads downhill for nearly 7.5 miles from its intersection with the Rammel Mountain Road.

Jackpine Creek: {D} This clearcut-scarred drainage flows northwest into Bitch Creek from the Rammel Mountain Massif. Terry Brattain made one of the few ski tours ever here. Approach from Hovermale Ridge, Jackpine-Pinochle Road, Coyote Meadows, or Rammel Mountain Road.

South Badger Creek: {C} Thick pine forests, absence of a trail and pitch, wildly meandering braided streams, and long distances make lower Badger Creek canyon a poor choice for ski travel. On the other hand, upper Badger Creek provides easy ski travel and leads to some terrific terrain, notably the south face of the Rammel Mountain massif, the west face of Dry Ridge Mountain, and north-side routes on Green Lakes Mountain. Badger Creek Canyon comes to a head at Pass 9,680-plus, the lowest point on the Teton Crest between Fox Creek Pass and Pass 9,600-plus, north of Glacier Peak.

From Idaho Highway 33 north, bear right five miles north of Driggs, where the road turns west into Tetonia. Continue another four miles, then turn right at the T and drive to the end of the road. Ask homeowners there for permission to park your car and ski across their property.

PEAKS AND BOWLS

Rammel Mountain (10,140 feet): This remote, challenging mountain—the highest non-divide peak north of Peak 10,643—is quite worthy of attention from ski mountaineers.

Although much of the Rammel Massif can be accessed from South Bitch Creek, the best approach is via Hovermale Ridge to Point 8,294 on the lower southwest ridge of Rammel Mountain. From there, the quickest, easiest route to the summit runs northeast from Point 8,935 toward the west face. Approaching the west face by way of Indian Meadows is easy, but it's long and crosses through thick forests.

West Face: {D} This 25-degree face is the Rammel's most accessible and most popular route.

Other potential routes: Two impressive southeast couloirs drop off the summit into upper South Bitch Creek. At least six relatively unexplored, northeast-facing glacial pockets, rimmed by wondrous bowls, abut the long ridge between points 9,789 and 9,592. Bear Canyon and the basin of Lake 8,660 offer the most extensive terrain. One couloir drops off the northwest ridge of Rammel to Lake 8,660 at the 9,800-foot level. Many bowls here are avalanche-prone.

Peak 9,840-plus: This conical peak, just west of Dead Horse Pass, offers superb terrain on its east and north faces. Access from South Badger Creek, Badger Creek High Route, or South Bitch Creek.

Dry Ridge Mountain (10,321 feet): Viewed from the summit of Mount Moran, this peak's triangular, planar southeast face could {E} inspire skiers to endure long approaches up Moran Canyon, South Badger Creek, South Bitch Creek, or Dry Ridge.

Potential ski routes include the vast bowls of the northeastern cwm, which forms the headwaters of South Bitch Creek. The 2,100-foot west side is a vast avalanche path that offers good skiing in safe conditions. Unfortunately, when snowmobilers Dan Schwendiman and Gary Ball were here, they hit the wrong place at the wrong time, propagating a mile-wide avalanche as they climbed toward Dead Horse Pass. Consistent warmth that week caused free water to weaken the snowpack. A week-long rescue effort drew hundreds to the scene by snowmobile, helicopter, and skis. The avalanche killed Schwendiman and broke Ball's leg.

HIGH ROUTES

Badger Creek High Route: {D} This safe, scenic high ridge is the primary western access to Dead Horse Pass and the bowls and basins southeast of Rammel Mountain.

Badger Creek Low Route: {C} From the saddle east of Point 8,160-plus, it's easy to descend on gentle, forested slopes southeast into Badger Creek south fork. From the bottom of Badger Creek, try to resist the temptation to continue to Teton Valley via the canyon. It is much easier and quicker to climb this route, then descend the Hovermale Ridge road.

South Badger Creek-Moose Basin: {E} Ray White, John Carr and John Connors used this route during a tram-to-Flagg Ranch-crest tour one June in the early 1970s. It's the safest and easiest route around the Doubtful/Glacier massif. From the north end of the Littles Peak-South Badger Creek route, cross over Dead Horse Pass and ski carefully down avalanche terrain for four miles and 2,000 feet to Hidden Corral Basin in South Bitch Creek. To regain the crest, climb steeply via Camp Lake to either Nord Pass or Pass 9,600-plus, north of Glacier Peak. To reach Moose Basin from Nord Pass, ski over the crest near some finger-like limestone spires between Moose Mountain and Peak 10,360.

South Badger Creek-Moran Canyon north fork: {E} Make a nice traverse into Moran north fork via a steep but short couloir below Pass 9,680-plus.

FRED'S MOUNTAIN REGION

Perpetual snowfall, sparse forests, high, windswept ridges, vast scenic plateaus, and ample snowbowls characterize this broad section of the Teton Range. The image immortalized on Grand Targhee Resort brochures is a skier slicing turns in profile down a deep powder slope, the Teton high peaks jutting in the background. The snow is so deep that it bulges around the sparse, cloaked trees of Mary's Nipple and Steve Baugh Memorial Bowl.

This region stretches from the north wall of Teton Canyon north to Dry Ridge Road and includes all crest points from the 10,686 Plateau to Green Lakes Mountain. Lengthy approaches relegate most skiing here to overnight trips.

For detailed reference to the Fred's Mountain Region, use USGS maps for Clawson, Granite Basin, Mount

Moran, and Rammel Mountain.

APPROACHES

Dry Ridge Road (Targhee National Forest Road No. 013): {C} From the 90-degree turn near Tetonia, Idaho, on Highway 33, head east for two miles, then turn left at the sign for Dry Ridge. Dry Ridge Road is the first right—about 1.25 miles north—but is not marked. There is no parking area, so shovel your own parking spot.

Follow snowmobile tracks on the ridge crest, around the north side of Crow's Nest to the South Badger/North Leigh divide. In the opposite direction, ski west and downhill for more than 10 miles to Teton Valley.

North Leigh Creek Canyon (Targhee National Forest Road No. 007, North Leigh Road): {B} Of the popular west-side canyons, this one lies farthest north. From the 90-degree turn near Tetonia, Idaho, on Highway 33, head east and follow signs to North Leigh Creek. You won't find a parking area at the end of the road, so shovel out your own spot.

The summer road allows easy flat-tracking from

Frequented both by backcountry skiers and avalanches, Steve Baugh Memorial Bowl adds yet another astonishing attraction to the view from Grand Targhee Resort in Alta, Wyoming.

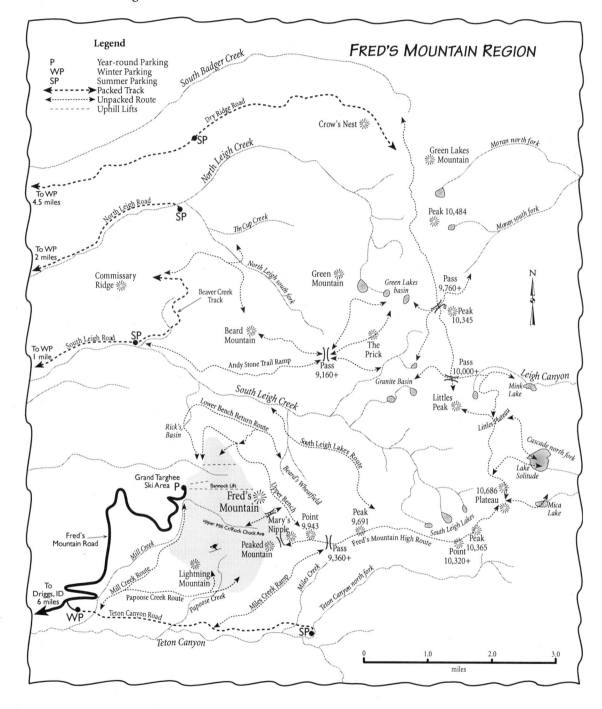

Legend

P	Year-round Parking
WP	Winter Parking
SP	Summer Parking
●–––––>	Packed Track
<···········>	Unpacked Route
––––––	Uphill Lifts

FRED'S MOUNTAIN REGION

South Badger Creek

Dry Ridge Road

Crow's Nest

Green Lakes Mountain

Moran north fork

SP

North Leigh Creek

Peak 10,484

Moran south fork

To WP
4.5 miles

North Leigh Road

SP

Tin Cup Creek

Green
Mountain

Green Lakes
basin

Pass
9,760+

N

To WP
2 miles

North Leigh south fork

Peak
10,345

Commissary
Ridge

Beaver Creek
Track

The Prick

Pass
10,000+

Leigh Canyon

Mink
Lake

To WP
1 mile

South Leigh Road

SP

Beard
Mountain

Andy Stone Trail Ramp

Pass
9,160+

Granite Basin

Littles
Peak

Littles Plateau

Cascade north fork

South Leigh Creek

Lower Bench Return Route

Rick's
Basin

South Leigh Lakes Route

Lake
Solitude

Mica
Lake

Beard's Wheatfield

10,686
Plateau

Grand Targhee
Ski Area   P

Bannock Lift

Fred's
Mountain

Upper Bench

Peak
9,691

South Leigh Lakes

Fred's
Mountain Road

Upper Mill Cr/Rock Chuck Ave

Mary's
Nipple

Point
9,943

Peak
10,365

Fred's Mountain High Route

Point
10,320+

Mill Creek

Peaked
Mountain

Pass
9,360+

To
Driggs, ID
6 miles

Mill Creek Route

Lightning
Mountain

Miles Creek Ramp

Papoose Creek Route

Papoose Creek

Miles Creek

Teton Canyon north fork

WP

Teton Canyon Road

SP

Teton Canyon

0	1.0	2.0	3.0

miles

the end of the plowed road to the fork of the canyon. Access to or from Dry Ridge on the sparsely forested south slopes poses little difficulty from anywhere along this road {D}. But thick forests on the south side of the canyon makes access to Commissary Ridge impractical.

If you are heading for the south fork, go all the way to the end of the road before turning south. Don't let false drainages that look like forks on the south side of the canyon fool you into leaving the road. The south fork accesses Green Mountain, The Prick, and the north facets of Beard Mountain.

North Leigh main fork leads to beautiful Green Lakes basin. Steep windward slopes and small cliffs extend a mile and a half above the basin between Green Lakes Mountain and Peak 10,484. You'll find wind-loaded bowls on the northeast sides of Green Mountain and The Prick.

Beaver Creek Track: {C} This short, wide draw is the primary approach to Beard Mountain and Rendezvous Ski Tours' Commissary Ridge yurt, and it offers excellent, easy ski terrain to boot. After a three-mile flat tour up South Leigh Creek, the well-worn track turns north up the west side of the Beaver Creek bottom.

Andy Stone Trail Ramp: {E} This ramp follows a bed of Bighorn Dolomite, providing relatively gentle access from South Leigh Creek to The Prick, Green Mountain, and North Leigh south fork. The ridglet on the south side of the ramp seems to be the easiest, safest route, though it is quite narrow and is strewn with brush and deadfall in places. The ramp is difficult to locate for skiers heading up from the bottom of South Leigh because of thick forest and low-angle terrain. Just ski along the base of Beard Mountain until you reach a small creek. Follow the creek up and left. All told, the Andy Stone Trail Ramp is not an enjoyable tour route, but it is useful for exiting the North Leigh high country.

South Leigh Creek Canyon (Targhee National Forest Road No. 008, South Leigh Road): {B} From the 90-degree turn near Tetonia, Idaho, on Highway 33, head east and follow the road until it bears right and uphill to a private residence. Park on the north side of the road, west of the fork, at the turn below the resi-

dence to avoid having your car towed. A good ski track leads up the road straight east from this turn.

Travel is easy for five miles in the lower canyon, until the ski track turns up Beaver Creek and snowmobile tracks turn around at the wilderness boundary. From here on, expect difficult trail-breaking.

The tedious approach up this canyon leads to South Leigh Lakes and Granite Basin. If you intend to ski the bowls at the head of South Leigh, approach from Grand Targhee via Fred's Mountain High Route.

Fred's Mountain Road: Plowed since the late 1960s, this often dangerously icy road climbs precipitously from Alta, Wyoming to the base of Grand Targhee Resort.

Mill Creek: {D} This popular, narrow canyon drains the mini-cirque between Fred's Mountain, Mary's Nipple and Peaked Mountain. Approach the mouth of the drainage where it meets the Teton Canyon Road at the old winter parking area. Access the draw at its midpoint by dropping gradually to the south from the base of Grand Targhee Resort. To approach the upper basin, ski south off the Bannock ski lift. An in-bounds cat-track runs along the north side of the creek.

In descending the lower canyon, skiers can follow a cat-track that traverses above the creek on the east side; it is used to return snowcat skiers to the resort. At the end of the cat-track, continue contouring south on the east side of the creek to avoid the narrow, thickly forested creek bottom. Then ski nice forested terrain into Teton Canyon by turning west down the ridge between Teton and Mill creeks. For a more pristine tour, drop into the creek from the summer trailhead, just south of the resort parking lot.

On Jan. 23, 1991, the "Mill Creek Four"—John Grassi, Skeeter Cattabriga, Ray Warburton and Don Lingle—tried to access the backcountry east of the ski area by ascending Mill Creek. They crossed into an area closed by the resort, were cited by the ski patrol, and faced criminal charges. The foursome was determined to fight the ticket in court but the resort dropped the charges before that became necessary.

Papoose Creek Route: {E} This steep draw

drains south from the Lightning Mountain/Peaked Peak saddle. During a descent of the southwest side of Peaked, avoid steep, removed lower Papoose Creek by heading west to a small col at 7,600 feet, then continuing into lower Mill Creek.

Miles Creek Ramp: {D} Following a feature similar to the Andy Stone Trail Ramp, this route connects Teton Canyon, near the boy scout camp, to Pass 9,360-plus, at the head of Beard's Wheatfield.

Teton Canyon: See Teton Canyon Region.

PEAKS AND BOWLS

Crow's Nest: This high point of Dry Ridge offers few skiing opportunities, except in the bowls on the northwest side. The south couloirs might make good runs if they weren't filled with avalanche debris.

Green Lakes Mountain (10,195 feet): Perched high at the remote head of Moran Canyon north fork, this obscure peak actually has been the site of some skiing. On Feb. 10, 1991, Tom Bennett and this author skinned up the rocky north ridge and postholed down a southwest tree chute to reach the South Badger/North Leigh divide.

Potential routes: The fantastic wind-loaded east-face snow pyramid sports bowls stretching north and south for miles. The northwest couloir extends nearly 1,000 feet into South Badger Creek, and angling north off the northeast shoulder is a nice route into South Badger Creek.

Peak 10,484: This multifaceted mountain is the highest peak in the headwaters of Moran Canyon. Potential routes include the southwest face of the south summit and the impressive triangular northeast face above Moran Canyon north fork. Approach from Green Lakes basin or Moran Canyon.

Green Mountain (9,614 feet): If this mountain wasn't so remote, it would be among the most popular beginner to intermediate areas in the range. Approach from North Leigh Creek, Commissary Ridge or South Leigh Creek via the Andy Stone Trail Ramp. If approaching from North Leigh, try to follow the summer Green Mountain Trail, which ascends a clearing on the north edge of the west face. If you follow the south fork too far, you'll encounter difficult, dangerous and steep gullies and headwalls.

West Face: {C} This broad, rolling face ranges from 10 degrees to 20 degrees for more than 1,200 feet.

Peak 9,974 (The Prick): Combined with Green Mountain, this elegant mountain comprises the largest open plateau on the west slope. Approach from North Leigh Creek, Beard Mountain via Beard Mountain High Route, or South Leigh Creek via the Andy Stone Trail Ramp.

West Ridge: {C} This classic, treeless spur drops 900 feet in one mile to Pass 9,160-plus.

Northwest Face: {C} Gently sloping nearly 1,800 feet in a mile and a half, this is the longest open face of its grade in the range.

Other potential routes: The south face offers several good spring runs into Granite Basin.

Peak 10,345: Nice bowls grace the northeast side of this lonely crest peak at the head of Moran Canyon south fork.

Commissary Ridge: Rendezvous Ski Tours owns and operates a yurt on this ridge west of Beaver Creek. An easy tour starts up Beaver Creek, gains the ridge, then follows it west until you can find a nice route back into South Leigh Creek. You'll find short, enjoyable shots on the north side of the ridge.

Beard Mountain (9,466 feet): Named for a ranching family living at the mouth of South Leigh Creek Canyon, this mountain is a skiers' favorite. Approach from South Leigh Creek via Beaver Creek. Two standard methods will get you to the summit: From the head of Beaver Creek, follow the north ridge of Beard easily to the summit; or zigzag straight up the south edge of the west face.

West Face: {D} This popular, broad bowl has a relatively short approach and a moderate pitch as it angles into Beaver Creek. Aspen groves make it a magical place to ski.

South Face: {E} This face is long, steep, and recommended only for spring skiing. Watch out for rocks and cliffs.

Northeastern Cwm: {E} The north and east sides of the mountain contain large avalanche bowls that empty into a beautiful, remote basin, which drains into North Leigh south fork.

Littles Peak (10,712 feet): This large, conical crest peak often is wind-scoured. Most skiing here has been ridge tour-ing. In the right conditions, how-ever, you can find excellent skiing on the south and west faces, and in the five gullies on the southwest side. Approach from South or North Leigh creeks, Granite Basin, and Leigh or Cas-cade canyon.

G r a n d Targhee Ski Area: Much to the chagrin of backcountry ski-ers, this superb lift-served ski area encompasses some of the best ski terrain on the west side of the Tetons. Approach from Fred's Mountain Road. The resort holds a U.S. Forest Service lease and governs use of the land within its permit area, which includes Mary's Nipple, and Fred's, Peaked and Lightning mountains.

Though it is not the highest peak of the group, Fred's Mountain (more than 9,880 feet) is the most prominent; it was opened to the public—served by two chair lifts—in 1969. Its original name, Mount Baldy, more accurately describes its broad, convex, sparsely forested west face.

Mary's Nipple is the highest summit of the group, at more than 9,920 feet, and sits at the head of Mill Creek, a mile southeast of the Bannock ski lift top station. Peaked (9,827 feet) and Lightning (8,452 feet) mountains opened to cat skiing in the early 1990s and since have been approved for chair-lift development.

The issue of backcountry access through the ski area has been controversial. Backcountry skiers covet Fred's Mountain Road and resort parking for the highest and quickest winter access from Teton Val-ley into the Tetons. Skirting the ski-area boundary to en-ter backcountry to the east is im-practical, so ski-ers cross through the resort's permit area. In the in-terest of safety, however, the re-sort limits uphill travel on Fred's Mountain and on Teton Vista Traverse.

Its "user policy" states that Targhee will not open or close permit-area boundaries but that it will control all use within its boundaries. So backcountry skiers who want to pass through the ski area must ask the ski patrol which routes are open to uphill traffic at the time.

Teton Vista Traverse cat track is the standard route from the resort base up Mill Creek. It traverses south from the base of Bannock Chair into Mill Creek, then climbs the north flank toward Mary's Nipple. But it usually is closed to uphill traffic during ski-area hours, especially on busy days.

This western aerial view shows the Grand Targhee Ski Area, including Fred's Mountain, Mary's Nipple, and Peaked Mountain.

Rock Chuck Avenue ascends the south flank of Mill Creek but is open to uphill travel only when the patrol has secured the area from avalanche danger. Triangle Flats Traverse cat track enters Mill Creek lower than Teton Vista Traverse, then gains the west ridge of Peaked Mountain. It also may be used to access the backcountry, but only when opened by the patrol and, even then, only before or after ski-area hours. Skiers also may purchase single-ride tickets and access the backcountry from Bannock Lift via Teton Vista Traverse if the Fourth of July/Rock Chuck Avenue areas and Mary's Nipple are open to the saddle.

In the late 1980s and early 90s, resort owners battled with Forest Service, area residents, and environmental groups about plans to expand the resort. Public opposition blocked proposed ridge-top residential development, but a 1994 Environmental Impact Statement paved the way for expansion of base facilities, as well as new lifts on Lightning and Peaked mountains.

Following is a handful of out-of-bounds areas located on Mary's Nipple and Fred's, Peaked, and Lightning mountains:

Lightning Mountain South Face: {D} This corn classic finishes at a small col at the 7,600-foot level on the Papoose Creek Route.

Peaked Mountain Southeast Face: {F} Ski this 3,000-foot bowl and one of two couloirs in early morning spring corn to the Miles Creek Ramp and Teton Canyon.

Mary's Nipple South Face: {F} Choose between two couloirs through the Bighorn Dolomite during this 3,000-foot early morning spring corn run to the Miles Creek Ramp and Teton Canyon.

Fred's Mountain Southeast Couloir: {F} This steep chute drops to the Upper Bench Return Route, just northwest of Point 9,628.

Point 9,770 East Face: {E} This steep, precarious sheet of snow plummets to the Upper Bench Return Route from the north end of Fred's summit ridge.

Lower Northeast Ridge: {F} This abrupt spur climbs from Point 8,522 to the northwest ridge of Fred's Mountain. Primarily, it is used to regain the ski area from the Upper Bench Return Route when severe avalanche conditions rule out traversing the North Avalanche Path safely. Even with severe exposure, dangerous sugar snow, and third-class rock climbing, this ridge often is the lesser of two evils.

North Avalanche Path: {E} Dropping north into South Leigh Creek from North Boundary, this extremely dangerous avalanche bowl is a ski run only for the most knowledgeable avalanche professionals. Luckily, only one fatal accident has occurred here. An avalanche sent a man and his dog over a 300-foot cliff and killed them near this formidable 1,700-foot run. After skiing to the edge of the cliff, the pair triggered the avalanche when they tried to zigzag back up.

Grand Targhee Nordic Center: Established in 1975, the Grand Targhee Nordic Center offers a full-service shop and rentals. Its myriad terrain and trails circle scenic Dry Creek Basin and Rick's Basin. Approach from Fred's Mountain Road.

Point 9,943: This handsome summit lies a mile southeast of Fred's Mountain. Approach via Fred's Mountain High Route or the Mill Creek-Upper Bench route.

South Face: {F} Ski this 3,000-foot face in early morning spring corn. Choose one of three couloirs through the Bighorn Dolomite to the Miles Creek Ramp and Teton Canyon.

Steve Baugh Memorial Bowl: {E} This classic, steep northwest face runs onto the Upper Bench Return Route. On April 7, 1993, Jeff Jung jumped the cornice above the bowl and triggered a large slab avalanche that buried all but his legs. His partner, Hollis McElwain, extricated him. The safest run avoids a steep avalanche bowl by following a line of trees directly northwest of the summit.

Peak 9,691: This elegant peak lies a mile west of Point 9,943. Approach via the Miles Creek Ramp or Fred's Mountain High Route. To make an adventurous loop back to the ski area or South Leigh Creek, use the Lower Bench Return Route or the South Leigh Lakes Route.

Beard's Wheatfield: {B} Sprawling nearly one mile square, first sight of this huge, treeless bowl shocks most skiers. But their excitement diminishes when they realize how gentle the slope is. If it was easier to access, Beard's would be a perfect beginner slope. But its location allows only experienced ski mountaineers to tour its vast open spaces.

West Peak-north face: {D} This 200-foot bowl offers prime powder yoyoing above Beard's Wheatfield.

The Great White Bed: {D} This 500-foot, convex, northwest face is the yoyoing treasure of South Leigh Creek.

Other potential routes: The mile-long, east-facing wall offers good spring yoyoing terrain. It ranges from 100 feet to 600 feet high and stretches between Peak 9,691 and Point 9,203. The fluted northeast bowl releases skiers into remote South Leigh Lakes.

Point 10,320-plus: This handsome snow-dome along the Fred's Mountain High Route is nestled between South Leigh Lakes and Teton Canyon north fork.

Potential routes: A 1,700-foot, south-facing snowdrift leads into Teton Canyon, while the north bowls lead 1,000 feet gently to South Leigh Lakes.

Peak 10,365: Some 3.25 miles east of Mary's Nipple, along the Fred's Mountain High Route, this peak offers at least three south-facing spring runs into Teton Canyon north fork and large north-facing bowls above South Leigh Lakes.

10,686 Plateau: This expansive plateau is the culmination of South Leigh Canyon. Most of its numerous west-facing bowls are wind-scoured, limiting skiing to ridge touring. Approach via Fred's Mountain High Route, South Leigh Creek, Cascade Canyon, or Teton Canyon north fork. See High Routes for the many tours that employ this plateau crossroads.

HIGH ROUTES

North Leigh Creek south fork-Commissary Ridge: {D} Use this route only in safe avalanche conditions to return to Commissary Ridge from the northeastern cwm of Beard Mountain. It follows the line of the summer trail that traverses steep avalanche slopes on the north end of Beard's north ridge.

Beard Mountain High Route: {F} Once deemed too technical to ski, this intricate route connects solitary Beard Mountain with the rest of the range. From the summit, ski east along the ridge until you reach a rocky knife edge. Traverse on exposed slopes on the south side and climb to the top of Beard's east summit. Remove your skis and downclimb through trees via a third-class chimney on the southeast side of the peak to a ramp, which is easy to follow west to the pass. Use caution during winter attempts of this route due to fragile cornices and steep, unconsolidated snow.

Pass 9,160-plus-Green Lakes basin: {E} or {F} Choose one of two dangerous options to exit east from the Beard Mountain massif. From the pass, either climb to the summit of The Prick or to the saddle between The Prick and Green Mountain. From the summit, Ray White and Bev Boynton downclimbed the steep cornice-capped northeast chute to reach upper Green Lakes basin in 1991. From the saddle option, ski a moderate wind-loaded slope into the basin.

Pass 9,160-plus-Granite Basin: {E} To exit southeast from the Beard Mountain massif, follow the summer trail across the steep south-facing avalanche slopes of The Prick into the basin.

Granite or Green Lakes basins-Moran Canyon south fork: {C} Just north of Peak 10,345 and a small lake, make an easy passage between the high plateaus of these west-side basins and the rolling paradise of bowls in Moran south fork. Beverly Boynton, Bob Graham, Matthew Goewert and this author used this route to access Cleaver Peak during two separate climbing attempts in January of 1992 and March of 1993.

Littles Peak-South Badger Creek: {C} This classic stretch of the Teton Crest traverse follows a sloping bench along the west side of Peak 10,484 and Green Lakes Mountain. From Littles Peak, make a descending traverse across the head of Granite Basin and drop into Green Lakes basin. From a bowl southwest of Peak 10,484, make an ascending traverse north to a bench, which you'll follow north a mile to South Badger Creek.

Mink Lake-Granite Basin: {E} Scott

Berkenfield, Ray White and Beverly Boynton used this route during two traverses between Leigh and South Leigh in the 1980s and 1991. White and Boynton traveled west to east. A cornice might hinder the crossing at Pass 10,000-plus, north of Littles Peak.

Littles Plateau-Mink Lake: {D} Forrest McCarthy and this author made this safe, fun descent on April 14, 1993, while retreating from a Teton Crest

traverse attempt in a blizzard. From the plateau southeast of Littles Peak, drop north down a shallow gully and turn west down a windblown shoulder into the head of Leigh Canyon. Spiral back east to arrive at Mink Lake.

10,686 Plateau-Littles Peak: {E} Use this high-ridge route to gain the northern Teton Crest from Grand Targhee. From the plateau, downclimb northwest on third-class rock and follow the sharp ridge to Littles Plateau. Ascend the easy south ridge of Littles Peak.

10,686 Plateau-Lake Solitude: {E} In April of

After a long day of yoyoing on Beard Mountain's west face, skiers can kick back in the alpenglow of dusk and check out their signatures from the Commissary Ridge Yurt.

1982, Peter Koedt crossed the range from Grand Targhee via Lake Solitude. He encountered third-class rock climbing while descending the northwest ridge of Point 10,686, then dropped into Cascade Canyon at the first col. Cornices often block easy passage.

10,686 Plateau-Mica Lake: {E} This classic link allowed Peter Koedt, Larry Young, and Tom Balben to make a moderate, direct traverse between Grand Targhee and Cascade Canyon south fork in February of 1983. From the shallow saddle between two high points in the plateau, the trio chose one of two gaps through east-facing cliffs and kicked steps down 200 feet of 50- to 55-degree snow slopes.

Lower Bench Return Route: {D} After skiing bowls above Beard's Wheatfield, this scenic, undulating Gallatin Limestone bench provides a long, strenuous, and potentially dangerous circumnavigation of Fred's Mountain to the ski-area base or South Leigh Creek. For speed and safety, attempt this only in firm or shallow snow and only under the most stable avalanche conditions. Be prepared for an adventure. It is safer and faster to return to Grand Targhee Resort by climbing Point 9,943 and traversing west to Mill Creek or Peaked Mountain.

At the bottom of Beard's Wheatfield, cross a V-shaped drainage, then turn west around Fred's northeast ridge and traverse under dolomite cliffs for almost two miles. During the traverse, you will turn around one more ridge and encounter thick forest and avalanche-runout zones. From the final clearing on the bench, make an ascending traverse through sparse trees, past some cliffs, and into a gully that leads to Rick's Basin. Climb to the top of Rick's Basin and cross the head of Dry Creek to reach the ski-area base. To reach South Leigh Creek, simply ski down an easy clearing from the final clearing on the bench.

Upper Bench-Lower Bench: {G} The three-mile-long Bighorn Dolomite cliff band that separates these two benches is a classic example of the obstacles that Teton skiers must overcome to link skiable areas. Gaps in this cliff that do not require technical skills are very few. On Nov. 15, 1994, Mark Limage, Wes Bunch, Russell Rainey and this author searched for a safe route through the cliff from the Lower to the Upper bench. Two possibilities on the west face of the cliff fizzled upon closer inspection. We continued on the Lower Bench Return Route around Point 8,945 and followed some fox tracks up a feasible but strenuous north-facing couloir just east of Point 8,522. Deep, late-season snow might make one of the west-facing options more practical.

Upper Bench Return Route: {E} After skiing runs like Steve Baugh Bowl, this scenic, undulating Bighorn Dolomite bench provides a long, strenuous, and potentially dangerous tour around Fred's Mountain and back to the ski-area base. Attempt this only in the most stable avalanche conditions and only if your party is prepared for an adventure. It certainly is safer and faster to return to Grand Targhee by reversing Mill Creek-Upper Bench or by climbing Point 9,943 and traversing west to Mill Creek or Peaked Mountain.

Schuss northwest down the bench under Fred's west-face cliffs and climb a short snowdrift to gain the northeast ridge of Fred's Mountain. Turn west and ski or traverse across a large bowl below Fred's north-face cliffs. This is where the tour enters severe avalanche terrain. Carefully gain the lower northeast ridge of Fred's near Point 8,522 and ascend the ridge to the top of North Boundary in the ski area. Expect severe exposure, dangerous sugar snow, and third-class rock climbing on this ridge.

Another option for finishing the route is to traverse west from Point 8,522, across two extremely avalanche-prone bowls, and regain the ski area at North Boundary Traverse, above Rick's Basin.

South Leigh Lakes Route: {D} Use this long, sloping shale and sandstone ramp for fun, scenic travel between South Leigh Lakes and South Leigh Creek.

Mill Creek-Upper Bench: {F} From the Bannock ski lift, traverse on a cat track into upper Mill Creek and drop over the saddle between Fred's Mountain and Mary's Nipple to the upper bench via a steep, narrow break in a cliff. Rocks might block passage in early season or during low snow years.

Fred's Mountain High Route: {E} Use this classic undulating ridge traverse to connect Fred's Mountain with the Teton Crest. From the saddle, make an ascending traverse east across the steep, south-facing avalanche slopes of Mary's Nipple and Point 9,943. In the early to mid-1980s, Clark Kido was caught in a slab avalanche while traversing here. Try this one only in the safest conditions.

Descend to Pass 9,360-plus at the top of Beard's Wheatfield and Miles Creek Ramp. Continue east on the ridgetop, then either contour across the north side of Point 10,320-plus or climb to its summit. Climb the west ridge of Peak 10,365 and ski its steep north face to a narrow ramp leading east. At the end of the ramp, climb to the 10,365/10,686 saddle and ascend a steep ridgeline north to 10,686 Plateau.

TETON CANYON REGION

This region encompasses two distinct areas, separated by the half-mile-deep chasm of Teton Canyon. Draining into this curving valley from the south and west lies the Peak 10,643 Massif. Bordered by the steep walls of Darby Canyon on the south and Teton Canyon on the north and east, this land of high plateaus, vast forests, and steep-sided creeks might be the Tetons' most detached mountain massif. As a result, most skiing here involves day trips focused on powder skiing and plateau touring. Spring Creek, Eddington Canyon and the Hogback Trail are the principal approach routes to the fantastic powder bowls of Chicken Knob and the beautiful windswept plateau of Peak 10,643.

Draining from the east into Teton Canyon, the rolling crest peaks between the 10,686 Plateau and

Grant Hagen (left) and Herman Seherr-Thoss revel in the scenery of upper Cascade Canyon. During this late spring 1942 tour, they skied into the middle fork, which they named Brown's Basin, in honor of Fred Brown.

Buck Mountain comprise the balance of this region. Much of the skiing in this region of the Teton Crest involves width traverses via Teton and Cascade canyons. But Table Mountain and other crest peaks to the north offer exceptional routes for downhill skiers too.

For detailed reference to the Teton Canyon Region, use USGS maps for Grand Teton, Mount Moran, Granite Basin, Mount Bannon, Clawson, and Driggs.

APPROACHES

Teton Canyon (Targhee National Forest Road No. 009): {D} This paradisiacal canyon is the longest, widest and flattest of any canyon in the range, other than South Bitch Creek. Its three main forks drain more than 12 miles of the Teton Crest. Long, horizontal cliffs and steep avalanche terrain limit skiing on the canyon walls. But Alaska Basin is a magical place for winter touring.

The flat lower canyon is popular for winter

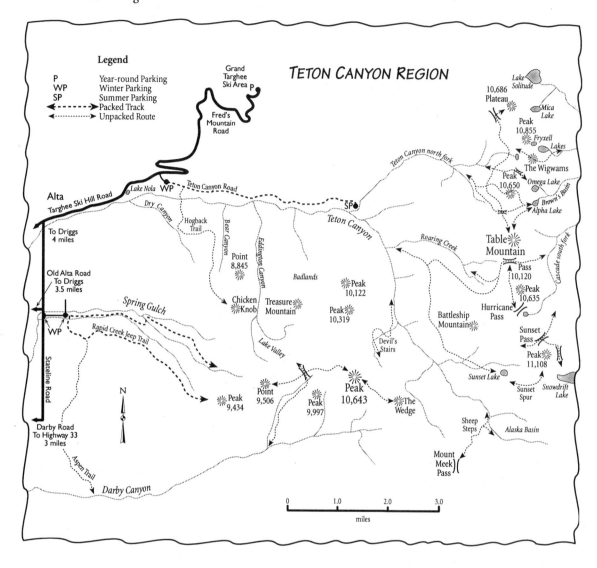

Legend

P	Year-round Parking
WP	Winter Parking
SP	Summer Parking
◄---►	Packed Track
◄·····►	Unpacked Route

TETON CANYON REGION

cross-country day ski trips. But the south-facing flanks of the canyon are sensitive wildlife winter ranges, so stay on the groomed road. Avoid taking dogs into the area and encourage two paths of travel, one for skiers and the other for snowmobilers. When the Teton Canyon road opens in spring, skiers access excellent skiing terrain in Teton Canyon north fork more easily by parking at Teton Campground.

A half mile east of Lake Nola and a half mile west of the first hairpin turn on the Fred's Mountain Road, turn right at the sign for Teton Canyon. Drop down a short hill to the big parking lot.

Hogback Trail: {D} This long route follows a summer trail that isn't labeled on the 1968 Mount Bannon map. Use it to approach Chicken Knob and Lake Valley from Teton Canyon. From the old parking area and cattle guard near the mouth of Mill Creek, strike south and cross Teton Creek on a footbridge.

Follow snowmobile and/or ski tracks up a shallow draw to a forested meadow. Begin a long, ascending traverse east to the "hogback" between Dry and Bear creeks, which you'll follow south to a vast forested plateau and Chicken Knob.

Bear Canyon: {D} Use this narrow, forested canyon for a direct approach to Alta Dena Bowl. This route is not used often.

Eddington Canyon (Lake Valley): {D} This steep canyon provides access to Peak 10,643, as well as the excellent east- and north-facing ski runs on the ridge between Chicken Knob and Point 9,506. Do not attempt winter or spring travel in this canyon unless snow conditions are stable. Both sides of the canyon are steep, with numerous avalanche paths. Avalanche paths on the huge, west-facing wall look much like man-made ski runs through the trees. These swaths are quite visible from various points in Teton Valley and have led many a tourist to mistake this for the Grand Targhee Resort.

The canyon is not steep at the bottom, but 1.75 miles up from Teton Canyon, a steep headwall and a long, narrow gully block easy passage into Lake Valley. Farther up the canyon, short cliff bands restrict skiers to the creek bottom.

During a January, 1984 snowmobile descent of Eddington Canyon, 21-year-old James Schultz launched off a cliff and landed in the creek, breaking the ice. Soaking wet, he began a difficult descent to Teton Canyon on foot. Tragically, though, Schultz died from exposure before reaching safety.

Aspen Trail: {C} This trail traverses west-facing slopes near the 6,700-foot contour for four miles between the mouths of Darby Canyon and Spring Gulch. It infringes upon sensitive wildlife winter range, and thus is discouraged as a ski route.

Spring Gulch: {D} This is the largest of the four relatively steep canyons or draws that drain the west side of the massif between Darby and Teton canyons. Spring Gulch provides entry to the Eddington Canyon headwaters (Lake Valley), Treasure Mountain, and Peak 10,643. A few short, shallow bowls near the head-

waters and on the south flank are the only attractions in the canyon itself.

Ascending the canyon is fast and easy because you usually will find a firm snowmobile track to the top of the canyon and beyond. On the other hand, descending the canyon is a hair-raising luge ride with few safe crashing zones. If you need to, leave the track and follow one of at least three creeks in the canyon without too much bushwhacking.

From Driggs, turn east on Targhee Ski Hill Road and continue straight at Cottonwood Corner onto Old Alta Road. Turn left at the first T intersection and drive around a pasture for two miles to another T. Turn right onto Stateline Road and drive 100 yards to a junction with the unmarked Spring Gulch Road, a one-lane-road that turns east along a line of trees and a fence. Shovel out a spot and park at this junction. Be warned that tires have been slashed here. If you are in a four-wheel-drive vehicle, you can park 200 yards up Spring Gulch Road at a 90-degree turn, but you'll still have to shovel out a parking space. Ski up snowmobile tracks along a fenceline to enter Spring Gulch.

Rapid Creek Jeep Trail: {C} This is a popular snowmobile track, leading to treeline below Peak 9,434. The west end of this trail crosses through private land. Approach as for Spring Gulch.

Roaring Creek: {D} At 10,120 feet, the pass at the head of Roaring Creek is the lowest point along the crest between the Mount Meek Pass area and the pass just north of Littles Peak. Ski vast, gentle bowls at the head of the drainage.

If you're approaching Roaring Creek from the Teton Canyon forks, ski up the south fork until you reach a treeless clearing that offers an unobstructed view of the cascades of the Roaring Creek mouth. The bottom 500 feet of Roaring Creek is challenging, both for upward- and downward-bound travelers. Avoid avalanche terrain and thick forests by following the spur just south of the creek.

Downhill travelers in the upper canyon should try to stay on the north side of the creek for a quicker, easier descent. When the creek gets steep near the bottom, cross to the south side and descend the forested spur.

PEAKS AND BOWLS

Peak 10,855: Many one-day traverses of the Tetons involve hours of climbing or flat-slogging but little opportunity for exhilarating descents. If you include this beautiful crest peak in a traverse between Grand Targhee and Cascade Canyon, however, you'll win your just reward. Approach from Cascade Canyon or Grand Targhee via Fred's Mountain High Route.

Fryxell Lakes Route: {E} or {F} From the east, Peak 10,855 appears to be no more than a gentle snow dome. In reality, though, it offers sustained moderate but exposed skiing for 2,700 feet, past the Fryxell Lakes and into Cascade north fork. Reach the lakes via the elegant southeast couloir or the east ridge.

(Early free-heel: Peter Koedt and Tom Schmidt; May 25, 1993. Early snowboard: Greg Brazelton; May 25, 1993.)

Southwest Face: {E} or {F} The same morning that Peter Koedt's party left Targhee for Peak 10,855, Tom Bennett left Jackson Hole with a car parked at Teton Canyon Campground. From the west, the sharp summit of Peak 10,855 and vast snow bowls and chutes dominate the view of Teton Canyon's north fork. After summitting via Fryxell Lakes, Bennett skied this impressive southwest face into Teton Canyon north fork.

(Early free-heel: Tom Bennett; May 25, 1993.)

Mica Lake Faces: {D} These mellow faces southeast of Mica Lake were skied in a wet spring storm from a camp at the Cascade forks.

(Early free-heel: Michael Keating, Dave Ellingson and Doug Marden; spring 1991.)

Other potential routes: The Petersen Glacier drops to Mica Lake, providing yet another route from the crest into Cascade Canyon. The northeast cwm is a large snow basin accessed via a couloir from the east ridge, or from the northeast shoulder. The east-ridge couloir drops 600 feet into the northwestern cwm, just west of rock tower 10,480-plus.

The Wigwams: Long believed too rocky to ski, skiers have discovered wonderful routes here in recent years. Approach from Cascade Canyon or Teton Canyon north fork.

South Wigwam South Face (10,840 feet): {F} This classic, triangular bowl drops 1,200 feet to Omega Lake from the sharp summit of the South Wigwam. You might have to negotiate short couloirs near the bottom of the face.

(Early free-heel: Tom Turiano; May 4, 1992.)

Other potential routes: The tiny, unnamed basin east of The Wigwams offers wonderful moderate terrain. After 650 feet, it joins with the Fryxell Lakes Route on Peak 10,855 for another 2,000 feet into Cascade north fork.

Peak 10,650: This Colorado Front Range-like mountain sits at the head of Teton Canyon north fork.

Southeast Face: {E} This beautiful clone of Rendezvous Bowl drops 1,000 feet to Alpha Lake and holds snow well into June. Grant Hagen and party dubbed the cirque—which holds Alpha and Omega lakes—Brown's Basin, to honor Fred Brown.

(Early fixed-heel: Grant Hagen and Herman Seherr-Thoss; spring, 1942. Early free-heel: Tom Turiano; May 4, 1992.)

Northwest Face: {D} Although the wind often scours this beautiful face, it's worth monitoring for that one day when it's powder. Peter Koedt and Kevin Dye skied the face during a circum-Wigwams loop from Cascade Canyon.

(Early free-heel: Peter Koedt and Kevin Dye; June, 1984.)

Table Mountain (11,106 feet): This breast-shaped mountain lies in the geographic center of the Teton Range. Views from the summit are spectacular in all directions—most notably, the sharp summits between Mount Owen and the South Teton tower to the east.

Skiers use a variety of approaches to the summit. Direct climbs from the heads of Teton Canyon north fork and Roaring creeks are relatively safe and efficient. Instead, you might choose to climb the entire west ridge from Teton Campground, or take it partway, after climbing steeply out of Teton or Roaring creek. At least two routes access the west ridge from Teton Canyon north fork. The best uses the northern spur of Table, just east of the massive granite buttress in the north fork. Another employs the avalanche-prone bowl just southeast of the summer trail switchbacks on the east face of Point 9,960-plus.

West Ridge: {D} This high, broad plateau extends more than three miles and 4,150 feet between Teton Campground and the Table Mountain summit. The upper ridge is relatively gentle and often wind-hammered but its position is fantastic. The lower west ridge broadens into a vast, forested mountainside with numerous faces and gullies—a powder or corn skier's paradise.

Northwest Face: {D} This is one of the finest runs on the west side of the range. High Mountain Heli-Skiing occasionally flew skiers to this bowl in the late 1970s and early 1980s. From the summit, ski a large bowl toward Teton Canyon north fork. Forested rollers below make excellent powder terrain.

The north and northwest faces of Table's west ridge are quite popular for late spring corn skiing. Watch out for huge cornices that hang precariously off the ridge.

Other potential routes: The northeast ramp is a steep, avalanche-prone face leading into Cascade south fork. The south ridge proper usually is wind-scoured. But just east of the ridge is a huge pillow of snow that is excellent for skiing in safe conditions. The south side of Table's long west ridge can serve up excellent spring corn.

Battleship Mountain (10,679 feet): This aptly named sedimentary remnant protrudes unaccompanied from the vast plateau near Hurricane Pass. Approach from Alaska Basin, Cascade Canyon, or Roaring Creek.

Battleship Bench: {E} This is a longtime favorite of Teton Valley skiers and High Mountain Heli-Skiing. Ski more than 3,800 feet from the west shoulder or the rise south of Hurricane Pass into Teton Canyon, through sparse forest, odd boulders and great powder. Approach from Roaring Creek, tagging Hurricane Pass en route to Battleship Mountain.

Ski the final 1,500 feet into Teton Canyon one of two ways. For a fantastic run in safe conditions, catch the west-facing avalanche paths next to Roaring Creek, and drop straight into Teton Canyon. If avalanche danger is high, opt for the forested spur just south of lower Roaring Creek.

Peak 11,108: This two-faced sedimentary peak is the northern culmination of The Wall of Avalanche Canyon. One view of the peak displays a sheer cliff face; from the other view, it is barely recognizable as a peak. Approach from Cascade, Teton, or Death canyon.

Potential ski routes: The north couloir is a 45-degree gap in cliffs, capped by a cornice at its broad top and bearing a narrow section about halfway down. Climb its 500 vertical feet directly from Cascade

Russell Rainey skins up firm windpack on the north face of Table Mountain. If you can catch it in safe powder, you'll be in heaven. The south-facing routes on Peak 10,650, Peak 10,855 and South Wigwam provide the backdrop.

Canyon or via the Sunset Spur from Alaska Basin. The Sunset Spur is a long, low-angle ramp rising above Sunset Lake to the scenic plateau above The Wall of Avalanche Canyon. The northwest face provides an exciting route back to Sunset Lake.

Dry Canyon: {D} Though this may seem to be nothing more than a vast expanse of forest, you can find skiable shots through the beautiful pines and aspens. Wait for good powder conditions and ski northwest from the top of the "hogback," directly into Dry Canyon. Approach from Hogback Trail.

Point 8,845: This is a subtle point three quarters of a mile north of Chicken Knob. Approach from the thick forests at the mouth of Bear Canyon or the Hogback Trail.

Alta Dena Bowl: {D} On the northwest side of this bump lies this 600-plus-foot clearing. Alta Dena Bowl is skied most commonly after skiers yoyo the east side of Chicken Knob.

This aerial view looks east toward Table Mountain (left) and the Roaring Fork headwaters (center). The High Peaks provide the backdrop for ski tours in this region.

Peak 9,279 (Chicken Knob): This insignificant bump is the primary attraction for powder skiers in the Lake Valley area.

East Face: {D} The interminable sparse forest on the west slopes of Chicken Knob give little inkling to the treasures on the east side—a one-mile wall of 25-degree slopes, some 200 feet to 1,200 feet high.

Treasure Mountain (9,841 feet): Approach this snow dome from Lake Valley.

Eddington Chutes: {E} These chutes are prominent from Teton Valley and, in stable conditions, offer fantastic west-facing runs angled at 35 degrees. Warning: Choose your chute carefully because some of the southern ones end in huge cliffs.

Southwest Face: {D} Gentle slopes, random cliff bands, and a long approach decry any potential skiing treasure here.

Badlands: {E} The northeast side of Treasure Mountain offers steep, gladed terrain with short, intermittent cliffs. This area is blocked from below by the large cliffs on the south side of Teton Canyon. Nonetheless, Lars Moller weaved a route—nearly 3,000 feet long—through these cliff bands and into Teton Canyon.

Point 10,122: This is the northern culmination of the long north ridge of Peak 10,643. Its north side is characterized by a prominent Glory Bowl-like face, which seems to offer potential for a superb spring descent. But cliffs at its base would force most skiers back to the summit to escape. A more reasonable north-side route drops gently northeast into a narrow draw that leads to a hanging basin above Teton Campground. You'll have to negotiate steep chutes, ledges—and possibly rappels—to descend into Teton Canyon. Approach from Lake Valley.

Peak 10,319: This broad snow cone sits just

more than a mile north of Peak 10,643. Ski vast, gentle bowls from the summit into Lake Valley, which also serves as the approach.

Peak 10,643: This broad mountain—a monarch of its massif—offers good downhill terrain, but the snow often is quite wind-scoured on south and west faces. Firm snow makes this a ridge walker's paradise. On occasion, you'll find powder on the north side of the southwest ridge. The quickest approach appears to be from Spring Gulch via Point 9,506-Peak 10,643.

West Face: {D} This three-mile-wide face offers all aspects except east as it tumbles gently into Lake Valley.

Point 9,997: This small but striking, conical peak stands at the head of Darby Canyon's north fork. You'll find excellent steep skiing on its north face. Approach from Darby north fork or Lake Valley, via the cone's sharp east ridge.

HIGH ROUTES

Table Mountain-10,686 Plateau: {E} During a winter traverse between the Jackson Hole and Grand Targhee ski areas in the early 1990s, Bill Dyer and Ted Dugan made this enjoyable high traverse around the west side of Peak 10,650. If you stay high, you'll encounter tricky couloirs through short cliffs on the southwest and northwest sides of Peak 10,650. From the upper north fork of Teton Canyon, Dyer and Dugan climbed to the 10,365/10,686 saddle and followed Fred's Mountain High Route to Grand Targhee.

Wigwam Notch Ramp: {F} This interesting passage climbs diagonally to the notch between the north and south Wigwams, from the tarn at the head of Teton Canyon north fork. If you're planning a traverse into Fryxell Lakes, expect third-, fourth-, or fifth-class terrain—depending on snow conditions—on the east side of the notch.

Teton Canyon-Omega Lake: {E} At the lowest point between Peak 10,650 and the South Wigwam, cross a challenging corniced pass, but only if avalanche danger is low.

Teton Canyon-Alpha Lake: {D} Pass between

these two cirques with minor difficulties. The easiest route harbors a cornice, just south of Peak 10,650. In June of 1984, Peter Koedt and Kevin Dye climbed Peak 10,650 and dropped easily into Teton Canyon via the northwest face.

Table Mountain-Alpha Lake: {E} In safe avalanche conditions, ski down the north ridge of Table and drop sharply into Cascade middle fork.

Roaring Creek-Battleship Bench: A long 100-foot cliff rings the south side of Roaring Creek, blocking passage onto the Battleship Bench. From Pass 10,120, make a descending traverse south toward this long, limestone cliff band. Traverse northwest under the cliff until you can climb southwest out of Roaring Creek onto the Battleship Bench.

Roaring Creek-Cascade south fork: {D} In the 1960s or 70s, Robert Hammer, Dean Millsap, and Joe Gale made a nice width traverse of the Tetons using this straightforward crossing.

Hurricane Pass-Roaring Creek Pass: {C} Use this route during true crest traverses. Traverse and climb high across the west face of Peak 10,635.

Sunset Lake-Roaring Creek Mouth: {C} A more scenic alternative to Teton Canyon, this inconspicuous passage follows a sloping bench around the south and west sides of Battleship Mountain. You'll follow either above or below a limestone cliff band the entire way.

Sunset Pass: {E} This scenic pass is just northwest of Peak 11,108. In April of 1940, Fred Brown, Betty Woolsey and Reddy and Willi Muller used this pass twice in two days to cross back and forth from Cascade into Teton Canyon.

Sunset Pass-Avalanche Divide: {E} In April of 1940, Fred Brown and Betty Woolsey made this exciting traverse across the slopes below the north face of Peak 11,108.

Point 9,506-Peak 10,643: {D} Follow this undulating route from the head of Spring Gulch to the summit of Peak 10,643.

Peak 10,643-The Wedge: {D} This scenic ridge presents no major obstacles, though you might have to do some easy rock scrambling and cramponing. On Dec. 17, 1991, this author underestimated the size of the cornices that loom over Teton Canyon to the east. About half a mile northwest of The Wedge, a bus-sized chunk of snow broke away between my feet. I avoided the 500-foot plunge—almost certain death—by diving for safety. These cornices are some of the largest in the range; give them a wide berth. The southwest side of the ridge, near Peak 10,643, usually is wind-scoured.

Devil's Stairs: {E} High Mountain Heli-skiing once took this wandering, wind-slabbed route on in powder. Follow the summer trail through the limestone cliff that rims Teton Canyon, to the shelf north of The Wedge.

Sheep Steps: {D} This common route follows the line of the summer trail between Mount Meek Pass and Alaska Basin. Snow conditions often are wind-slab, TG, or sastrugi.

DARBY CANYON REGION

Surrounded by Fox Creek Canyon on the south, Darby Canyon on the north and the Death Canyon Shelf cliffs on the east, this region might be the most well-guarded in the range. And that challenge is what drives skiers to explore the region from adjacent areas, including Rendezvous Mountain, Open Canyon, and Buck Mountain.

Darby Canyon is popular for good reason. Six grandiose peaks of Madison Limestone stand at the headwaters of the canyon, embodying the highest stretch of the Teton Crest between Rendezvous Peak and Table Mountain. You can ski at least one elegant, treeless face from each summit, and vast snow bowls abound on the lower peaks.

For detailed reference to the Darby Canyon Region, use USGS maps for Mount Bannon and Driggs, Idaho.

Tom Turiano crosses the head of Darby main fork toward The Wedge during a two-day traverse between Open Canyon and Spring Gulch. The Wedge offers steep skiing in a world of otherwise mellow peaks.

APPROACHES

Darby Canyon: {D} This beautiful canyon offers immense touring possibilities, though it is nearly surrounded by cliffs and slopes too steep to ski safely.

Five miles north of Victor, turn east on the marked Darby Canyon Road (Targhee National Forest Road No. 012). Park a half mile from the mountains, where this plowed road ends. Be sure to park out of the way of snowmobile trailers. Ski east to the T, then turn right and follow the road around a pasture and into the canyon.

The canyon's eight-mile-long north wall rises more than 2,000 feet, with slopes averaging 35 degrees, broken only by the north fork draw. Avoid the west end of the wall, as it is sensitive wildlife winter range. At the east end of Darby Canyon, a gently sloping Bighorn Dolomite bed surface rises to an abrupt end at a five-mile-long, 600-foot dropoff—a remarkable geological phenomenon. In the upper main fork of the canyon, expect frustrating encounters with long, vertical cliff bands 10 feet to 20 feet high, unless you employ careful

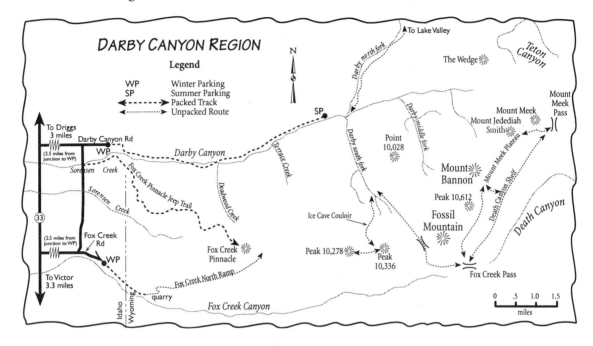

route-finding. In some spots, you can jump or climb these bands. Underbrush, deadfall, and a meandering stream make travel in the trailless main-fork canyon bottom an arduous undertaking.

Branching south from the main fork of Darby Canyon are at least five drainages, culminating along the lengthy east/west ridge that forms the northern boundary of Fox Creek Canyon. To approach the south fork and Fossil Mountain, ski up the main fork and cross a footbridge just past the summer parking area. Try hard to follow the summer trail through the forest and in the lower south fork because cliff bands block the creek bed. Stay high on the east side of the canyon to avoid a cliff band about a mile from the forks. Use caution crossing beneath the massive avalanche slope on the west face of Point 10,028.

Deadwood Creek: {D} Along with an unnamed neighboring draw to its east, Deadwood Creek provides more reasonable access into Terrace Creek Basin than does Terrace Creek. But both V-shaped draws are steep, thickly forested, and have intermittent cliff obstacles.

Terrace Creek: {E} Travel in this draw is not recommended unless snow conditions are bombproof. Skiers must wind through large cliff bands and extremely steep avalanche slopes that intersect the creek at the 7,800-foot level. During the winter of 1993, Jim Olson and friends switchbacked up the forested ridge east of the difficulties in lower Terrace Creek. Terrace Creek Basin is beautiful, but flatness limits its skiing potential. Only the west face of the north shoulder of Peak 10,278 offers appropriate terrain.

Fox Creek Pinnacle Jeep Trail: {D} Also known as Zohner's Pipeline Road, this long, winding snowmobile track starts at the mouth of Darby Canyon and, in five miles, takes you to treeline near Fox Creek Pinnacle.

Sorensen Creek: {D} This is not recommended for travel because it has private land at its base, minimal snow cover, and thick undergrowth.

Fox Creek North Ramp: {C} Use this broad Bighorn Dolomite ramp to access the extensive west ridge of Fossil Mountain and the Terrace Creek headwaters from Fox Creek. From the quarry, just more than a mile from the end of the plowed road in Fox Creek, skin up a road—switchbacking, climbing, and traversing through aspen groves and meadows—to the saddle east of Fox Creek Pinnacle.

Fox Creek Canyon: {C} Use this long, forkless canyon to access Fox Creek Pass and the north and south ramps of Fox Creek. Three miles north of Victor, Idaho, turn right at the road marked for Fox Creek. As you enter the canyon, park just past the Highland Way switchback, where the plowed area ends. Stay off of the south-facing slopes above the canyon; they are sensitive wildlife winter range. About a third of a mile up the snowbound road, step over a gate and continue up the road rather than following the sign to the parking area and trailhead.

Farther up the canyon, the north wall is quite steep and bears at least 20 avalanche paths in five miles. Many gawk at these stunning couloirs, all but one or two of which end in impassable cliff bands. The south side of the upper canyon is a jumble of huge cliffs, tiny cirques and thick forest. Only with the perfect conditions and route would skiing be enjoyable and safe here. Touring in the canyon bottom is not popular because of the thick willows and its V shape. The headwaters, however, offer an expansive, treeless plateau that is superb for touring.

About a mile from the end of the plowed road, you'll encounter a gravel quarry and weir, owned by the LDS Church. Through the years, various state permitees of this operation have met with opposition from local residents, environmental groups, and the Teton County Commission, but the operation continues.

PEAKS AND BOWLS

Point 9,348 (Fox Creek Pinnacle): This earthy hump on the west end of the ridge between Darby and Fox Creek canyons offers enjoyable downhill skiing on its northeast-facing bowl and north-facing chutes. Approach via the Fox Creek North Ramp or the Fox Creek Pinnacle Jeep Trail.

Peak 10,278: Accessed most easily from the Fox Creek North Ramp via its west ridge, this peak offers a mile of 250-foot slopes off the west side of its north shoulder. The long northwest arm also presents moderate gladed terrain.

Peak 10,336: In 1988, Tom Bennett tried to descend to Teton Valley from the summit of Fossil Mountain via its entire west ridge. To avoid the fourth- and fifth-class climbing on the east ridge of this craggy peak, he contoured steep firm snow on its south side. One step from the corniced ridge, Bennett's edges gave way and he slid 100 feet on the hard crust into Fox Creek Canyon before self-arresting. Approach from the Fox Creek North Ramp.

Northwest Face: {D} Nearly 1,000 feet of 20-degree slopes lead to the bench above the ice cave. Climb back out or plunge into Darby south fork via the Ice Cave Couloir.

(Early free-heel: Terry Brattain; late 1980s.)

Point 10,028: This elegant peak is at the north end of Fossil Mountain's long northwest ridge. Early, spring morning crust would make its west face a spectacular 2,000-foot ski run. Approach from Darby south fork.

Fossil Mountain (10,916 feet): This sphinx-shaped castle of Madison Limestone is the focal point of west-slope ski mountaineering. Approach from Fox Creek Pass or Darby south fork.

West Face: {D} This classic 600-foot powder bowl culminates at Fossil's northwest cliffs, forming the head of Darby south fork.

(Early free-heel: Jim Olson et al, early 1990s.)

Southwest Face: {E} Often wind-hammered or sun-crusted, this 1,000-foot exposed snow platter is the primary ascent and descent route.

(Early fixed heel: Callum Mackay, Robbie Fuller and Ray White; January, 1973. Early free-heel: Jay Moody et al; March, 1986.)

Other potential routes: The east face offers a remote backcountry challenge for extreme skiers.

The Wedge (10,360-plus feet): This sharp, sphinx-shaped peak of Madison Limestone offers steep skiing in a world of otherwise mellow peaks. Approach from Teton Canyon, Darby main fork, or via Peak 10,643-The Wedge.

Wedge Couloirs: {F} Northwest and southeast of The Wedge are two long, steep gullies leading northeast onto the shelf above Devil's Stairs. The lower slopes of these couloirs exceed 40 degrees; attempt them only in the most stable snow conditions.

(Early free-heel: Terry Brattain and Linda and Mike Merigliano; early 1980s.)

Other potential routes: The southeast ridge offers the primary route from the summit. Terry Brattain and Mike and Linda Merigliano ascended The Wedge during their tour from Darby Canyon to Peak 11,094 in the early 1980s. They encountered some steep post-holing in a chimney while climbing toward the upper ridge from the saddle between The Wedge and Point 9,830.

Mount Meek (10,681 feet): This peak of Darby

Fossil Mountain is the monarch of the southern Teton Crest. The 1,000-foot exposed snow platter of the southwest face (left) provides a moderate ski route from the summit.

Formation limestone slopes modestly above the head of Darby main fork and towers precipitously above Teton Canyon. Approach from Darby main fork or via the Mount Meek Pass-Mount Meek.

South Slope: {C} This face of drifts, sastrugi, and dwarf trees leads to Mount Meek Plateau.

(Early free-heel: Tom Bennett and Tom Turiano; Jan. 28, 1989.)

Other potential routes: The west slope offers often wind-scoured, sparsely treed skiing into Darby main fork. An impressive couloir pitches into Teton Canyon from near the summit.

Mount Jedediah Smith (10,610 feet): Overshadowed by mounts Bannon and Meek, this graceful nunatak offers nice skiing on all flanks. Approach from Darby main fork or Mount Meek Plateau.

East Face: {E} This ever-steepening avalanche face is a spectacular place to ski.

(Early free-heel: Terry Brattain and Mike and Linda Merigliano; 1980s.)

Mount Bannon (10,966 feet): One of the highest peaks of the Teton Crest, this pyramid has seen surprisingly little skiing activity. Approach from Mount Meek Plateau or Darby main fork.

Southeast Face: {E} This 900-foot, treeless snow face reigns as one of the nicest spring runs in the range. In winter, it often is wind-hammered.

(Early free-heel: Tom Turiano and Tom Bennett; Jan. 28, 1989.)

Other potential routes: The southwest face is steeper and bigger than the southeast one, and a band of limestone near the bottom offers only two passages.

Peak 10,612: At the head of the seldom-visited middle fork of Darby, between Fossil Mountain and Mount Bannon, this snow cone receives little attention from skiers. Nonetheless, the east, west, and northwest aspects offer nice terrain.

HIGH ROUTES

Darby forks-Lake Valley: {E} This avalanche-prone route follows Darby north fork between Darby and Eddington canyons. The bottom section of the draw is quite steep, with intermittent cliff bands blocking easy passage.

Peak 10,278-Peak 10,336: {E} You'll encounter short sections of third-class scrambling on the east ridge of Peak 10,278.

Ice Cave Couloir: {G} This difficult route squeezes through the Madison Limestone cliffs at their shortest point, just southeast of the Ice Cave. During his tour in the 1980s, Terry Brattain encountered a 30-foot third-class downclimb, a 50-degree couloir, and an avalanche-prone slope.

Fox Creek Pass-Darby South Fork: {E} This route might have been skied first in the spring of 1967, when Bill Briggs and Peter Koedt led a group from the tram to Darby Canyon.

From Fox Creek Pass, head west—on the north side of the canyon—one mile on uneven terrain until just past Fossil Mountain. Climb a 35-plus-degree gully to the pass west of Fossil. The north side of this pass is gentle.

Mount Meek Pass-Mount Meek: {F} Tom Bennett and this author pioneered this very steep, exposed route from the Death Canyon Shelf near Mount Meek Pass to the south shoulder of Mount Meek during January of 1989. We encountered 50-degree couloirs and hanging snowfields. Attempt this only under the most stable snow conditions.

Mount Meek Plateau-Death Canyon Shelf: {F} Two routes connect these scenic benches. The best route—directly east of Mount Bannon—is a 40-degree couloir that drops 500 feet to the Death Canyon Shelf. A quarter of a mile southeast of that couloir lies a steep, avalanche-prone face with intermittent cliffs; it also leads between the shelf and the plateau. Attempt these routes only under the most stable snow conditions.

Death Canyon Shelf: {C} This is the unmistakable classic passage of the Tetons. In mid-February of 1938, Fred Brown, Allyn Hanks and Howard Stagner made the first recorded ski traverse of the shelf. Elegant views of the high peaks to the north and Spearhead Peak to the south will charm you on this 1,000-foot wide, relatively flat passageway that cuts across the sedimentary cliffs of the Death Canyon headwaters between Fox Creek Pass and Mount Meek Pass.

Fox Creek Pass-Mount Meek Plateau: {F} During the 1980s, Mike and Linda Merigliano found this exciting 600-foot passage southeast of Fossil Mountain while trying to gain Mount Meek Plateau from Fox Creek. On Dec. 17, 1991, John Fettig, Steve Stenger, Jim Olson and this author followed in their tracks during a tour from Open Canyon to Spring Creek.

Smart route-finding will help you handle this route's short cliffs, chutes, drifts, dwarf tree forests, and 35- to 40-degree slopes. Attempt it only under the most stable snow conditions because of hollow and wind-loaded snow.

GAME CREEK REGION

I ts treasures hidden from Teton Valley by high forested ridges, the Game Creek area once was a secret powder stash for Teton Valley skiers. During the last decade, however, the region has popularized, with ski yurts near Plummer Canyon and Baldy Knoll. The ridges and bowls of Alpenglow Ridge are some of the most elegant in the range.

For detailed reference to the Game Creek Region, use USGS maps for Victor, Driggs, Rendezvous Peak, and Mount Bannon.

APPROACHES

Fox Creek Canyon: See Darby Canyon Region.
Fox Creek South Ramp: {D} This ramp follows a bed of Bighorn Dolomite from Fox Creek Canyon to

The Clement brothers traverse the west face of Point 10,024 toward Acid Ridge and admire their tracks on Zimbabwe, which is the north face of Point 9,550 and is perfect for yoyoing on moderately steep, forested terrain.

the west ridge of Housetop Mountain. It provides the quickest access to Baldy Knoll, Rendezvous Ski Tours' yurt, and the expansive bowls of upper Game Creek. Leave Fox Creek at the weir, just more than a mile from the end of the plowed road. Cross the creek on snow-covered boulders just below the weir or on a footbridge 100 yards upstream. Follow a road swath as it switchbacks and traverses through forest and small meadows. Eventually, you'll reach a big sloping meadow. Skin to the top of the meadow and contour east across steep, thickly forested slopes to a small basin below Baldy Knoll. Climb south to the west ridge of Housetop.

Game Creek Canyon: {C} This canyon—steep-sided and inconspicuous at its mouth—conceals ski terrain of most exposures at its headwaters and flanks. To view its sparsely forested, rounded peaks and bowls, drive across Teton Valley to Pine Creek Pass.

To reach the canyon mouth, turn northeast off Idaho Route 33 onto the Old Jackson Highway. This road makes an immediate 90-degree turn northwest.

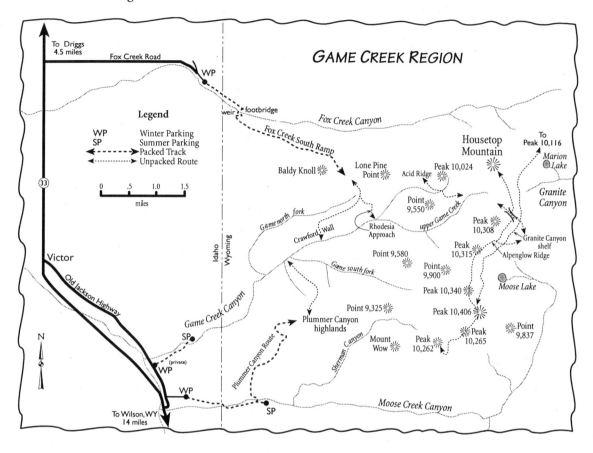

Follow it past Moose Creek Road and some houses, and drive over a small hill. Park 50 yards from the bottom of the hill, near the intersection with unmarked Game Creek Road. Sometimes, this intersection is plowed wide enough to accommodate one car. If not, shovel out a parking spot to avoid trouble.

Ski northwest a quarter mile up Game Creek Road, past a small ranch. (Residents plow one lane on this road in winter.) At the point where the plowed road turns sharply right and up a hill, bear left on an unplowed road that leads to a circle at its end. Cross the creek on a concrete weir, climb a short hill, and follow the line of the summer trail through meadows and forest on the north side of the canyon. Expect moderate deadfall, underbrush, thick forest, steep canyon walls, and multiple stream crossings through the lower and middle canyon. To minimize effects, try to follow the summer trail. Don't venture onto the south-facing slopes near the canyon mouth, as they are prime wildlife winter range.

The upper canyon splits into four primary forks. The steep, forested north fork provides tedious access to and from Baldy Knoll. Branching north from the main fork of Game Creek is a major tributary that drains the mini-cirque east of Point 10,024 and Point 9,550 (Acid Ridge and Zimbabwe). The main fork of the canyon culminates at Pass 9,960-plus and the south face of Housetop Mountain. The remote south fork accesses a trio of high, rounded crest peaks, such as Peak 10,406.

Despite direct approaches from the forks of Game Creek to these headwater areas, the standard approach to the upper canyon follows the Fox Creek South Ramp.

Plummer Canyon: {D} This steep, V-shaped draw drains from the north into Moose Creek, about a mile east of Moose Canyon parking area. Plummer Canyon is the best access to the rolling ski terrain and spectacular aspen and pine forests of the Peak 10,262 massif. Use this draw to approach the Rendezvous Ski Tours' Plummer Canyon yurt as well. The yurt was installed in 1987, removed during permitting conflicts, then resurrected in 1991.

Cross Moose Creek on a slippery log near the Moose Canyon campground, and ski west to the inconspicuous mouth of the canyon. Trees have been cleared near the creek for a summer trail so ski travel is enjoyable up or down, though snow conditions often are difficult. Near the top of Plummer Canyon, switchback on the face to west of the creek to avoid excessive steepness, and gain a broad ridge at 8,000 feet.

Sherman Canyon: {E} The headwater of this drainage is the primary playground of Plummer Canyon Yurt skiers; it contains bowls, faces, and glades of all exposures and difficulties. On the other hand, the lower section of this canyon is for adventurous expert skiers only. Extreme narrowness, thick forest and underbrush, as well as a fairly steep pitch, are cause for creative route-finding and maneuvering. At one point, you must traverse a narrow, sloping ledge across a cliff band. For these reasons, treasures of the upper basin are best accessed from Plummer Canyon. Cross exciting log jams in Moose Creek, just east of the mouth of Sherman Canyon, for access or escape. The stream at the mouth itself cuts abruptly through a shell-like limestone formation.

During the first half of the 1990s, the soil of the Sherman and Game Creek highlands destabilized as a result of overgrazing by domestic and wild animals. On July 15, 1954, a violent flood caused major land and property damage in Teton Basin, partly because of weak mountain soils. During the mid- to late 1960s, a massive cooperative effort by local, state and federal interests aimed to alleviate downstream flooding and excessive erosion by contour-trenching the Sherman and Game Creek headwaters. Be prepared for big bumps when you ski over the trenches.

Moose Creek Canyon: See Mount Glory Region.

PEAKS AND BOWLS

Baldy Knoll (8,880-plus feet): This pillar of westside skiing is best approached from Fox Creek South Ramp. A yurt bearing the knoll's name sits near a row of trees, just south of the saddle that is east of the knoll. Built in 1988, it is owned and operated by Rendezvous Ski Tours.

Bunny's Bowl: {C} This wide-open slope south of the Baldy Knoll yurt is a classic beginner run.

Back Door Bowl: {D} This nice north-facing bowl drops north into a small basin from the saddle east of the knoll.

Baldy Bowl: {D} This northeast side of Baldy Knoll is a favorite powder run for yurt skiers.

Valley View Bowl: {C} This scenic run drops easily northwest—from Baldy Knoll to the Fox Creek South Ramp.

Point 9,286 (Lone Pine Point): Game Creek north fork culminates at this insignificant bump. Approach from Fox Creek South Ramp.

Southwest Face: {B} You'll find terrific easy terrain on this treeless face.

North Face: {E} Find plenty of steep, avalanche-prone shots through the trees. Catch this one only in safe conditions.

Northwest Face: {D} Dropping from the west ridge of Lone Pine Point toward Fox Creek Canyon, you'll catch more wonderful shots through the trees.

Point 10,024: This east peak of Housetop Mountain is a centerpiece of skiing in the Game Creek region and a popular destination of Baldy Knoll yurt skiers.

Acid Ridge: {C} Skiers "tripping" to Jackson Hole once used this west ridge of Point 10,024.

Southwest Face: {D} Easier to find in perfect corn than powder, this elegant, forested face leads

1,400 feet, at 30 degrees, into a northern fork of Game Creek.

East Face: {D} This classic powder bowl drains into a northern tributary of Game Creek. Watch for dangerous wind-slab conditions.

North Face: {D} Though skiing directly off the north side of Point 10,024 would be suicidal, you'll find great powder skiing half a mile west of the summit, off the north side of a small hump on the ridge.

Point 9,550: This is the southwest spur of Housetop Mountain. Approach from Acid Ridge or Game Creek main fork.

Southwest Face: {E} This 2,000-foot open face or ridge was a favorite corn run of High Mountain Heli-Skiing. This author and seven clients made an early ski ascent here on March 9, 1994.

Zimbabwe: {E} Christened by Tom Warren, this north face of Point 9,550 is perfect for yoyoing on moderately steep, sparsely forested terrain.

Housetop Mountain (10,537 feet): This monarch of the Game Creek region is not only the highest summit but is flanked by the biggest bowls, steepest faces, and most scenic ridges. Approach from Granite Canyon, Game Creek main fork or, most commonly, the long west ridge and Fox Creek South Ramp.

West Ridge: {D} During a historic tour by avalanche professionals and guides in 1968, Juris Krisjansons, Robbie Fuller, Harry Frishman, Ray White, Dean Moore, and Bob Sartar skied from the tram to Housetop and into Fox Creek via this classic undulating ridge. During the descent, Krisjansons set off a 100-yard-wide, two-foot-deep slide on the north side of the ridge. Luckily, he was able to grab a tree and watch the torrent rage by, losing only one ski pole. The group skied down the slide path and found Krisjansons' pole atop more than 10 feet of debris.

(Early fixed-heel: Juris Krisjansons, Robbie Fuller, Harry Frishman, Ray White, Dean Moore, and Bob Sartar; 1968.)

South Face: {E} You can make more than 200 turns during a 15-minute run of this classic 1,500-foot, 35-degree bowl.

East Face: {F} This spring corn classic offers 700 feet of 40-degree skiing to the bench above Marion Lake. On March 8, 1994, Bill Iorio skied a steeper east-facing chute farther south.

Peak 10,308: This craggy peak may seem to offer nothing for skiers, but at least one route has been snuck through the cliffs. Approach from Game Creek main fork or Granite Canyon.

Southeast Couloir: {F} From near the summit, ski a straight-sided chute to the bench above Granite Canyon middle fork.

(Early free-heel: Mike Best; late December, 1991.)

Other potential routes: The northwest ridge leads to an inconspicuous chute that drops abruptly into Game Creek. The north face offers four avalanche-prone, cornice-capped couloirs that fall north into Game Creek from the northwest ridge.

Peak 10,315: This elegant crest peak sees very little skiing. Most commonly, skiers traverse its north and south ridges during an Alpenglow Ridge tour. Nonetheless, this peak does harbor some striking lines. Approach from Game Creek main fork, Granite Canyon shelf-Peak 10,315, or Moose Lake.

East Face: {F} You'll encounter intermittent cliffs during a descent of this steep, avalanche-prone slope above Moose Lake.

(Early free-heel: Mike Best; late December, 1991.)

Other potential routes: The aesthetic northwest ridge leads into Game Creek main fork—or drop southwest or north via couloirs into obscure main-fork side basins.

Point 9,580: This insignificant bump is a subsidiary summit of Point 9,900. Approach directly from Baldy Knoll yurt via Rhodesia Approach, Game Creek main fork, or the long scenic ridge that divides the forks.

Rhodesia: {D} This northwest face of Point 9,240-plus is a classic High Mountain Heli-Skiing run that offers 1,800 feet of 25-degree gladed slopes into Game Creek main fork.

Northwest Face: {E} This aesthetic avalanche gully and face would tender excellent skiing in safe conditions.

Point 9,900: This large subsidiary summit along the northwest ridge of Peak 10,340 has negligible skiing opportunities on its cliffy, avalanche-prone flanks. During extremely rare favorable conditions, however, cornice-capped chutes on the north face would be a steep skier's dream.

Peak 10,340: This huge, rarely visited snow cone offers elegant faces and ridges of all aspects. But most flanks usually are wind-hammered. Skiers commonly traverse its north and south ridges during an Alpenglow Ridge tour. Approach from Game Creek south fork.

East Face: {F} Skiers encounter sparse short cliffs and chutes during a descent of this steep, avalanche-prone slope above Moose Lake.

(Early Free-Heel: Mike Best; late December 1991.)

Peak 10,406: Protruding slightly east of the crest, this high peak sits on the divide between Moose Creek and Game Creek south fork. The remarkable view north from the summit reveals a mile-wide gap of lowland between the sedimentary peaks of the crest and the igneous high peaks. This phenomena extends nearly 20 miles to Paintbrush Divide. Approach from Game, Moose, or Granite creek.

Potential routes include the airy 800-foot southeast face, which Tom Bennett, Forrest McCarthy and this author climbed on Dec. 21, 1993, en route to Peak 10,262 from the tram. Attempt this face only when avalanche danger is low because of the wind-loaded slopes hanging above 500-foot cliffs. The often wind-hammered 1,700-foot west bowl leads into Game Creek south fork, and the sometimes wind-loaded north ramp provides relatively safe passage between the crest and Moose Lake cirque.

Peak 10,265: Aside from Housetop Mountain, this dome offers perhaps the best skiing of any crest

point in the Game Creek headwaters. Approach from Game, Moose, or Granite creek.

West Ridge: {D} Used several times by High Mountain Heli-Skiing, this long, undulating ridge leads 1,600 feet into Game Creek south fork.

Southwest Face: {D} Quite often the only powder in a sea of sastrugi, this 600-foot bowl offers the nicest skiing in the vicinity.

(Early Free-Heel: Tom Turiano and Harry Beach; January, 1991.)

Point 9,040-plus (Plummer Canyon highlands): The flats and flanks of this high, aspen and pine plateau are among the primary playgrounds of Plummer Canyon yurt skiers. Approach from Plummer Canyon.

North Side: {D} and {E} Numerous 600-foot shots lead through forest and meadows toward Game Creek.

East Side: {E} This magical, mile-wide face wanders through open bowls and aspen groves for 1,000 feet into Sherman Canyon. Spring serves up the best snow.

This aerial of Game Creek main fork from the west shows Housetop Mountain dominating the skyline. The powder skiing treasures of Zimbabwe and Rhodesia flank the canyon farther down.

Northwest Face: {C} Vast meadows of easy terrain lead 600 feet in a mile from the summit to the yurt.

Point 9,235: Two snow domes sit at the northern head of Sherman Canyon. Approach from Plummer Canyon.

South Bowls: {D} Treeless bowls almost 500 feet high and a quarter of a mile wide grace these upper slopes of Sherman Canyon.

North Escarpment: {E} This mile-wide, 1,500-foot, 35-degree gladed wall above Game Creek south fork has been neglected by backcountry skiers since High Mountain Heli-Skiing enjoyed the steep and deep here in the late 1970s. Understandably, most skiers who see the escarpment conjure images of voluminous snow sliding at high speed, pulverizing everything in the way and piling 70 feet deep in the south fork canyon bottom. It happens. Ski this treasure only in the safest spring powder.

Point 9,780 (Mount Wow): Stunned by the fantastic terrain, snow quality and views from the summit, first-time visitors to Mount Wow certainly make the appropriate exclamation. Glenn Vitucci and Carole Lowe let out so many "Wows!" in the area that they decided to name the mountain accordingly. Approach from upper Sherman Canyon via Plummer Canyon.

West Face: {C} This classic intermediate run offers nearly 1,800 feet of gentle, gladed terrain into Sherman Canyon.

North Face: {E} Several gladed, convex shots lead north from the summit nearly 700 feet into upper Sherman Canyon.

Peak 10,262: This southernmost peak of Alpenglow Ridge is isolated by cliffs on the north and west and by steep slopes on the south. Approach from Game Creek south fork, Alpenglow Ridge or, most commonly, from upper Sherman Canyon via Plummer Canyon.

Northwest Face: {D} Sloping gently to the summit from upper Sherman Canyon, this face is the primary ski route on Peak 10,262 and offers loads of options. Expect somewhat wind-affected snow.

North Couloir: {F} This 500-foot gully drops steeply from near the summit into Game Creek south fork. It is the easternmost of the many couloirs that cleave the long, north-facing dolomite cliff of Peak 10,262. Confident in the snow stability, Dave Moore coerced his five hesitant partners to ski the route by jumping in first himself.

(Early free and fixed heel: Dave Moore, Dave Coon, Gail Jensen, Bob Wagner and two others; Dec. 23, 1994.)

Point 9,837: On Jan. 2, 1992, tightly turning ski tracks were observed on the steep east face of this insignificant ridge near Moose Lake. At the bottom of the face, the tracks ended abruptly at a cliff's edge. There were no landing, traverse, or boot tracks!

HIGH ROUTES

Crawford Wall: {E} During a guided tour to the Plummer Canyon yurt in April of 1994, John Crawford spotted this alternative to the tedious Game Creek north fork for traversing to the Baldy Knoll yurt. Nearly a mile up the main fork, climb the steep, south-facing, forested slope above. Climb a short broken cliff near the bottom, then make a long ascending traverse northeast under some cliffs near the top to gain the long southwest ridge of Lone Pine Point. Follow this ridge until you can ski across a steep-sided gully to the Baldy Knoll yurt. This route is not recommended because of inconsistent snow on the north side of Game Creek Canyon.

Rhodesia Approach: {F} During a guided tour from the Baldy Knoll yurt, this author used this steep and narrow, avalanche-prone gully to descend into Game Creek and access Rhodesia. Again, this route is not recommended.

Alpenglow Ridge (Housetop Mountain-Peak 10,262): {F} Aside from occasional snow drifts, precarious cornices, and rocky sections, this classic, undulating, scenic crest traverse is one of a kind in the Tetons. Surprisingly, there has been no known tour of the entire ridge. Harry Beach and this author skied only part of the ridge—between peaks 10,315 and 10,265—in January of 1991. And, on Dec. 21, 1993, Tom Bennett,

Forrest McCarthy, and this author skied the section between peaks 10,406 and 10,262.

Two perplexing sections of the six-mile route warrant description: First, bypass the cliffs and gendarmes of Peak 10,308 by transferring between the Granite Canyon shelf and the ridge crest. Second, the crux of the traverse is between peaks 10,265 and 10,262. Ski the fantastic southwest face of Peak 10,265 into the basin east of Peak 10,262. Beneath prime avalanche terrain, traverse delicately south, just above a 400-foot cliff, to the southeast ridge of Peak 10,262, and follow this easily to the summit. A second, possibly safer route, follows one of two 50-degree, north-facing couloirs west of the northeast ridge of Peak 10,262.

Acid Ridge-Upper Game Creek: {D} This classic traverse offers a quick, safe route from the saddle west of Point 10,024 to the headwaters of Game Creek main fork. From the saddle, climb 100 feet along Acid Ridge and begin a half-mile traverse to Pass 9,400-plus at the west end of Zimbabwe. Then drop easily into upper Game Creek. In the reverse direction, this route provides excellent passage back to Acid Ridge after a descent of the south face of Housetop.

Granite Canyon shelf: {B} This gently rolling four-and-a-half-mile bench of Darby Formation and Bighorn Dolomite provides a safe, easy avenue between peaks 10,406 and 10,116.

Upper Game Creek-Granite Canyon shelf: {E} This 9,960-plus-foot pass is the safest, easiest route between Granite and Game Creek canyons. On the wind-loaded east side, use one of two spurs above Granite middle fork to gain the crest.

Granite Canyon shelf-Peak 10,315: {E} Follow the relatively safe line of the Teton hydrologic crest from the shelf to gain the north ridge of Peak 10,315. But don't attempt this unless avalanche danger is low. In January of 1991, Harry Beach had an exhausting experience trying to get edge grip on impenetrable wind slab while climbing this spur from the shelf. About 20 feet below the flat ridge, his edges gave way and he slid at least 400 feet back to the shelf. He made the ridge on his second try.

Plummer Canyon highlands-Game Creek forks: {E} Although many steep bowls and gullies connect these locations, the safest, easiest route descends north from the Plummer Canyon yurt on a gentle, gladed promontory. From the end of the point, follow a steeper, heavily forested broad ridge to the Game Creek forks.

RECOMMENDED ROUTES

Light Touring

Jackson Hole Nordic Center {K}-{D}
Grand Targhee Nordic Center {K}-{D}

Class K:
Jenny Lake Track
Jackson Lake-from Signal Mountain Lodge, Colter
    Bay, or Lizard Creek
Teton Canyon Road

Class A:
Darby Canyon
Moose Creek
South Leigh Creek

Class B:
Old Pass Road
Death Canyon Track to Phelps Lake overlook

Class C:
Ski Lake Track
Taggart and Bradley lake tracks

Class D:
Spring Gulch

Day Downhill

Class C:
Albright Peak-lower east slopes
Burnt Wagon Gulch
Moby Dick-west ridge to Coal Creek
Mount Wow-west face (from Plummer Canyon yurt)
Nancy's Run
Point 10,075-east ridge

Class D:
25 Short-northeast ridge
Beard Mountain-west face
Fossil Mountain-west face
Housetop Mountain-west ridge
Laurel Swath
Moby Dick-southwest face
Mount Glory-west ridge to Lord Calvert's to Coal
    Creek

Owl Peak-east ridge
Point 10,333-northeast ridge
Taylor Mountain-Powder Reserve
Table Mountain-west ridge or northwest face

Class E:
Amphitheater Lake Buttress-east face
Jensen Canyon
Maverick-east face
Mount Glory-Glory Bowl
Peak 10,686-east side
Pinedale Canyon
Point 9,943-Steve Baugh Memorial Bowl
Rock Springs Canyon
Wimpy's Knob-east face

Class F:
Laurel Canyon
Taylor Mountain-south face

Day Loops and Traverses

Class D:
Death Canyon-Teton Canyon
Phillips Ridge-Ridge Tour
Teton Canyon-Miles Creek Ramp-Beard's
    Wheatfield-Lower Bench Return Route

Class E:
25 Short-Snow Devil Ridge-Peak 10,696-Maverick
    Buttress
Avalanche Canyon-Cascade Canyon
Avalanche south fork-No Wood Basin-Death
    Canyon
Cascade Canyon-Roaring Creek-Teton Canyon
Mount Glory-Taylor Mountain
Peak 10,450-Fox Creek Pass-Fossil Mountain-Darby
    south fork
Peak 10,450-Housetop Mountain-Fox Creek
Spring Gulch-Peak 10,643/Chicken Knob-Eddington
    Canyon

Stewart Draw-Avalanche Canyon
Teton Pass-Teton Village

Class F:
Waterfalls Canyon-Ranger Peak-Quartzite Canyon

Ski Backpacking

Baldy Knoll Yurt {B}-{E}
Commissary Ridge Yurt {C}-{E}
Plummer Canyon Yurt {C}-{F}

Class D:
Darby Canyon and forks
Moose Basin Area
Snowshoe Canyon south fork
South Leigh Creek-Granite Basin-Leigh Canyon
South Leigh Creek-Granite Basin-Moran Canyon
Talus Lake and Webb Canyon highlands
Upper Berry Creek

Class E:
Cascade Canyon and forks
Moran Canyon and forks
Moran Canyon-Dry Ridge
Open Canyon-Fox Creek Pass-Mount Meek Plateau-
    Peak 10,643-Spring Gulch
Teton Crest Traverse
Upper South Bitch Creek

Class F:
Eagles Rest/Doane/Ranger traverse

Classic Steeps

Class E:
Mount Hunt-south and east sides
Prospectors Mountain-Banana Couloir
Static Peak-southeast face
Veiled Peak-northeast bowl

Class F:
Albright Peak-east face
Buck Mountain-east face
Disappointment Peak-east face/Spoon Couloir
Rockchuck Peak-east face
The Jaw-east face

Class G:
Cody Peak-Once Is Enough
Cody Peak-Twice Is Nice
Middle Teton-Glacier Route
Mount Moran-Skillet Glacier

Mount Owen-Briggs' and Boomer's Route
Mount Wister-east ridge/southeast couloir
South Teton-southeast face
Teewinot Mountain-east face

Class H:
Buck Mountain-Bubble Fun Couloir
Cody Peak-Central Chute
Grand Teton-Briggs' Route
Grand Teton-Ford Couloir
South Teton-southeast couloir

Notes And Sources

Introduction *pp. 13-16*

Geological history derived from Love and Reed, *Creation of the Teton Landscape; The Geologic Story of Grand Teton National Park.*

How to Use this Book *pp. 17-20*

Skier Grade System adapted from William Briggs' *"Classification Chart."*

Teton Skiing Guide *pp. 21-32*

Example of "cataclysmic collapse" drawn from *Jackson Hole News* articles, "Atlas shrugs off the new year," 1/6/82, p.21, and "9 days later ... Grand avalanche revisited," 1/13/82, p.5. Accounts of climbers killed in moats published in *Jackson Hole Guide*, "Bright, Cheerful Day Held No Hint of Tragedy," 6/24/71, p.1; and *Jackson Hole News,* "Man killed in mountain accident," News, 6/23/82, p.12, references Richard Schaffer death. Geological history of Jackson Hole's lakes derived from Love and Reed, *Creation of the Teton Landscape.* Information about lake-ice formation drawn from interviews and correspondence with Jeff Rader and Dan Burgette; Bohren's *The Freezing of Lakes*; and Marchand's *Life in the Cold, An Introduction to Winter Ecology.*

Details of lake-ice anomalies gathered via interviews and correspondence with Jeff Rader and Dan Burgette and from Strung, "When Ice Is Safe," *Field and Stream*, 2/89, p.87. Information about lake-ice travel derived from interviews and correspondence with Jeff Rader and Dan Burgette; Strung, "When Ice Is Safe," *Field and Stream*, p.87; Richey, David, "Ice Safety and Rescue," *Outdoor Life*, 12/77, p.120; and Strung, "Are You Walking On Thin Ice?" *Outdoor Life*, date not available, p.42. Accounts of skiers and climbers killed in "slides for life" derived from: Thuermer, "The Grand claims Dan McKay," *News*, 7/14/82, p.A1; *Accidents in North American Mountaineering*, (Dan McKay death); Thuermer, "Mark Stewart killed skiing Teewinot," *News*, 5/8/85, p.3; Heller, "Skier killed in Teewinot death slide," *Guide*, 5/7/85, p.A1 (Mark Stewart death); Abendroth, "Teewinot claims first fatality of summer season," *Guide*, 5/18/94, p.A3 (Arlo Morrill death); Thuermer, "1,000-foot plunge kills Idaho climber," *News*, 6/15/94, p.9A (Bill McDonald killed in slide on Owen-Spalding). Other examples of solo skiers getting into trouble were drawn from: Simpson, "Search saves skier from death in Phillips canyon," *Guide*, 2/20/91, p.A13; and "Patrolmen rescue youth who skied out of bounds," *Guide*, 3/13/91, p.A8. Alpine starts referenced from Swift, David, "High Country Skiing-The discipline of corn snow," *News*, 4/28/82, p.21 (with comments from Robbie Fuller and Rod Newcomb, writer aims to educate late Glory Bowl skiers of aesthetics and avalanche awareness).

Effects of skiers and snowmobiles on wildlife drawn from Freddy, David, et al, *Reponses of Mule Deer to Disturbance by Persons Afoot and Snowmobiles*; and Teton Basin Ranger District, Draft Winter Travel Map. Other information about sensitive wildlife areas and closures derived from: Grand Teton National Park documents, including: 1977 Environmental Assessment, Alternatives for Management of Winter Recreational Activities; 1984 Compendium to 1977 Environmental Assessment; 1988 Backcountry Management Plan; 1990 Compendium to 1988 Backcountry Management Plan; and a memo from Mason Reid to Denny Ziemann, "Mystic Isle Closure." A letter from Brad Exton of the Teton Basin Ranger District, Targhee National Forest, provides information about west-side wildlife areas and closures. Related information was drawn from the Targhee National Forest Draft Winter Travel Map and 1988 Teton Valley Community Task Force documents, including: Teton Canyon to Fox Creek Recommendations on Management of Wildlife Winter Range and Winter Recreation; Teton Canyon Recommendations on Management of Wildlife Winter Range and Winter Recreation.

Snowmobile and snowplane history drawn from Platts, *The Pass: Historic Teton Pass and Wilson, Wyoming*; and "Snowmobiles Open New Era of Winter Sports," *Guide*, 1/9/69. Skijoring references: 1977 Environmental Assessment, Alternatives for Management of Winter Recreational Activities, GTNP, p.31; and Thuermer, "Going to the Dogs," *free snow*, Fall 1994, p.8.

A Historical Perspective *pp 33-50*
John Colter history derived from Harris, *John Colter; His Years in the Rocky Mountains*. Webbs and skis data derived from: an interview with Bill Resor; *John Colter; His Years in the Rocky Mountains*; and "Treasures of the Past," a video provided by Teton Valley Arts and Humanities and Teton Valley Historical Society. Historical information about postal delivery in the area taken from: "Neither Snow Nor Rain..." *Teton Magazine*, Winter-Spring 1970. p.12; and Platts, *The Pass: Historic Teton Pass and Wilson, Wyoming*. "The Town Hill," *Teton Magazine*, c. mid-1970s, p.21, describes skis, boots, and poles of the early 1900s. Rosy Rosencranz data drawns from: Payne's, *Make It Wyoming; Biographical Sketch of Rudolph Rosencrans;* "Rosy of the Rangers," *The Denver Post*, Empire Magazine, 2/55; and "Rosy Celebrates Ninetieth Birthday," *Guide,* 12/23/65. Personal interviews with Bob Kranenberg and James Braman brought to light their historic roles in Teton skiing, while Hill and Simmons were featured in the *Jackson's Hole Courier* article, "150 mile ski trip requires 8 days," 1/26/39, p.1. Patricia Petzoldt's *On Top of the World; My Adventures with my Mountain-Climbing Husband,* offered information detailing Paul Petzoldt's Teton adventures. *The Town Hill* tells about Mike O'Neil, ski jumping, and added to the *News'* "Jackson Hole SKi Club 50th Anniversary supplement and *The Grand Teton*, "Jackson Hole Winter Sports Association Holds Initial Meeting of Year 1932-33" (1/17/33, p.2.), in providing information about Jackson Hole Ski Association early races and gear. *The Town Hill* and *Courier* articles "Dartmouth Ski Team to Spend Christmas in Jackson Hole," 12/9/37; "Dartmouth Ski Team to Practice on Teton Pass," 12/23/37; "200 Persons See Crack Dartmouth Ski Team Perform on Teton Pass," 12/30/37 track activities of the Dartmouth Team, while information about the Hoback Boys was derived from the 1/26/39 *Courier* article, "Hicks Boys Steal Show At Ketchum Ski Meet Sunday," as well as *The Town Hill*, and an interview with Jim Huidekoper.

The extent of Fred Brown's early tours is drawn from: *The Town Hill*; Woolsey's *Off The Beaten Track*; and interviews with Mike Yokel, Jack

Durrance, Jim and Virginia Huidekoper, Bob Kranenberg, Ted Major, Muggs Schultz, and Betty Woolsey. Personal interviews with Yokel and Jim and Virginia Huidekoper also provided information about Brown's youth, personality and work, while data about his racing activity was drawn from "Fred Brown is Wyoming's combined downhill and slalom champ," *Courier*, 2/23/39. Elkins' *The Complete Ski Guide*, gives information about Teton Pass Ranch; *American Alpine Journal*, Vol. 2, 8:543, 12/19/35 tells of Allyn Hanks and Dudley Hayden's 1933 ski tour into the Tetons; and information about the earliest Teton skiing foray was derived from an interview with Bob Kranenberg; Hanks and Brown shot a super-8 video of skiing in Cascade south fork, and watching the video in 1934 inspired Kranenberg to ski in the Tetons. Details of Brown's other tours were drawn from: "Skiers Find Warmer Temperatures at Higher Elevations," *Courier*, 2/24/38, p.1; Woolsey, *Off The Beaten Track*, (p.192-193).

Information about first winter ascent of Grand Teton derived from Bonneys' *Guide to the Wyoming Mountains and Wilderness Areas* and a preview of Renny Jackson's unpublished history of Teton mountaineering, and stories of early park skiers come from personal interviews with Bob Kranenberg, Bill Briggs, Pete Hayden and Blake Vandewater. Fritz Brown column derived from: "Choice and Care of Skiing Equipment," *Courier*, 1/7/37; and "Climbing Technique," 1/28/37. *The Town Hill* p.47,48,51-54,56-65, and an interview and correspondence with Ted Major offer information about early Snow King. Data about early skiing and tows on Teton Pass drawn from *The Town Hill* and Bonneys' *Guide to the Wyoming Mountains and Wilderness Areas*. Barracato's "Historic Teton Valley," published in the 1993-94 Teton Valley, Idaho Winter Guide offers information about early lift-served skiing in Teton Valley, while ski equipment of the 1940s and 50s is derived from interviews and correspondence with Peter Koedt, Ted Major and various others. An interview with Paul Imeson tells of Grover Bassett.

Sheep Creek ski cabin data drawn from: Thuermer, "Need for use of Elk Refuge could curtail visits to unique mountain Ski Cabin retreat," *News*, 1/8/86, (access to cabin could be blocked by expansion of elk wintering grounds); Eastridge, Diane, "B-T may rescind ski cabin closure," *Guide*, 1/3/91, p.A1, (local skiers denied permits to go to cabin and complained); Thuermer, "Forest eyes closing Goodwin ski cabin," *News*, 1/16/91, p.3A (gives ski cabin chronology and cites elk-herd wintering grounds and conflict with Wilderness Act as reasons for ski-cabin closure); Eastridge, "Ski Club granted cabin for season's remainder," *Guide*, 1/16/91, p.A18 (Forest Service grants limited access to cabin); Eastridge, "Forest official says ski cabin may yet stay," *Guide*, 2/13/91, p.A3 (cabin viewed as pre-existing use and thus defies Wilderness Act); interviews with Walter Kussy and Neil Rafferty. Information about Betty Woolsey derived from Woolsey, *Off The Beaten Track*; Lunn, Arnold, *The Story of Skiing* (racing and mountaineering); Hayden, Roger, "Locals...First Tracks," *Jackson Hole Magazine*, Winter 1993-94; Woods, Rebecca, "Pioneers of Skiing Jackson Hole," *Jackson Hole Skier Magazine*, 1991/92; interviews with Betty Woolsey and Muggs Schultz.

Interviews and correspondence with Frank Ewing, Rod Newcomb, Bill Briggs, and Inga and Peter Koedt provided information about Ewing; Dick Pittman and Jake Breitenbach story drawn from "Dick Pittman, Ski Patrolman, Killed Thursday in Avalanche," *Guide*, 3/19/64, and from interviews with Frank Ewing and Rod Newcomb. INEL foursome story derived from interviews with Robert Hammer and Bill Barmore. Details of the first descent of Buck Mountain drawn from correspondence with Barry Corbet and Eliot Goss, and Bonneys' *Guide to the Wyoming Mountains and Wilderness Areas*, which cites the exploit as a 6/60 ski ascent by Barry Corbet). 1960s winter mountaineering data derived from: interviews and corrrespondence with Peter Lev, Rick Horn, Peter

Koedt, Frank Ewing and Rod Newcomb; *Guide*'s "Petzoldt's NOLS Boosts Winter Activity," 1/2/69; "2nd Team Marches Against Blizzardy Grand Teton," 1/2/69 (using snowmobiles to approach from Moose, the team attempted east ridge and failed, then tried and failed again in 2/69), and "Winter Mountaineering Becomes Popular," 2/27/69. "Petzoldt's NOLS Boosts Winter Activity" also provides accounts of NOLS ascents.

Jackson Hole Ski Area: McCollister background derived from interviews with Paul and Mike McCollister and Oliver, Peter, "It's a Hole New Ball Game in Jackson," *Skiing*, 12/93. Early Peak 10,450 explorations drawn from interviews with Jim Huidekoper, John Harrington, and Rod Newcomb. Lift openings detailed via interviews with Jerry Balint and John Bernadyn; and early ski-area setting drawn from correspondence with Ray White. Grand Targhee Ski Area data derived from Harris, Darryl, "Wyoming's New Idaho Ski Area," *Teton Magazine*, Winter-Spring 1970, p.14; Dewell, Thomas, "Grand Targhee Resort turns 25," *News*, 11/16/94; and interviews with Jim Huidekoper, Bill Rigby, John Harrington, and Targhee ski patrolmen. Free-heel skiing ban at Grand Targhee detailed via an interview with Jim Day; "Skiing single and skinny," *News*, 2/21/80 (includes interviews with all three resorts about Grand Targhee ban on free-heel skis); Woods, Becky, "Skiers pressure Targhee to allow pin bindings," *Guide*, 3/12/81; "Grand Targhee not free yet," *News*, 3/25/81; "Targhee will allow X-C skiers," *Guide*, 3/26/81.

Ski activity and tours by Peter Koedt, Jerry Balint, Ray White, and Pepi Stiegler drawn from personal interviews and correspondence with Koedt, Balint, John Bernadyn, White, Stiegler and Bill Briggs. Information about Briggs' skiing derived from: interview and correspondence with Briggs; "New Director of Snow King Ski School is Bill Briggs," *Guide*, 11/3/66; Cook, John Byrne, "Bill Briggs, Extreme Pioneer," *Jackson Hole Skier*, 1994. Details of the first descent of Grand Teton from: "Briggs to lead ski descent of Grand Teton," *News*, 4/

8/71; "Briggs Skis Down Grand Teton," *News*, 6/17/71; "Come On, Make Some Good Tracks: First Ski Descent of the Grand Teton," *Teton Magazine*, Winter-Spring, 1972; "Grand Teton, first ski descent," *AAJ*, Vol.18, 46:132-133. Briggs' motives detailed in Turiano, Thomas, "Kamikaze Klassics," *Rock and Ice Magazine*, January/February 1991; Briggs' literary works from: Skiers Manual I and II; *Guide* column, as well as Whitney Thurlow correspondence. Interviews and correspondence with Jorge Colòn, Wade McKoy, Mark Wolling, and Davey Agnew detail Colòn's ski activity, while a Mike Quinn interview tells of AAI/Mike Quinn experience. Information about unorthodox equipment drawn from interviews with Bob Stevenson, Ray White, Jorge Colòn and others. Ski activity of Bob Stevenson, Chuck Schaap, Davey Agnew, Peter Wuerslin, and Jim Roscoe derived from personal interviews.

"Crash and Burn" story told in interview with Jim Day, while Jeff Crabtree and Peter Koedt detailed Crabtree's crest taverse. Frank Venutti story derived from a personal interview with Bill MacLeod; John Carr information drawn from interviews and correspondence with Carr and Ray White; and climbing-ranger history derived from Jim Olson interview. Mountaineering Outfitters history drawn from an interview with store clerk and correspondence with Ron Watters; mountain "maggot" history taken from correspondence with Ron Watters and Day interview. Davey Agnew, Ben Franklin, Ron Watters, and John Borstlemann provided information about Gregg Amalong and westside skiers, while Bob Stevenson and Rick Liu told of the obsession with turning, and Day offered details of Teton Pass telemarkers. Stories of Day, Dave Titcomb and Tom Russo come from interviews with Day and Cindy Duncan. "Nordic Patrol rescues skier in Coal Creek," *Guide*, 3/22/79, tells story of when Art Becker broke his leg, Bob Stevenson stayed with him, and Alice Stevenson and another skied out to get help. Stories of NOLS deaths drawn from 1/25/74 GTNP memorandum to superintendent, "NOLS Winter Accident, 1-16-74"; "Superintendent's Board of Inquiry Report. Deaths of Bart Brodsky, Michael Moseley, and David Silha," NOLS Winter Accident, 1-16-74," GTNP, 1/29/74; Huidekoper, Virginia, "Avalanche, Tetons claim three," *News*, 1/24/74.

Seasonal park employee upgrade information drawn from interview with Jim Olson; avalanche forecast hotline data from interview with Gary Poulson; American Avalanche Institute data from interview with Rod Newcomb; avalanche transceiver history from interviews with Rod Newcomb, Ray White, and Dean Moore; skiing guide services from interviews and correspondence with Peter Koedt, Dave Miller, Chi Melville, and Jim Day, as well as Teton County Historical Center data; 2/11/82 *Teton Valley Winter Recreation Guide* article gives history of Teton Mountain Touring; 11/17/66 *Guide* article, "Winter Survival Program Tuesday," tells of Dick Person and Juris Krisjansons' avalanche program and Person's "Skiing Unlimited." Interviews and correspondence with Ron Watters, Glenn Vitucci and Carole Lowe provide data about Kirk Bachman and Rendezvous Ski Tours, respectively, while information about Serendipity Bump and Gelunde competitions was derived from: Woodin, Rip, "Gelande-'77," *Guide*, 4/7/77; Beedle, Steve, "Serendipity sends Snow King toward summer," *Guide*, 4/7/77; and "Freestyle," *News*, 4/20/77.

Extreme skiing data derived from: interviews with Larry Bruce and Steve Shea; Beedle, Steve, "Ski Season Never Ends...not even in July," *Guide*, 7/13/78 (mentions Jeff Rhoads and Brad Peck's descent of the Grand as well as filming of *Fall Line*); "'Fall Line', a film on extreme skiing, climbing, shot here," "Breashears: 'The Kloberdanz Kid,'" *News*, 7/4/79; McKay, Dan, "Round of Chuters," *Powder Magazine*, 2/83, reprinted in *Jackson Hole Skier Magazine*, 1993, and describes jumping into Corbet's Couloir; McKay, Dan, "Skiing in the Hole," *Guide*, 3/8/79, tells of Bill Danford and Joe Larrow launching into Corbet's Couloir; *Rhthyms*, Solomon film. Steve Shea and

Robin "Boomer" McClure data obtained via personal interviews with Shea, Bill Briggs, Dave Miller and others, plus accident report audio tape, courtesy of Briggs; "Matterhorn claims two," *News*, 7/27/77; and "The end of the dream," *Guide*, 7/28/77 (includes Bill Briggs eulogy). Post-season skiing off tram derived from interviews and correspondence with Mark Wolling, Jim Roscoe, Gregg Martell, Steve Lundy, Joe Larrow, Mike Quinn and Larry Detrick; and "Local skier rescued after fall on Rendezvous Mountain," *News*, 6/6/79, (post-season skier injured in Four Shadows). Modern downhillers portrayed via interviews and correspondence with Theo Meiners, Brian Bradley, Richard Collins, Mike Fischer, Greg Miles, Jim Duclos, Jay Moody, Les Gibson, and others; Rick Wyatt data via interviews with Wyatt, Jeff Newsom and Renny Jackson; Jeff Rhoads data via interviews and corrrespondence with Jeff and Kellie Rhoads; Beedle, Steve, "Ski Season Never Ends...not even in July," *Guide*, 7/13/78 (mentions Jeff Rhoads and Brad Peck's descent of the Grand); "I Skied Grand Teton-Rhoads," *Idaho State Journal-Enjoy Magazine*, 1/26/79; Rhoads, Jeff, "Teton Descent," *The Intermountain Skier*, 4/79. Dan McKay portrayed via interviews and correspondence with Wade McKoy, Joe Larrow, Steve Shea, Skeeter Cattabriga, and Jim Kanzler; McKay, Dan, "Speed thrills...If the Gros Ventre isn't fast enough," *Guide*, 5/8/80; McKay, "Buck Mountain on skinny skis," Thuermer, "Sportsman Dan McKay's last story," *News*, 7/8/87; McKay, "Round of Chuters," *Powder Magazine*, February 1983, reprinted in 1993 *Jackson Hole Skier Magazine*; Thuermer, "The Grand claims Dan McKay," *News*, 7/14/82; Woodall, Bob, "Dan McKay believed in trying all the way," "Local skier killed on Grand," *Guide*, 7/15/82; *Accidents in North American Mountaineering*, Vol.4, No.6, Issue 36.

Figling data derived from interview with Roland Fleck; Swift, David, "Is Jackson Hole ready for figling?" *News*, 6/2/83. Monoskiing data drawn from interviews with Davey Agnew and Jerry Balint; snowboarding data from interview with Dustin

Varga; Peter Carman's supergaiter from interview with Russell Rainey; and the Mountain Noodle from interview with Chi Melville; Chavez, Chris, "Don't be a noodle, try skiing a Noodle," *Guide*, 2/7/90 (mentions Clair Yost first skiing on the pass in 1974). Chouinard cable binding data drawns from interview with Rick Liu, and SuperLoop binding from interview with Russell Rainey; Dostal, John, "Behind the Brand...SuperLoop," *Cross Country Skier*, January/February 1994. "Ski marketing programs get mixed receptions," *News*, 1/22/86, tells of Jackson Hole becoming a destination resort; Peter Wuerslin data and Marty Vidak/Peter Quinlan tours derived from personal interviews. Mike Best data drawn from personal interview and from Thuermer, "Avalanches hit record numbers," *News*, 3/4/92, which told of Best being carried over cliffs on Glory Bowl during full moon ski on 1-17-92.

The Routes *pp. 51-178*

Northern Range pp. 51-58

Ashton-Flagg history and Huckman avalanche data derived from Allen's *Early Jackson Hole*; Grassy Lake Road closure drawns from Thuermer, "Grassy Lake Road and camps to stay closed," *Jackson Hole Daily*, 4/26/94; Forellen Peak-east ridge tour detailed in Barnett's *The Best Ski Touring in America*.

Ranger Peak Region pp. 59-66

Jackson Lake Dam history drawn from Righter's *Crucible for Conservation; The Struggle for Grand Teton National Park*; Jackson Lake levels from Love, topo/relief map of GTNP, chart on lake level fluctuations; *News*, 1/11/84 (says Bureau of Reclamation has map of levels). Fonda/Wilcox deaths detailed in "Two Park Rangers Dead After Fall Thru Ice on Jackson Lake," *Guide*, 3/17/60; Dickenson, Russell, GTNP memorandum to superintendent, 4/4/60. Colter hot springs data derived from "Low H_2O level exposes hot springs," *Guide*, 8/4/77 and 10/13/77 (Note that hot springs extend some 1,700 feet along Teton fault, on the west shore of Jackson Lake, north

of Colter Canyon mouth; water temperature was 161.1 degrees Fahrenheit and flowed at 200,000 gallons per second). Gustavus Doane story derived from Bonney, *Battle Drums and Geysers* (Doane's journal of travel through Jackson Hole). Information about Peak 10,686 forest fire of July, 1974 drawn from Campbell GTNP Freedom of Information Act correspondence, 3/5/93.

Snowshoe Canyon Region pp. 67-72
No entries.

Mount Moran Region pp. 73-80

Mystic Isle closure derived from 1984 Compendium to 1977 Environmental Assessment, GTNP, and Mason Reid memo to Denny Ziemann, 10/15/92. Spalding Bay closure from "Motorboat launching banned at Spalding Bay," *Guide*, 4/18/93. Thor Peak-Standard Route drawn from Dewell, Thomas and Turiano, Thomas, "Four skiers conquer Thor Peak," *News*, 6/2/93; Dostal's "Behind the Brand...SuperLoop" (mentions Russell's nordic descent of Thor). Mount Moran-Skillet Glacier data derived from: Manley, Fletcher, "Skiing the Skillet: First Ski Descent of Mount Moran," *Teton Magazine*, Winter-Spring 1970; *AAJ*, 37:411,419; Thuermer, "Four injured climbing in Grand Teton Park," *News*, 8/4/93; Thuermer, "Three swept 2,000 feet in avalanche," *Jackson Hole Daily*, 7/30/93, (detail astonishing summer avalanche on Skillet Glacier). Peak 10,952-east couloir data drawn from: Turiano, Thomas, "Cleaver Peak's elusive summit," *News*, 2/9/94. Cleaver Peak: Ibid; Clelland, Mike, "Teton relief," *News* letter to editor, 2/16/94; Turiano, "Pure attempt," *News* letter to editor, 2/16/94. (Corrects error in "Cleaver Peak's elusive summit," which alleges that Bev Boynton used a snowmobile during her attempt, which she did not.)

Mount Saint John Region pp. 81-86

In "Spring Avalanches: The mountains are alive," *News*, 4/23/80, climbing ranger Ralph Tingey describes spring-avalanche dangers at Hanging Canyon and cites examples of how immense they can be. Data about early Paintbrush Canyon ski tour to Holly Lake drawn from interview with Bob Kranenberg, while Beaver Dick Lake data references Thompson and Thompson's *The Honor and The Heartbreak*, and Symmetry Spire-Symmetry Couloir is drawn from "Bright, Cheerful Day Held No Hint of Tragedy...Three Die In Park's Worst Disaster," *Guide*, 6/24/71 and "Man killed in mountain accident," *News*, 6/23/82 (Richard Schaffer death).

The High Peaks pp. 87-106
Teton Park Road plowing history derived from *Courier* articles of 2/16/39 and 11/2/39. Snowmobile approaches drawn from "2nd Team Marches Against Blizzardy Grand Teton," *Guide*, 1/2/69, and interviews with Peter Koedt and Frank Ewing. Garnet Canyon history and big avalanche from *AAJ*, Vol.2, 8:543, 12/19/35; Bonney, *Guide to the Wyoming Mountains and Wilderness Areas*, "Atlas shrugs off the new year," *News*, 1/6/82 and "9 days later...Grand avalanche revisited," 1/13/82. Glacier Gulch history drawn from Renny Jackson correspondence, while information about Glacier Gulch avalanche derived from: Huidekoper, Virginia, "Avalanche, Tetons claim three," *News*, 1/24/74; Anderson, Emory J., "3 Mountain Hikers Dead In Teton Avalanche," *Guide*, 1/24/74; Peter Hart's 1/25/74 GTNP memorandum to superintendent; "Superintendent's Board of Inquiry Report-Deaths of Bart Brodsky, Michael Moseley, and David Silha, NOLS Winter Accident, 1-16-74," GTNP, 1/29/74; Williams and Armstrong, *The Snowy Torrents-Avalanche Accidents in the United States 1972-79*. Cascade Canyon patrol cabin data derived from GTNP document, 5/91; South Teton-southeast couloir infomation from Simmons, Drew, "Snowboarder blazes trails on Teton Range slopes," *News*, 6/19/91. South Teton-Frishman Couloir detailed in "Well known valley climber dies climbing Middle Teton," *Guide*, 1/22/81; *Accidents in North*

American Mountaineering, Vol.4, No.5, Issue 35 (Harry Frishman death, 1/19/81).
Turiano, Thomas. "Kamikaze Klassics," portrays the Middle Teton-Glacier Route, while Bonneys' *Guide to the Wyoming Mountains and Wilderness Areas* tells of Bill Briggs raving about skiing in Dartmouth Basin, though Briggs denies ever skiing there. (In the 1940s, Dartmouth Basin referred to upper Cascade south fork, rather than the steep draw west of the Lower Saddle, as it is known today.) Grand Teton-Briggs' Route data is derived from: "Briggs to lead ski descent of Grand Teton," *News*, 4/8/71; "Come On, Make Some Good Tracks," *Teton Magazine*, 1972; "Briggs Skis Down Grand Teton," *News*, 6/17/71; *Intermountain Skier*, Vol.II, Issue II; Woodall, Bob, "Grand Teton becoming popular descent," *Guide*, 6/21/79 (photo of Joe Larrow); Stump, David, "Meiners, Zell join elite corps of Grand skiers," *Guide*, 6/8/88; "Grand Teton, first ski descent," *AAJ*, Vol.18, 46:132-133. Story of Dean Moore derived from Rohde's, "He's not climbing walls, he's climbing mountains...A visit with Dean Moore," *Guide*, 1/18/79. Information about the *Fall Line* video provided in: "'Fall Line', a film on extreme skiing, climbing, shot here," *News*, 7/4/79, and Beedle, Steve, "Ski Season Never Ends...not even in July," *Guide*, 7/13/78. Data about Kim Anderson fall drawn from Thuermer, "Briggs misses Grand ski descent anniversary," *News*, 6/22/83. Stephen Koch-first snowboard descent derived from: Thuermer, "Koch first to snowboard Grand Teton," *News*, 6/14/89; Chavez, Chris, "Believe it or not, he snowboarded the Grand," *Guide*, 6/14/89; Turiano, "Passages Through Walls of Stone," *Jackson Hole Skier Magazine*, 1992/93; Turiano, "Koch 'Boards the Grand," *Jackson Hole Skier Magazine*, 1989/90; Turiano, "Expedition Notes," *Snowboarder Magazine*, 11/89; Sheehan, Casey, "Snowboarder Cuts Grand Teton Down to Size," *Powder Magazine*, 11/89; Interviews with Stephen Koch. Rick Wyatt's first free-heel descent drawn from Thuermer, "Nordic skier descends The Grand," *News*, 6/16/82;

Thuermer, "Briggs misses Grand ski descent anniversary," *News*, 6/22/83; and interview with Wyatt. Mike Rettig's free-heel attempt told in "Briggs misses Grand ski descent anniversary," *News*, 6/22/83. Jeff Rhoads' first descent of Ford Couloir is detailed in "I Skied Grand Teton-Rhoads," *Idaho State Journal-Enjoy Magazine*, 1/26/79; Rhoads, Jeff, "Teton Descent," *The Intermountain Skier*, 4/79; Beedle, Steve, "Ski Season Never Ends...not even in July," *Guide*, 7/13/78 (mentions Jeff Rhoads and Brad Peck's descent of the Ford Couloir); and interview with Jeff Rhoads.

News article of 6/15/94, "1,000-foot plunge kills Idaho climber" tells of climbers killed in falls on Owen-Spalding route, while "Snowboarder blazes trails on Teton Range slopes" details snowboarding the Owen-Spalding route. The story of the first descent of Black Ice Couloir is told in Dewell's "Two ski Grand's Black Ice Couloir," *News*, 6/15/94; "Surf Mountaineering," *Rock and Ice Magazine*, Cliff Notes, September/October 1994; Simmons, Drew, "Not Afraid of the Dark," *Couloir Magazine*, Oct/Nov 1994. The story of Dan McKay's death is derived from: Thuermer, "The Grand claims Dan McKay," *News*, 7/14/82; Woodall, Bob, "Dan McKay believed in trying all the way," "Local skier killed on Grand," *Guide*, 7/15/82; *Accidents in North American Mountaineering*, Vol.4, No.6, Issue 36. East Ridge avalanche deaths portrayed in: the National Park Service Case Incident Record of 4/26/79, which details the deaths of Tim Drew and Jerry Lucas; "Spring Avalanches: 'The mountains are alive,'" *News*, 4/23/80, in which climbing ranger Ralph Tingey describes spring avalanche dangers and cites several examples of how enormous they can be; "Grand Teton claims lives of two men," *News*, 5/2/79; Williams and Armstrong, *The Snowy Torrents*.

Mount Owen-Koven Couloir referenced in "Snowboarder blazes trails on Teton Range slopes," *News*, 6/19/91; "Mount Owen Stories," *Ski*, summer of 1976. Mount Owen-Briggs' and Boomer's Route data derived from: "Mt Owen, first ski descent," *AAJ*, 49:134-135 (says descent started 150 feet below summit); "Skiing Mount Owen" and "Briggs, McClure are first to ski Mt. Owen," *News*, 6/27/74; "Skiers Make First Descent Of Mt. Owen," *Guide*, 6/27/74. *News* article of 5/8/85, "Mark Stewart killed skiing Teewinot" and *Guide* articles, "Skier killed in Teewinot death slide," 5/7/85, and "Teewinot claims first fatality of summer season," 5/18/94, tell of climbers and skiers killed during slides for life on Teewinot. Teewinot northeast shoulder avalanche data drawn from "Spring Avalanches: 'The mountains are alive,'" *News*, 4/23/80, in which climbing ranger Ralph Tingey describes spring avalanche dangers and cites examples of the tremendous size they can achieve.

Buck Mountain Massif pp. 107-116

Beaver Creek fire: information derived from Gerty, Mary, "Taggart/Bradley trail reopens through burn area," *News*, 12/18/85 (fire started 8/30/85). Avalanche Canyon data drawn from Woolsey's *Off The Beaten Track*; and *News* article, "30 Years Ago in the Tetons," 4/29/71. Albright Peak (Peak 10,552) referenced in "Avalanche sweeps skier 2,000 feet," and "Marden struggled for his life in avalanche," *News*, 1/15/92. Static Peak data: derived from Stump, Dave article and photo, *Guide*, 4/24/80; *1988 Backcountry Management Plan*, GTNP, which bans humans from Static Peak from Nov. 1 to April 30. Buck Mountain data drawn from: Bonneys' *Guide to the Wyoming Mountains and Wilderness Areas*, which cites exploit as a 6/60 ski ascent by Barry Corbet; "Buck Mountain on skinny skis" and "Sportsman Dan McKay's last story," *News*, 7/8/87; Thuermer, "Climbers flock to peaks claim Grand, others," *News*, 12/31/85 (States that Bob Graham climbed east ridge of Veiled and the east face of Buck from Avalanche Canyon, which probably means he climbed and skied the lower northeast couloir of Buck). Mount Wister story derived from "Board of Inquiry Report into the death of Bruce Melliger," GTNP, 2/20/85 (Melliger was killed 2/3/85).

Open Canyon Region pp. 117-122

Open Canyon avalanche drawn from Dewell, "Search finds no victims after Teton Pass slide," *News,* 2/93 (mentions the avalanche in upper Open Canyon). Death Canyon data references Murphy, Richard J., "Death Canyon: For ski tourers a promise of adventure," *News,* 3/21/74. Mount Hunt information drawn from: McKay, Dan, "Skiing in the Hole...Tallyho," *Guide ,* 3/22/79 (tells about Mark Wolling, Jorge Colòn, Dan McKay, and Tocho Silva skiing Mount Hunt in 3/79; praises Colòn as strong hiker and calls east face "Grunt" and southeast face "Gums' Gulch"). A 4/25/84 *News* article tells of Carson Hubbard.

Rendezvous Mountain pp. 123-134

During a personal interview, Wade McKoy provided data about Cody Peak for the author in telling about skiing Twice Is Nice and Once Is Enough. Other related data was derived from: Barry, Jim, "First Tracks: Concentration," *Guide,* 1/28/82, (focuses on Once Is Enough); "Local skier rescued after fall on Rendezvous Mountain," *News,* 6/6/79 (tells of skier injured after fall in Four Shadows); and a 4/8/92 *News* article, which tells of the first descent of Shirley's Snowfield. Information about Green River avalanche accidents was drawn from: "Avalanche Catches Richard Ream," *Guide,* 4/2/70, which tells of a Richard Ream Weekend at Teton Village that raised $2,725 to help Ream with medical bills; "Skier recalls 92 minutes of burial," *News,* 12/16/92; Thuermer, and Welch, Craig, "Skier survives avalanche burial," *News,* 4/8/92; and Simpson, David, "Skier is rescued after 90 minutes under avalanche," *Guide,* 4/8/92. Deaths in upper Rock Springs canyon are portrayed in 4/6/94 *News* and *Guide* articles that tell of a ski accident that took the lives of two young skiers. For Jackson Hole Ski Patrol history, the author drew on: "Ski patrol pioneered avalanche technique," *News,* 12/16/92; "Hunting for avalanches," *News,* 2/28/79, which describes morning avalanche-control procedures,

focusing on the three Howitzer cannons; Thuermer, "Patrolmen discover quirks in radio transceivers," *News,* 1/15/86, which discusses interference of metal objects and electronic devices in effectiveness of beacons; as well as interviews with Jim Kanzler, Gary Poulson, Jerry Balint and John Bernadyn. Further interviews with Peter Lev and Rod Newcomb provide data about the Dick Porter and S&S avalanches. "Hunting for avalanches," *News,* 2/28/79, describes three close calls during avalanche blasting, with added close-call information derived from interviews with Balint and Bernadyn. Stories of 1986 avalanches derived from: Thuermer, "Snow avalanche sweeps six, kills one," *News,* 12/4/85; and a 12/5/85 *Guide* article, both telling of the death of Paul Driscoll; "Massive slide strips Rendezvous," *News,* 12/11/85 (big bomb); Thuermer, "Storm pummels valley, kills one," *News,* 2/19/86 (death of Tom Raymer); Flynn, Janet, "Memorial set for 'the Ranger,' Tom Raymer," *Guide,* 2/20/86; and "Raymer remembered as sportsman, adventurer," *News,* 2/19/86. Less-tragic avalanche information is drawn from: "Skier rescued from area avalanche," *News,* 3/11/71 (Jeff Roberts incident); Thuermer, "Skier recalls 92 minutes of burial," *News,* 12/16/92; Thuermer and Welch, "Skier survives avalanche burial," *News,* 4/8/92, p.A1; Simpson, "Skier is rescued after 90 minutes under avalanche," *Guide,* 4/8/92.

Jackson Hole ski area recent history and future is derived from: Burdick, Christine, "Ski lift upgrades coming, but not for another year," *Guide,* 5/18/94; Dewell, Thomas, "New quad will replace Thunder chair at area," *News,* 5/18/94; Oliver, "It's a Hole New Ball Game in Jackson."

Headwall avalanche activity portrayed in: Sellett, Michael, "Ski Area opens lifts; operations near normal," *News,* 2/26/86; Thuermer, "Avalanche, slide was biggest ever at Village," *News,* 2/26/86 (features avalanche of 2/24/86); Flynn, "Avalanches slam village, valley," *Guide,* 2/18/86; Conover, Adele,

"Weather triggers major slide at ski resort," *Guide*, 1/31/90 (tells of Headwall avalanching during ski area hours on Super Bowl Sunday).

Granite Canyon Arch: Stump, "Welcome to the outer limits of..." *Guide*, 4/10/80, (provides photos and story of first descent of Arch Couloir).

Mount Glory Region pp. 135-142

Teton Pass travel history derived from: Platts, *Historic Teton Pass*; Platts, "High Adventures on Teton Pass," *Teton Magazine*, 1990. Teton Pass avalanche history drawn from: "... Pass Not Yet Open...," *Courier*, 3/1/17 (notes that 50 pounds of dynamite failed to induce an avalanche because of temperature drop); Mitchell, Kurt, "Gunning for Glory," *News*, 1/15/86; Heller, Jean, "O'Jack, Thompson survive burial in Pass avalanche," *Guide*, 2/18/86; Kessler, Nancy, "Pass avalanche close call," *News*, 2/19/86 (motorists O'Jack and Thompson waited at bottom of Glory Bowl for a snowplow to clear a small slough; then a big avalanche hit—18 feet deep, 160 feet wide); "Teton Pass still closed, opening expected at end of next week," *News*, 2/26/86 (it took nearly three weeks to clear 25 feet of debris, 300 feet wide); Thuermer, "State wrestled Highway 22 for years," *News*, 12/23/92 (provides a comprehensive history of avalanche control on Teton Pass).

Phillips Canyon rescue is detailed in "Search saves skier from death in Phillips canyon," *Guide*, 2/20/91. Information about Glory Bowl avalanches provided in: "Glory Bowl Slides on Easter," *News*, 4/13/77; "Old 'Glory' Rides Again," *Guide*, 4/14/77, p.1; "Avalanches hit record numbers," *News*, 3/4/92. Little Tuckerman's avalanche data derived from "Search finds no victims after Teton Pass slide," *News*, 2/93; Twin Slides avalanche data from: Nelson, Fern K., *This Was Jackson's Hole*; Snowshoe Bowl avalanche data from: Thuermer, "Father, son survive burial in avalanche," *News*, 1/23/91; Taylor Mountain-Poop Chute data from: Sarthou, Jacques, "One Up from Glory," *Teton Magazine*, Winter-Spring 1973.

Rammel Mountain Region pp. 143-146

Dry Ridge Mountain avalanche data drawn from: Thuermer, "Avalanches hit record numbers," *News*, 3/4/92 (tells story of 2/29/92 Dry Ridge avalanche, which caught snowmobilers Dan Schwendiman and Gary Ball, killing Schwendiman and breaking Ball's leg); Thuermer, "Avalanche kills snowmobiler," *News*, 3/4/92; Thuermer, "Avalanche victim found dead of a broken neck," *News*, 3/18/92; Thuermer, "Avalanche deaths haunt valley history," *News*, 12/9/92.

Fred's Mountain Region pp. 147-156

Mill Creek "Powder Four" case data derived from: Thuermer, "Skiers consider fighting out-of-bounds ticket," *News*, 2/6/91; "Charges to be dropped against four Targhee skiers," *News*, 6/19/91; and interview with Skeeter Cattabriga. Interviews with Grand Targhee ski patrol and Hollis McElwain provided information about the Steve Baugh Bowl accident. Grand Targhee backcountry access data was derived from: an interview with Jim Day; "Skiing single and skinny," *News*, 2/21/80 (Targhee expels Lowell Gillespie for skiing with a single ski, mounted with two sets of bindings; Lowell goes to court. Article also talks about ban of free-heel skis); "Grand Targhee not free yet," *News*, 3/25/81; Woods, Becky, "Skiers pressure Targhee to allow pin bindings," *Guide*, 3/12/81; "Targhee will allow X-C skiers," *Guide*, 3/26/81; "Skiers consider fighting out-of-bounds ticket," *News*, 2/6/91; "Charges to be dropped against four Targhee skiers," *News*, 6/19/91; and interview with Targhee Mountain Manager Larry Williamson. Information about the Grand Targhee Resort expansion controversy derived from: the Final Environmental Impact Statement of the Grand Targhee Resort Master Development Plan; Thuermer, "Alliance may fight OK for Targhee expansion," *News*, 5/25/94; Hayden, Roger, "Targhee gets green light as appeals end," *News*, 8/3/94. An interview with Grand Targhee ski patrollers provided data about the North Avalanch Path and Clark Kido accidents.

Teton Canyon Region pp. *157-164*

"Driggs snowmobiler dies of exposure," *News,* 1/11/84, tells of the Eddington Canyon snowmobile accident, noting that James Schultz was 21 years old. Sunset Pass-Avalanche Divide data derived from: Woolsey, *Off The Beaten Track*; Huidekoper, "30 Years Ago in the Tetons," *News*, 4/29/71.

Darby Canyon Region pp. *165-170*

A *News* article, "Salt Lake operator touts his Fox Creek quarry," by Matt Testa, provides data about the Fox Creek Quarry, circa summer, 1993.

Game Creek Region pp. *171-178*

Flooding and contour trenching data derived from: Targhee National Forest Draft Proposal for Trail Creek Watershed Improvements, 1/5/66. Mount Wow information from: McKoy, Wade, "A Room with a View," *Jackson Hole Skier*, 1994 (story about guided yurt tour between Plummer and Baldy yurts. The featured group skied Mount Wow). A 3/4/71 *News* photo features someone on the summit of Peak 10,406. Housetop Mountain-west ridge route data derived from: DuMais, Richard, *50 Ski Tours in Jackson Hole and Yellowstone*.

GLOSSARY

alpine 1. Pertains to skiing with a fixed-heel and rigid boots. 2. Describes precipitous mountain terrain that is above treeline.

alpine touring 1. Backcountry skiing with alpine equipment. 2. Backcountry skiing with alpine boots and bindings that have a releasable and lockable heel.

amphitheater A large bowl with at least 180 degrees of aspects.

anchor An implement that attaches a rope or person to a mountainside.

apron A wide, often convex, hanging snowfield that forms a band across a mountainside.

arete 1. A sharp ridge or vertical corner. 2. A ridge that separates glacial cirques.

avalanche debris Piles of snow left at the bottom of avalanche paths after snowslides.

avalanche hazard reduction Efforts aimed at reducing avalanche dangers.

avalanche runout zone Gentler terrain at the base of an avalanche path, where debris collects.

backcountry Away from roads, chair lifts and civilization.

basin A generally flat valley, rimmed on three sides by mountains or ridges.

batholith A mass of igneous rock.

bed surface The smooth plane on which an avalanche slides.

belay Means of protecting oneself or another from a fall.

bench A relatively flat area above or below a cliff or sheep slope.

bergschrund The crevasse that separates the top of a glacier from snow or rock above it.

bindings Devices that attach ski boots to skis.

bivouac Camp out with very little camping equipment.

boot track Footsteps in snow that provide easy hiking.

bowl A concave snowfield.

bushwhacking Difficult non-trail hiking with obstacles such as shrubs, weeds and trees.

buttress A rocky or earthy ridge, spur, or tower with an apex.

cache Gear stored in the mountains for later use.

carve A technique whereby skiers balance on ski edges while turning, so as to minimize slip.

cat-track A road cut into the mountainside for grooming machines.

chasm A dramatic gorge.

check A technique whereby skiers torque skis and skid across their direction of travel for speed control.

chimney A crack wider than six inches in a rock face.

chockstone A block jammed into a crack in a rock face.

chute A wide chimney filled with snow or ice.

cirque A valley rimmed on three sides by mountains or ridges.

climax avalanche An avalanche whose bed surface is the ground.

climbing skins Straps attached to the base of skis to allow skis to slide forward but not backward during hill climbing.

contour 1. A line on a map to designate areas of equal elevation. 2. To remain at the same elevation while traveling across a mountainside.

corn Granular snow formed by repeated melt-freeze metamorphosis.

cornice An overhang of snow formed by wind transport of snow.

couloir A narrow gully of ice or snow surrounded by rock walls or dense trees.

craggy Rocky and cliffy.

crampon Spikes fastened to boots to provide grip on ice and firm snow.

creep The slow, flowing movement of snowpack down a slope.

crest A high ridge that forms the hydrologic divide of a mountain range.

crevasse A stress-induced crack in glacier ice.

crust A thin, cohesive slab of snow.

crux The most difficult section of a route.

cwm (pronounced coom) A large bowl bound by mountain ridges.

deadfall Fallen trees.

diabase A dark, igneous rock.

diagonal stride Cross-country skiing technique involving opposite poling and striding.

dogleg A distinct, obtuse change in direction.

double falline A falline that differs from the direction of the run.

double-rope rappel A situation in which a rappel is longer than half a rope length, thus requiring that two ropes be attached so that they can be retrieved later.

draw A large gully.

dynamic ski maneuvering Controlled manipulation of skis while accelerating, with little chance to slow down immediately.

escarpment Long hillside.

exposure 1. The state of being exposed to weather elements. 2. Manifestation of an unsurviveable drop below while employing procedures to avoid falling. 3. Aspect.

extreme Activities that employ practiced methods to overcome obstacles beyond one's facilities and comprehension, where mistakes could result in severe injury or death.

falline The path an object takes when gravity is the sole force acting upon it.

fault scarp The exposed face of the uplifted portion of a thrust fault.

fifth class A climbing grade representing an ascent that is exposed and difficult enough that the leader places running protection while being belayed from below; this class includes 15 primary levels of difficulty.

figls Very short skis born in Europe and used during descents from early-season rock climbs.

figure-eight 1. An eight-shaped metal ring used for rappelling. 2. Interlocked ski tracks that form the shape of an eight.

firn See neve.

fixed-heel Skiing with bindings that lock skiers' heels to their skis.

flank Sides of a mountain or drainage.

flat-tracking Cross-country skiing on a flat ski track.

fluted Pertains to a mountain face that is riddled with vertical, narrow snow ribs.

flying buttress A buttress that appears totally detached from a mountain.

fourth class A climbing grade representing an ascent that is steep and exposed and on which the strongest climber anchors above and belays partners with rope.

free-heel Skiing with bindings that attach ski boots only at the toes, allowing skiers' heels to rise freely.

frost wedging Process of erosion whereby melting and refreezing of water in rock cracks causes fractures.

full track An avalanche that slides as far as possible.

gandy wagon Horse-drawn sleigh.

gendarme A rock tower along a ridge.

glade A sparse forest.

gneiss A metamorphic rock comprising much of the Teton high peaks.

gully A steep, narrow drainage.

hanging snowfield A snowfield that ends at a cliff.

headwall A steep face representing the easiest route to or from a location.

headwaters The source of a drainage.

herringbone A climbing method whereby skiers waddle back and forth between inside edges with skis in a V-shape.

horn 1. A mountain that forms at least a triple divide. 2. A protruding rock that can serve as an anchor.

hummock A dome of rock or earth, or a tuft of vegetation.

hydrologic crest The longitudinal divide of a range, at which water flows in opposite directions.

ice axe A mountaineer's tool for ice and snow climbing.

igneous Rocks solidified from a molten state.

kickturn A method of changing direction on skis without changing location.

knife-edge A sharp arete, ridglet, or ridge.

lee slope A slope that faces away from the wind source.

loop Ski tours that return to the starting point without crossing the same ground twice.

loose-snow avalanche An avalanche with no self-cohesion.

manky A rock-climbing term that refers to untrustworthy anchors.

massif High land between major valleys.

meadow A relatively flat, treeless expanse.

moat 1. The gap between a snowfield and a rock face. 2. A hole in a snowfield, formed by water erosion from beneath it.

monoski A wide ski on which bindings are mounted next to each other along the latitudinal axis of the board.

moraine A residual ridge of earth, placed by a glacier.

mouth The opening at the downstream end of a canyon or draw.

neve Dense, uniform snow that has undergone numerous melt-freeze cycles.

nordic Pertains to skiing with a free-heel.

notch A gap between two towers on a ridge.

nunatak An earthy mass left standing in the middle of a glacier.

objective hazard A hazard over which mountaineers have no control, other than timing of self-exposure.

outlet The point at which a stream drains a lake.

pillow An area of deeply wind-loaded snow.

piton A metal wedge that is hammered into rock cracks for an anchor.

plateau A relatively flat area that is elevated above surrounding valleys and basins.

posthole To break through the snow surface while walking.

powder Light, dry snow.

probe To search for a buried avalanche victim with a long pole.

probe pole Ski poles that can be adapted into avalanche probes.

ramp An angled bench that connects two points easily.

randonnée A rigid boot/binding system in which the bindings allow skiers to lock or release their heels.

rappelling Using a rope and friction device to descend a mountainside.

relief Vertical distance.

rib A narrow ridge in the midst of a face.

ridglet A small ridge.

rime A granular deposit of icy snow, which can stick to vertical rock faces.

route-finding Finding and following the safest, easiest, and quickest route.

runnel A U-shaped groove on steep snow, formed by loose-snow avalanches and/or running water.

saddle A large, relatively flat low area on a ridge between two peaks.

sastrugi Bizarre wind-sculpted snow formations.

schuss *See* straight run.

scoop A steep, concave, symmetrical glacial valley.

second class A climbing grade that refers to scrambling with frequent use of hands for balance, where the chance of being injured in a fall exists.

sedimentary Rocks formed by sediment deposition.

self-arrest A technique to stop one's motion during a slide on snow.

self-arrest grips Ski-pole hand grips with sharp, protruding fangs that aid in self-arrest.

serac A large detached block of glacial ice.

shot A less-obvious ski route.

shoulder A relatively flat area on a ridge.

side-hilling Traveling across a steep hillside.

skin To climb a slope with climbing skins.

skins *See* climbing skins.

slab A cohesive layer of snow.

slab avalanche The release and sliding action of a slab of snow.

slings Strap-like webbing used for technical climbing.

slough A small avalanche.

snowboard A single ski with bindings mounted in surf position.

snowcat An oversnow vehicle used to groom slopes and haul skiers and equipment.

spire A jutting peak of rock.

spur An earthy buttress with no apex.

starting zone The area of a slope where an avalanche is most likely to release.

stem christy A ski technique in which skiers initiate turns with a stem and finish with a skid.

stopper A metal wedge placed in rock cracks for an anchor.

straight run Pointing skis straight and letting them go with no braking action.

sugar Dry, granular, non-cohesive snow.

suncrust A thin layer of snow rendered cohesive by sun-induced melt-freeze metamorphism.

suncups Bizarre cups, spikes and bumps formed on snow surface by intense sun.

swath A treeless corridor through forest.

switchback 1. To climb or descend a slope by traversing back and forth across the slope. 2. The vertex or leg of a route that makes the traverse.

talus Rocks and boulders in a boulder field.

tarn A lake in a cirque or basin.

technical Requiring specific practiced techniques and equipment.

TG snow Dry, large, multifaceted, sugar-like snow

crystals formed by temperature gradient induced vapor movement within the snowpack, usually creating a dangerous sliding layer.

third class A climbing grade that refers to scrambling with constant use of hands for balance, where the chance of injury or death in a fall exists.

track 1. The path that an avalanche took. 2. A snow trail broken by a skier or snowcat.

trail-breaking The strenuous action of being the first skier to ski or walk through virgin snow.

traverse 1. To move laterally across a slope. 2. To travel across the length or width of a mountain range or mountain.

tree skiing Skiing through forested areas.

triple divide The point where three headwaters meet.

tour An outing.

V-shaped Fluvial drainages that usually are steep-sided and difficult to travel in.

vertical Perpendicular height difference between two points.

webbs Snowshoes.

wedge Modern term for snowplowing with skis.

whoomp The startling sound of one snow layer suddenly collapsing on a weaker layer.

wind-affected Altered by wind.

windblown *See* wind-affected.

wind-hammered A process whereby wind destroys snow crystals and makes snowpack dense.

wind-loading A process whereby wind transports and deposits snow on lee slopes.

wind-scoured Removal of all snow down to earth by wind.

wind slab A cohesive layer of snow formed by wind-loading.

windswept Areas where wind has removed snow.

windward The direction from which wind blows.

yoyo To ski a slope and then climb back up repeatedly.

yurt A Mongolian style domicile used for semipermanent backcountry refuges.

BIBLIOGRAPHY

Books

Allen, Marion V. *Early Jackson Hole*. Redding, CA: Press Room Printing, Inc. 1981.

American Alpine Club. *Accidents in North American Mountaineering*. The American Alpine Club: Vol.4, No.6, Issue 36/Vol.4, No.5, Issue 35.

Barnett, Steve. *The Best Ski Touring in America*. San Francisco: Sierra Club Books. 1987.

Bonney, Orrin H. and Bonney, Lorraine. *Guide to the Wyoming Mountains and Wilderness Areas*. Denver: Sage Books. Second, Revised Edition. 1965.

Bonney, Orrin H. and Bonney, Lorraine. *Battle Drums and Geysers*. Chicago: Sage Books/The Swallow Press. 1970.

DuMais, Richard. *50 Ski Tours in Jackson Hole and Yellowstone*. Boulder, CO: High Peak Books. 1990.

Elkins, Frank. *The Complete Ski Guide*. New York: Doubleday, Doran & Company, Inc. 1940.

Harris, Burton. *John Colter; His Years in the Rocky Mountains*. Casper, WY: Big Horn Book Company. 1983.

Love, John D., and Reed, John C. Jr. *Creation of the Teton Landscape; The Geologic Story of Grand Teton National Park*. Colorado University Press, Moose, WY: Grand Teton Natural History Association. 1968.

Lunn, Arnold. *The Story of Skiing*. London: Eyre & Spottiswoode, Inc. 1952.

Marchand, Peter J. *Life in the Cold, An Introduction to Winter Ecology*. University Press of New England. 1987.

Nelson, Fern K. *This Was Jackson's Hole*. Glendo, WY: High Plains Press. 1994.

Payne, Helen C. *Make It Wyoming; Biographical Sketch of Rudolph Rosencrans*. Teton County Historical Society. Circa 1954.

Petzoldt, Patricia. *On Top of the World; My Adventures with my Mountain-Climbing Husband*. New York: Thomas Y. Crowell Company. 1953.

Platts, Doris B. *The Pass: Historic Teton Pass and Wilson, Wyoming*. Wilson, WY. 1988.

Righter, Robert W. *Crucible for Conservation; The Struggle for Grand Teton National Park*. 1982.

Thompson, Edith M. Schultz, and Thompson, William Leigh. *The Honor and The Heartbreak*. Laramie, WY: Jelm Mountain Press. 1981.

Williams, Knox, and Armstrong, Betsy. *The Snowy Torrents-Avalanche Accidents in the United States 1972-79*. Jackson, WY: Teton Bookshop Publishing Company. 1984.

Woolsey, Elizabeth D. *Off the Beaten Track*. Wilson, WY: Wilson Bench Press. 1984.

Newspapers

Idaho State Journal-Enjoy Magazine. "I Skied Grand Teton-Rhoads." 1/26/79.

Jackson Hole Daily. Jackson, WY. Various issues. *See* Notes and Sources.

Jackson Hole Guide. Jackson, WY. Various issues. *See* Notes and Sources.

Jackson Hole News. Jackson, WY. Various issues. *See* Notes and Sources.

Jackson's Hole Courier. Jackson, WY. Various issues. *See* Notes and Sources.

The Denver Post Empire Magazine. Payne, Helen C. "Rosy of the Rangers," Denver, CO. 2/55.

Periodicals

American Alpine Club. *American Alpine Journal*. New York: American Alpine Club. Vol.2, 8:543. 12/19/35. Vol.18, No.46/No.37/No.49.

Barracato, Debbie. "Historic Teton Valley." *Teton Valley, Idaho Winter Recreation Guide*. Driggs, ID. 1993-94.

Bohren, Craig. "The Freezing of Lakes." *Weatherwise*. 12/86.

"Come On, Make Some Good Tracks." *Teton Magazine*. Jackson, WY. 1972.

Cook, John Byrne. "Bill Briggs, Extreme Pioneer." *Jackson Hole Skier Magazine*. Jackson, WY. 1994.

Dostal, John. "Behind the Brand...SuperLoop." *Cross Country Skier Magazine*. Jan./Feb. 1994.

Edgerly, Bruce. "Bobs, Dogs and Valkyries." *Snow Country Magazine*. 1/95.

Freddy, David, et al. "Responses of Mule Deer to Disturbance by Persons Afoot and Snowmobiles." *Wildlife Society Bulletin* 14(1). Colorado State University. 1986.

Grand Teton, The. Jackson, WY.

Hayden, Elizabeth Wied. "Neither Snow Nor Rain..." *Teton Magazine*. Jackson, WY. Winter/spring 1970.

Hayden, Roger. "Locals...First Tracks." *Jackson Hole Magazine*. Jackson, WY. Winter 1993-94.

Manley, Fletcher. "Skiing the Skillet: First Ski Descent of Mount Moran." *Teton Magazine*. Jackson, WY. Winter/spring 1970.

McKay, Dan. "Round of Chuters." *Powder Magazine*. Dana Point, CA. 2/83.

Oliver, Peter. "It's a Hole New Ball Game in Jackson." *Skiing Magazine*. 12/93.

Rhoads, Jeff. "Teton Descent." *The Intermountain Skier*. 4/79.

Richey, David. "Ice Safety and Rescue." *Outdoor Life*. 12/77.

Sarthou, Jacques. "One Up from Glory." *Teton Magazine*. Jackson, WY. Spring 1973.

Sheehan, Casey. "Snowboarder Cuts Grand Teton Down to Size." *Powder Magazine*. Dana Point, CA. 11/89.

Simmons, Drew. "Not Afraid of the Dark." *Couloir Magazine*. Simi Valley, CA. Oct./Nov. 1994.

Strung, Norman. "Are You Walking On Thin Ice?" *Outdoor Life*. Date not available.

Strung, Norman. "When Ice Is Safe." *Field and Stream*. 2/89.

"The Town Hill." *Teton Magazine*. Jackson, WY. 6/73.

Thuermer, Angus. "Going to the Dogs." *free snow*. Seattle, WA. Fall 1994.

Turiano, Thomas. "Expedition Notes." *Snowboarder Magazine*. Dana Point, CA. 11/89.

Turiano, Thomas. "Kamikaze Klassics." *Rock and Ice Magazine*. Boulder, CO. Jan./Feb. 1991.

Turiano, Thomas. "Passages Through Walls of Stone." *Jackson Hole Skier Magazine*. Jackson, WY. 1992/93.

Woods, Rebecca. "Pioneers of Skiing Jackson Hole." *Jackson Hole Skier Magazine*. Jackson, WY. 1991/92.

Films, videos

Fall Line. Bob Carmichael. 1979.

Rhythms. Salomon film.

Treasures of the Past. Teton Valley Arts and Humanities and Teton Valley Historical Society.

Manuscripts and other unpublished documents

National Park Service. Various Grand Teton National Park documents. *See* Notes and Sources.

Teton Valley Community Task Force documents: *Teton Canyon Recommendations on Management of Wildlife Winter Range and Winter Recreation* and *Teton Canyon to Fox Creek Recommendations on Management of Wildlife Winter Range and Winter Recreation*. 1988.

U.S. Forest Service. Draft Winter Travel Map. Teton Basin Ranger District, Targhee National Forest.

OTHER READING

Avalanche Awareness

LaChapelle, Ed. *The ABC of Avalanche Safety.* Second Edition. Seattle: The Mountaineers. 1985.

Moynier, John. *Avalanche Awareness; A Practical Guide to Safe Travel in Avalanche Terrain.* Chockstone Press. 1993.

Tilton, Buck. *The Basic Essentials of Avalanche Safety.* Merrillville, IN: ICS Books. 1992.

Backcountry Skiing Technique

Barnett, Steve. *Cross-Country Downhill and Other Nordic Mountain Skiing Techniques.* Seattle: Pacific Search Press. 1979.

Briggs, William. *The Skier's Manual.* Volumes I and II.

Cliff, Peter. *Ski Mountaineering.* Seattle: Pacific Search Press. 1987.

McMullen, John. *The Basic Essentials of Snowboarding.* Merrillville, IN: ICS Books. 1991.

Parker, Paul. *Free-Heel Skiing.* Chelsea, VT: Chelsea Green Publishing Company. London: Diadem Books, Ltd. 1988.

Townsend, Chris. *Wilderness Skiing and Winter Camping.* Camden, ME: Ragged Mountain Press. 1994.

Watters, Ron. *Ski Camping.* San Francisco Chronicle Books. 1979.

Mountaineering Technique

Mountaineering: The Freedom of the Hills. Seattle: The Mountaineers Books. Fifth Edition. 1992.

Selters, Andy. *Glacier Travel and Crevasse Rescue.* Seattle: The Mountaineers. 1990.

Local Guidebooks

DuMais, Richard. *50 Ski Tours In Jackson Hole and Yellowstone.* Boulder: High Peak Books. 1990.

Ortenburger, Leigh, and Jackson, Reynold. *A Climbers' Guide to the Teton Range.* Ortenburger and Jackson. 1992.

Watters, Ron. *Ski Trails and Old Timers' Tales.* Moscow, ID: Solstice Press. 1978.

Wilkerson, James. *Medicine for Mountaineering.* Seattle: The Mountaineers. 1975.

Wilderness Medicine

Lentz, Martha, Macdonald, Steven, and Carline, Jan. *Mountaineering First Aid.* Third Edition. Seattle: The Mountaineers. 1990.

Other

Masia, Seth. *Ski Maintenance and Repair.* 1987.

PHOTO CREDITS

ABOUT THE AUTHOR

Tom Turiano was born Nov. 26, 1966 and was raised in Fairport, a suburb of Rochester, New York. His love for skiing began at age 4, when he first took to the slopes. He spent his youth skiing at Bristol Mountain in the Finger Lakes Region.

Tom's first experience in Jackson Hole was while on a family trip during the summer of 1980, at which time he vowed to return again.

In 1984-85, Tom spent a year studying geology at the Colorado School of Mines, but left prematurely to pursue the mountain life in Jackson Hole. It was in Colorado that Tom got his first taste of ski mountaineering and rock climbing.

When he arrived in Jackson Hole in September of 1985, Tom was in awe of the Tetons but too cautious to explore them. Between 1985 and 1987, Tom climbed and skied extensively in the Gros Ventre, reaching the summit of all but two or three peaks in that range. He spent four years working with Bill Briggs at the Great American Ski School, during which time he learned philosophies of ski instruction, mountaineering and guiding. There he also met mountaineer Tom Bennett, who abruptly whipped him into a mountaineer, taking him on his first Teton ski tours.

Since those first arduous tours in the spring of 1986, Tom has devoted every winter and spring to that endeavor. He has skied from more than 100 Teton summits, traversed the range more than 20 times, and logged nearly 4,000 miles of touring. Literally spending more time in the mountains than not, it seemed to Tom that he should produce something tangible from those efforts. Herein are the results.

Tom currently guides climbing and skiing tours with the Exum Mountain Guides and Rendezvous Ski Tours and is a part-time ski instructor at the Jackson Hole Ski Area.

INDEX

Snow King gelunde jumping.

Teton Pass: Telemark Bowl, December 1950.

Neil Rafferty with his ski jitney, 1950s-1960s.